To Hazel:

If you are in
in Real Estate, Read this

If you aren't interested in Real
Estate Investment, Read this book

because you're a relative.

Dennis M. Brown

Investing in Real Estate:

How To Do It Right

Dennis M. Brouner

LONGMAN FINANCIAL SERVICES PUBLISHING INC./CHICAGO

a Longman Group USA Company

While a great deal of care has been taken to provide accurate and current information, the ideas, suggestions, general principles, and conclusions presented in this book are subject to local, state, and federal laws and regulations, court cases, and any revisions of same. The reader is thus urged to consult legal counsel regarding any points of law—this publication should not be used as a substitute for competent legal advice.

Library of Congress Cataloging in Publication Data

Brouner, Dennis M.
    Investing in real estate.

    1. Real estate investment.   I. Title.
HD1382.5.B76 1985   332.63'24   85-24020
ISBN 0-88462-638-5

Sr. Acquisitions Editor: Ivy Lester
Development Editor: Karen Berger
Copy Editor: Chris Benton
Cover/Interior Design: Ophelia Chambliss-Jones
Production Coordinator: Marguerite Duffy

CONTENTS

THIS BOOK IS DEDICATED TO

Brian and Amy, who had to sacrifice the most so that it might be written; and to Larry Schorno, who always wanted to see his name in print somewhere other than on a post office wall.

INTRODUCTION

Many books have been written on real estate investment, and the last thing this country needs is another such book. However, conspicuously absent from the bookshelves is a book that points out the hazards to be encountered and, hopefully, avoided in real estate investment. I wish that such a book as this had been published at the time when I first considered seeking my fortune through real estate. Unfortunately, the books available on the subject then and now are of two general types. The first type is the "get rich" books. Whether they are the "get rich quick" or "get rich more slowly" kind of books, their prevailing theme is the opportunities available in real estate investment. It is not surprising that these books tend to be best-sellers. People like to read about how they can get rich. The books offer very little in the way of concrete advice and accomplish very little more than offering encouragement to the novice to enter the field. Of greater concern is the fact that they offer very little in the way of prudent caution. They revel in examples of the fortunes made in real estate, with barely a mention of the fortunes lost. They also neglect to consider the many business considerations of the investments. When you buy a piece of income property, you are buying a business, and there are many business concerns that you will have to address.

The other books published in the field are the more technically oriented books, generally written to address a narrower aspect of real estate investment. Included among the subjects are real estate taxation, real estate financing, real estate negotiation, real estate accounting and bookkeeping, real estate law, real estate agencies, and real estate management, to name just a few. These books are generally directed at a narrow audience. Accountants will want to read about real estate accounting, lawyers will want to read about real estate law, and the rest of us will have very little interest in these areas. Since the books are addressed to professionals in particular fields, they tend to be technical in nature and deadly boring. They are written at a level above the head of the novice investor and are therefore of very little use.

So, this is the sorry state of affairs in the published literature on real estate investment. Either you are told that you are going to get rich, and you are encouraged to go precariously forward into the vast unknown to seek your fortune, or the technical advice you seek is written in a language that is beyond your comprehension. As a consequence, there are the plungers who throw caution to the wind and make investments, and there are the cautious noninvestors who, because of the uncertainties and their inherent risk aversion, never begin to invest. The former group may or may not be successful. They are to be commended because they gave it a shot; they took the risk in search of a reward. For some, the rewards are very great, and for that reason many will follow and attempt to emulate their success. The latter group represents a vast lost opportunity. Many will grow old wondering what might have been. They will kick themselves for opportunities missed but will fail to recognize that they have only themselves to blame. Instead, they will blame anything or anyone else. Circumstances are an ever-popular source of blame. There is an endless variety of circumstances that can "prevent" a person from investing in real estate if that person is looking for the excuse. Another source of blame is the other person: the reluctant spouse, the concerned child or parent, the sibling who has a lot of experience and cautions against the investment.

If you ask a friend to review an investment for you, he or she will tend to recommend against it, or at the very least, express concern. The reason for this is that your friend doesn't want to be blamed later when the investment doesn't work out. It is a lose-lose proposition. If the investment proves successful, you will credit the investment and not the friend; however, if the investment doesn't work, you will blame the friend for recommending it. A professional friend or acquaintance is in a slightly different position. The lawyer, accountant, stockbroker, real estate agent, or other professional is frequently paid to provide you with investment advice, and that will affect the advice given. Chapter 12 of this book is devoted to seeking and using professional advice. That chapter discusses the need for professional help and the difficulty in acquiring quality help.

Throughout the book, you will find that I express my opinions and generalizations without restraint. To me they are facts. I have lived the relationships, confirmed the stereotypes, and judged the prejudices. Therefore, when I tell you that appraisals are entirely worthless, you should know that I believe that they are entirely worthless. I will take the time to explain the reason for my evaluation, but since there is a whole profession devoted to the production of these worthless documents, you may expect some dissent to be expressed. Those expressing dissent might be advised to write their own book to express their point of view. Alternatively, they might choose to sue me for expressing my opinion. My right to freedom of expression will compete with their privilege to avoid criticism of the various professionals. The suit would be frivolous, but that doesn't really matter. One thing you will discover in real estate or in any other field is that we have become a litigious society. You don't even have to have a serious claim to bring suit and put your adversary to the time and expense of defending the suit. The defendant who chooses to ignore you does so at his or her own peril and risks a default judgment of whatever you claim. The potential for litigation, which is addressed in this book, is just one of the many risks you face when investing in real estate.

So, why is this book being written? It is being written to fill the void in the "how to" books. It is an attempt to allow the reader to avoid some of the pitfalls and problems that I have encountered. It is the advice of a seasoned soldier to a new recruit or the sharing of war stories with those on a similar path. It is designed to save you money and grief. And, although it may sound conceited to say so, I believe it should be considered required reading for anyone seriously considering an investment in real estate.

For whom was the book written? It is intended for the popular press, and is meant to be read by real estate novices and experienced investors alike. I would like to think that, as an experienced investor reads a passage describing an individual I have encountered or a circumstance I have experienced, a knowing smile will cross his or her face as he or she reflects on a similar person or situation. But the book will be particularly valuable to the novice. The price of the book is a very economical way to acquire the experience reflected in the text. Investors will pay for the knowledge

at one point or another in their investment careers. It is my hope
that they pay the relatively small price of the book rather than the
large cost of a poor investment.

Why should you read this book? So far, I have told you that you
should read the book because it's good for you. If you want children to question the food they are eating, tell them, "It's good for
you." They probably won't eat another bite. There must be more
presented here than stuff you should read or stuff you should
know. Fortunately, I feel there is a lot presented here that you will
find interesting and enjoyable. I hope most people will *want* to
read the book rather than just feel that they *should* read it.

The book is upbeat. There are fortunes to be made in real estate. Real estate is a valuable part of nearly every investment portfolio. Real estate is an excellent tax shelter and can be an
income-producing hedge against inflation. There are more rags-
to-riches stories associated with real estate than with any other investment. More leverage is available in real estate than in other
investments. And capital financing—whether debt, equity, or
some hybrid—is generally available to anyone with something to
offer the investment community. Finally, real estate offers something approaching an equal-opportunity source of wealth, regardless of the investor's race, sex, or ethnic background. Actually, the
last statement is not quite accurate. What real estate offers are
unique opportunities *as a result of* one's race, sex, or ethnic background. For example, women make most of the home-buying decisions in this country and are often more comfortable dealing
with a female real estate agent. Also, people tend to be more comfortable investing their money with a person of racial or ethnic
background similar to their own. Thus, the opportunities are there
if a person is determined to make use of them and change what
might be regarded as a liability into an asset.

This is not to say that the book is naive. It is an interesting phenomenon that we all start out completely ignorant of everything.
Through our growth and maturation process we become less naive
about some things, until we reach the point where we often deny
our original ignorance. I do not deny the fact that there was a time
when I was completely ignorant of real estate investment and of
life in general. I am now less naive about real estate investment. I
hope to share some of this found knowledge. However, my mo-
tives are hardly altruistic. It would seem only poetic justice to
profit from my mistakes.

REAL ESTATE INVESTING $\boxed{1}$

In our society, no one can avoid being involved in real estate investment in some capacity. When you are born, if your parents own the house in which they live (or own part of it, with the finance company or bank owning the balance), you will have a future interest in that property. You may expect to retain that interest, which will probably grow in value, until you are a teenager and your parents determine that the only way to control your disruptive behavior and teach you a lesson is to disinherit you. At about that time, you will probably determine that it is in your best interest to replace that property interest with a leasehold interest of your own. From that point on, unless economic considerations drive you back home to a hasty reconciliation with Mom and Dad, you will have some current interest and legal rights in real estate. You will continue to have some kind of interest in real estate until you die. At that time, you may be cremated or buried. You will not, however, own that plot of land in which you are buried. It is a popular misconception that the person buried in a particular grave owns the grave. That is not true. Dead people cannot own real estate. They can, however, control real estate to some extent, so it could be said that they have property rights. For example, you could state in your will that your son is to receive the family house when he completes medical school. Provided that this doesn't violate the property rights of a surviving spouse, this would be a perfectly valid disposition. You would have to provide for ownership rights until the son completes medical school, and you should recognize the possibility that the anticipated event may never occur. However, property rights are one way for persons long dead to control, or at least influence, the actions of the living. So, your property rights begin at birth and extend beyond your death.

The property rights we have considered thus far are the rights associated with property consumption. That is, as a consumer you need shelter, and you purchase and use that shelter. You may purchase its use on a daily, weekly, monthly, or annual basis, or you may acquire an ownership interest in the property that you are using for your personal shelter. It is not necessary to buy the house in which you live as your first real estate investment. In fact, the house in which you live may be a very poor investment, and you might be far better off renting it, investing the money you would otherwise put into the down payment in income property.

HOME OWNERSHIP VERSUS RENTAL

Now, you may think I have gone too far. Surely, it is heresy to suggest that something as basic to the American way of life as ownership of the family home is unnecessary and, worse, a waste of opportunity. But the family home need not be owned. Anything that can be purchased can also be leased, so it is important to consider whether the desired shelter can best be acquired through an ownership interest or through a leasehold interest. However, it is a fact that nicer homes generally don't make good rental properties. For example, a house that would require a mortgage payment of $1,200 per month (after a 20 percent down payment) would in many cases not rent for more than $800 per month. After income tax considerations, the cost differential is reduced since interest on the mortgage is deductible and at this writing rent payments are not. In our example, if the taxpayer/property owner is in the 35 percent marginal income tax bracket, his or her monthly expenditure for shelter will be lower through property ownership than through renting. Here is a simplistic example:

	Renting	Ownership
Monthly payment	$800	$1,200
Income tax savings	-0-	420
Net monthly cost	$800	$ 780

In this example, besides assuming that the taxpayer is in the 35 percent tax bracket, we assume that the payments are interest only and entirely deductible. In a long-term mortgage, the assumption that the payments are entirely interest, with nothing going to reduce the principal debt, is only a slight exaggeration. The higher the marginal income tax bracket, the more property ownership is favored over renting. Consider the following table.

Marginal Tax Bracket	Rental Cost	Net Ownership Cost	Favored	Dollar Advantage
20%	$800	$960	Renting	$160
25	800	900	Renting	100
30	800	840	Renting	40
35	800	780	Ownership	20
40	800	720	Ownership	80
45	800	660	Ownership	140
50	800	600	Ownership	200

This table also assumes that the entire $1,200 mortgage payment is deductible interest. Another assumption that is not so obvious is that the entire interest deduction results in tax benefit. Interest expense is an itemized deduction and will result in tax benefit only to the extent that, when combined with the other itemized deductions, the amount exceeds the zero bracket amount (formerly called the *standard deduction)*. I believe this is a reasonable assumption, since most people paying either $800 in rent or $1,200 in mortgage payments will have little difficulty in accumulating enough other itemized deductions to make the entire interest expense deductible for tax benefit.

The monthly after-tax cash flow analysis is a valuable starting point in our consideration of the costs and benefits of property ownership, but it fails to consider the investment aspects of ownership versus rental. The investment aspect of rental? Yes, because while renting itself does not result in investment in most cases, rent will absorb only a minimum of capital, and the remainder may be used for investment. This investment potential is what is often referred to as the *opportunity cost* associated with the use of the money. In other words, every time you use investment capital, you give up the opportunity to use the money for other purposes. To the extent that other uses would result in a return on investment, the use of the capital can be said to have a cost.

So, to consider fully the costs and benefits of home ownership versus rental, you must consider the investment worth of the house versus the various alternative investments. The other investments might include other real estate, stocks, bonds, commodities, collectibles—you name it. The alternatives are endless. So, how do you make a comparison? Probably the best way to start is to consider how good an investment the family home has been historically. In general, it has been a very good investment. The government and private lenders have made it possible to acquire property in the form of a family home with significant leverage. In English, that means that the home can be bought with very little money down. Since the primary investment benefit from home ownership is appreciation in value as a result of inflation and market conditions, the lower the down payment, the higher the return on investment.

Although the relationship between leverage and return will be explored in more detail later, a quick example will illustrate how leverage affects return. If you bought a house for cash instead of with a conventional mortgage with 20 percent down, and the property appreciated at a rate of 6 percent, you would experience a 6 percent return on investment, while the leveraged purchaser would experience a 30 percent return. For those who are not comfortable with percentages, it is helpful to use a dollar explanation. For example, assume the house cost $100,000 and could be bought either for cash or with 20 percent down. If the house appreciates at 6 percent per annum, its value at the end of one year will be $106,000. The $6,000 appreciation would be a 6 percent return on a $100,000 cash investment. But, if you bought the property for 20 percent down, or $20,000, the $6,000 appreciation would be a 30 percent return on investment.

The rate of return would be reduced, perhaps significantly, by transaction costs. In future years, the rate of return would be compounded by inflation. And the longer the holding period, the less significant the transaction costs. All of this will be considered in more detail later. The purpose of mentioning these matters here is simply to indicate that the traditional investment in the family home has proven to be a good one. However, it should be noted that, like other investments, the family home is subject to cyclical market fluctuations. If, for any reason, you must sell at a time when the market conditions are not as good as they were at the time you purchased, it is quite possible that you will lose money on your family's home. Also, because you will have real estate commissions and other costs to pay on the transaction, you are probably ill-advised to consider a real estate acquisition with a planned holding period of less than two years. Finally, you should recognize the sobering fact that the same considerations that are usually applied to rental property do not necessarily apply to the family home. For example, it is generally considered advisable to buy income property that is of less value than the surrounding property. The theory is that, if you fix up the acquisition, the surrounding property will help increase the value of the property. That might be a well and good theory for rental property, but you might have a hard time convincing your spouse of the advantages of acquiring and living in the lowest-value house in the neighborhood. The value of the home is supported by such intangibles as the value of the neighborhood, the quality of schools, and the general economic condition of the area, all of which are beyond the control of the individual property owner.

There is far more real estate to consider than the traditional family home. And generally, when you discuss your real estate investments, you are discussing your property holdings other than the family home. The property can range from raw land to highrise office towers. Your form of ownership can range from individual ownership, where you make all the ownership decisions, to limited partnership ownership, where you make virtually none of the business or investment decisions.

Starting from the basic and working our way to the more complex, the first property we should consider is raw land.

RAW LAND

Raw land is the precious metal of real estate investments. It has value because it is of limited supply. To quote Will Rogers, land is of value because "they ain't making any more of it." Raw land is also like precious metals in that it is frequently nonproductive and is not without carrying costs. Raw land may be bought from tiny lots of a few square feet (or even a few square inches in novelty purchases) to large ranches of thousands of acres. Land is always bought for its use, whether that use is current or a predicted, planned, or hoped) for future use. If the land is productive, either farmed by the owner or leased to others for that purpose, it may be expected to generate income for the owner. However, if the land is nonproductive, it will only cost the owner money to hold the property until it is sold. While most land is productive, most land that is purchased for speculation is nonproductive. It is a speculative investment. Ideally, you would purchase the property and sell it to a developer a week later for twice the price. What usually happens is something short of this ideal.

The first adjustment from the ideal occurs in the holding period. Unless the land is purchased for a specific purpose—either to be developed by the purchaser or by the purchaser in conjunction with others or to be purchased with the resale purchaser identified—the holding period can be a long and costly ordeal. This is because, even if the property is purchased for cash, the owner must pay the property taxes and the other costs necessary to its maintenance. The longer the holding period, the higher the costs and the lower the rate of return. The rate of return is reduced because of the additional costs associated with the property and because the delay in the sale reduces the present value of that receipt. The concept of present value, simply stated, is that cash is worth more now than at a future date. You would prefer to spend it now, or, if it were invested, it would generate interest for an increased nominal amount. In other words, $10,000 one year from now is not worth $10,000 today. Instead, the value must be discounted to reflect its present value. If your investments earn a 10 percent return, you would have to invest approximately $9,090 to have $10,000 in one year. Therefore, the present value of $10,000 one year from now, discounted at 10 percent, is $9,090; $10,000 in one year can be considered worth $9,090 today.

The second adjustment from the ideal lies in the likely resale price of the property. Occasionally, you will guess very well and make a killing on your land speculation. More often, your clairvoyance will fail for one reason or another. You will probably make money on your land speculation, but if you do nothing productive with the land, nothing to develop or improve the land, the rate of return you realize probably will not be spectacular.

BARGAIN PURCHASES
So, how do you make money on raw land? Well, the first thing to do is to identify a bargain purchase. If similar property in the area is selling for $10,000 per acre and you have negotiated a purchase price for $5,000 per acre, the chances are that you are making a bargain purchase. However, you must ask yourself, "Why am I getting such a good deal?" or "*Am* I getting such a good deal?" To determine how good a deal you're really getting, examine the property in detail:

- What defects are there in the property you are considering?
- Is the property landlocked so that it does not have access to a public road, thus substantially reducing its development value?
- Is the property without utilities or running water?

- Is the property zoned restrictively, thus preventing its development?
- Are the property rights on your parcel subordinate to the rights on an adjoining parcel through easement, contract, or other mechanism?

This is, of course, not an exhaustive list. The point is to be cautious, investigative, and even suspicious of the seller and the representations made about the property. It is important that you know as much as or more than the seller about the property.

Used car dealers always seem to have a car that was owned by a little old lady, who drove it only to church on Sunday. It is the cream puff, the bargain deal. The land equivalent is the ignorant seller who doesn't know what the property is worth. The seller is claimed to have acquired the property years ago, for a bargain price by today's standards, and can't believe it's worth what we know it is. In considering the believability of this story, note the following items.

1. Who is representing the seller? Does a sophisticated agent offset the seller's supposed ignorance?
2. Have other parcels been sold by this seller, thus increasing the seller's level of sophistication?
3. Who is the seller, anyway? Property ownership is a matter of public record. If you are suspicious of the representations made by the seller's representatives, it might well be worthwhile to investigate whom they represent. This information doesn't necessarily make a purchase good or bad, but it does shed light on the veracity of the information you are receiving.
4. Another part of the public record is the history of the property, including the prior owners, and the original balances of prior or existing loans or other encumbrances. This may yield valuable information as to the historical appreciation of the property, and perhaps prior problem ownerships as evidenced by foreclosures, liens and the like.
5. The public record includes other information that can be valuable if you know how to read it. For example, tax stamps might yield information as to prior purchase prices. If the rate of the tax is 55¢ per $500, or $1.10 per $1,000 of purchase price, and the prior sale has $55 of tax stamps affixed to the deed, you can determine that the prior price was $50,000.
6. Is the story relevant? Remember that the prior history of the property has only limited relevance when considering its future profitability.

LOOK FOR THE PATH OF DEVELOPMENT

Buy property in the path of development. This is hardly new or startling advice. Many of this country's private fortunes were built from this simple advice. Sometimes it is relatively easy to identify the path of development. Look for the new housing developments, the new warehouses, the new shopping centers. The shopping centers will be built in new commercial districts on arterials with good highway access. The warehouses will be on level land serviced by rail. The housing developments will be on wooded hillsides near the new shopping centers and new warehouses but preferably with a view of neither. If you buy property similar to that being developed around you, and you obtain a "bargain" purchase, chances are pretty good that you will make money. But remember that not every lot is developed. There are vacant lots surrounded by skyscrapers. Also, property is developed to different extents. The parcel across the street from the shopping mall may never be developed for retail purposes. It may be sought as an employee parking lot, or worse, it may be taken by the eminent domain of the local government for use by the bus company as a park-and-ride lot. Should either of these or many other possible events take place, it is unlikely that the property will realize the profit you had anticipated.

Speculating on raw land is a gamble. You may make a fortune, and you may lose a fortune. As you will see, there are more secure ways of making your fortune in real estate.

DEVELOPING PROPERTY

A first possibility is to do more than merely buy and sell land on speculation. If you take action to improve the property, you will be the master of your destiny. Your success or failure will depend on your skill or the combined skills of you, your partners, and your employees. If, at this point, you're thinking, "But I have no skill or experience in property development," then, for goodness sake, don't develop anything. You are virtually certain to lose money on your first project. And, depending on the magnitude of that loss, you may not have the resources for a second project.

As an alternative, you may get into the development business by going into partnership with a competent developer. The difficulty, of course, lies in locating a competent developer in need of an incompetent partner. Competent developers are difficult enough to find, and if they are truly competent, they are seldom in need of a partner. Also, wishing upon someone a partnership with a developer seems cruel indeed. The only thing worse I can think of would be a partnership with a stockbroker or an insurance agent.

DIVIDING THE PROPERTY

You should be aware that improving the property need not mean launching into some massive construction project. You could simply take your cue from the retailers and break bulk. The typical retailer buys by the case or truckload, marks the product up 100 percent, and sells the items individually. Many people have made a fortune in real estate the same way. They identify property being sold in 40-acre parcels that may be legally and profitably divided into one-acre lots. Dividing the property may involve nothing more than changing the legal descriptions, or it may involve constructing roads, bringing utilities and water to the property, and perhaps more. When you are making improvement decisions, you must always ask yourself what will improve the property, by how much, and with what degree of certainty. Finally, you must ask yourself what the degree of risk is. Translation: How much does it cost? In case of doubt, do nothing. Make only those improvements that have a high profitability of substantially improving the value of the property at a modest cost and always allow yourself a substantial margin for error. Eventually, with experience, this will become less of a problem, but initially you will probably find yourself constantly underestimating the cost of the improvements. It just doesn't seem that they should cost as much as they do. So, be cautious and do as little as possible.

CHANGING THE SALES UNIT

A variation on the concept of breaking bulk is the concept of changing the sales unit. You will find this to be a recurring theme in real estate. As it relates to raw land, the investor buys the land by the acre or some suitable large unit and sells the property by some other unit. Typical smaller units include sales by the square foot or what seems to me to be the ultimate contrivance to overprice property: sales by an amount per apartment unit that may be legally constructed on the property. The property may be zoned for a medium-density 15 units per acre and may sell for $6,000 per unit. The price, if stated at $90,000 per acre, would seem excessive to the builder; however, when stated at a cost per unit, it seems more acceptable. A similar example exists for property purchased by the acre and sold by the square foot. It is not uncommon to see property sold by the acre for, say, $20,000 per acre and shortly thereafter (a few months or a few years) selling for commercial purposes at about $4 to $5 per square foot. At first blush, the profit in this transaction may not be apparent, but remember that there are 43,560 square feet in an acre. Thus, at $4 per square foot, the property that was purchased for $20,000 per acre would be selling for in excess of $170,000 per acre—not a bad markup, if you can pull it off. However, the picture is not quite that rosy. Remember, you must correctly predict the path of development, where land values will be increasing rapidly. Also, when you buy land by the acre, you are buying much land that does not have much commercial value just to obtain those few acres of highway frontage. But, with the kind of markup frequently realized in these transactions, you don't need to convert all the land from farm to commercial use to realize a substantial profit. Finally, that portion of the land that you do not improve or sell to someone for commercial purposes is not likely to suffer a significant diminution in value as a result of being located near the new development. In other words, you will make money on the land that is sold for development and not lose money on the land that isn't. At some point, you must realize that not all of your land will be developed in the near future, so you may, without reluctance, sell it and avoid the carrying costs.

INCOME-PRODUCING PROPERTY

The vast majority of privately owned property is productive in some capacity. Generally, it is income-producing. However, as we shall see later, it may produce profits without producing an operating income.

There are two types of income associated with raw land: the appreciation due primarily to inflation and the changing uses of the land, and the income associated with development or improvement of the land. Income-producing property may also realize these types of income. But, in addition, income-producing property, or income property for short, may also produce three types of income: operating cash flow, debt amortization, and income tax shelter.

OPERATING CASH FLOW

Operating cash flow is the amount of cash that is left over each month after paying all the bills on the property. Frequently, this is stated before or after debt service. But for now, assume you collect the rent; pay all the operating expenses for the property, including debt service; and, after doing all that, you have money left over. That is your monthly cash flow from the property.

DEBT AMORTIZATION

Debt amortization is the paydown on the mortgage indebtedness on the property. If the property maintains its value, the debt paydown represents the amount of increased ownership of the purchaser. If the cash flow from the property is adequate to pay the operating expenses and service the debt, you as purchaser will increase your ownership of the property courtesy of the income from the property. In other words, the tenants will help the landlord acquire the property.

INCOME TAX SHELTER

Income tax shelter is a little more difficult to explain since it involves something common in the tax law, a "fiction." Basically, the fiction is that, while the property may be producing cash flow and appreciating in market value, the tax law allows you to treat the property as though it is losing value or depreciating. Further, it allows you to take these fictional losses and use them to offset income from other sources, thus reducing your taxable income and your tax bill.

The tax advantages associated with real estate have varied over the years and may be expected to vary in the future. There has hardly been a time in our history when the tax law has not favored real estate over other investments, including other traditional tax shelters like oil and gas and property leasing. But real estate enjoys particular advantages now. Since 1981, buildings have been depreciable over 15 years regardless of their "useful lives." In 1984, the depreciation period was changed to 18 years, which is less advantageous than 15 years but is still a substantial tax shelter.

Also, the accelerated cost recovery system, introduced in 1981, allows for the use of accelerated methods of depreciation. By *accelerated depreciation,* we mean that a greater percentage of the cost of the building will be written off in the early years of ownership. Thus, you may realize the tax advantages of building ownership very quickly.

But an alarming development has occurred as a result of the significant tax advantages enjoyed by improved property ownership. Since real property enjoys such a preferred status in the tax law, many investors are purchasing it for its tax shelter benefits, at the expense of the traditional benefits of cash flow and even appreciation. It would be a mistake to ignore the tax advantages, and I am not suggesting that anyone do that, but *don't buy property solely for its tax advantages.* Remember that the government giveth and the government can taketh away. This is especially true when a fiction is involved and with the government budget deficits running what they have been. Among the suggestions considered recently for changing the tax law are: changing the depreciation period from 15 to 20 years (the change to 18 years was a legislative compromise), applying the at-risk rules to real estate, and treating publicly traded partnerships as corporations for tax purposes. Other possible changes are limited only by the imagination of our elected representatives and the realities of the political environment. At this point, I do not expect you to understand the significance of the changes I have just indicated. Also, please don't misinterpret my mentioning them as a prediction that the proposed legislation will pass and become law. It would be a mistake to underestimate the housing lobby and the other real estate lobbies. Also, average congressmen and senators are reasonably well off, make a decent living, and probably have investments that include real estate tax shelters. They have an interest in the maintenance of a favorable tax law. My point here is that the tax law is tenuous and subject to change. Investing solely for the tax advantage is a mistake.

THE IMPORTANCE OF CASH FLOW

NEGATIVE CASH FLOW

Negative cash flow results when the costs of operating the property, including debt service costs, exceed the rental income from the property. If an apartment building is generating $10,000 in rental income, $4,000 in operating costs, and $8,000 in debt servicing, it will have a negative cash flow of $2,000 per month. Negative cash flow is a negative income on the property. Rather than producing income for you, your property is costing you money to maintain the investment.

How much negative cash flow is OK? Well, how much can you afford to lose? This is something of a rhetorical question, but it illustrates the point that many people currently subscribe to the theory that a certain amount of negative cash flow is all right. I do not agree with that reasoning, but I have witnessed how it evolved, and I understand it. Cash flow from property is but one advantage of property ownership. The other primary advantages are appreciation and tax shelter. As previously mentioned, the tax advantages of property ownership have seldom been better. As to appreciation, it will tend to vary with the rate of inflation. After all, inflation is the primary cause of appreciation. During the late 1970s and early 1980s, inflation was high and real estate was so favored as a tax shelter that the cash flow from property was reduced to a minor consideration. Eventually, investors began to question if cash flow was necessary at all. It became common to see property sell for 25 percent down and break-even cash flow. Finally, if cash flow was unnecessary, it made sense that negative cash flow was OK if it bought additional tax shelter or leverage-generated appreciation. Investors were correct in analyzing all the benefits of the investment and considering the rates of return after tax. But the error comes in analyzing the risk and the reason for appreciation. In considering the risk, the investor seldom considers the possibility of changes in the tax law. But, as previously discussed, the tax law can and will change. However, your accountant may advise you that generally you don't have to concern yourself with changes in the tax law since the changes in the tax law are usually applied prospectively only. So, if you buy property that may be depreciated over 15 years, and the law changes so that the property may be depreciated over no fewer than 18 years, you may continue to depreciate your property over 15 years. But, if the property is being purchased primarily for the tax advantages, and those advantages diminish for a new purchaser, you can't expect the purchaser to be willing to pay as much for the property as you were willing to pay. So, the risk of tax changes for existing owners is that they may adversely affect the resale value of the property.

When investors and their advisors discount the importance of cash flow, they disregard the reason for property value and appreciation. Investments in real estate are no different from other investments, in that they are made to generate a return. The return may be composed of several elements, including cash flow, tax savings, debt amortization, and appreciation. The amount you are willing to pay for the investment depends on the income you expect it to generate. The tax shelter and cash flow benefits are early benefits of ownership. Appreciation is a more speculative later benefit of ownership. Both debt amortization and appreciation are benefits that generally will not be realized until the property is sold or refinanced. I cannot accept the thinking that cash flow is not important to appreciation.

THE GREATER FOOL THEORY

Those who discount the need for cash flow are also likely to endorse the "greater fool" theory. Basically, this theory holds that what you pay for property is not really that important. You may pay too much for the property and not negotiate the best terms, but you shouldn't really be concerned. You may be a fool, but you can be sure that some greater fool will come along who is willing to pay even more and at worse terms than you. During periods of high inflation, this theory almost works. It has been said that poor investments have a way of correcting themselves if you can wait long enough. What this is really saying is that the value of the property may catch up with your purchase price. But the worth of an investment is a relative thing. There is no substitute for the work required to identify a bargain purchase. And you can make far more money through intelligent purchases than through any other element of property ownership. The advantages may not be fully realized for years to come, but they exist nonetheless.

As to the question of the existence of a greater fool, please note that there will always be persons of greater and less intelligence than you. One of those with less intelligence, less diligence, or less sophistication than you may come along with enough money to make your bad purchase look like a piece of genius. But don't count on it. We use up fools quickly since, as the cliché indicates, they are soon separated from their money. Hopefully, after reading this book you will be a little less naive and won't have to take you turn being someone else's greater fool.

MAKING MONEY IN REAL ESTATE INVESTMENTS

So far, we have considered the opportunities available in land speculation and land development. We will not reconsider that information here, except to mention its limitations. Land speculation is not without its costs—both the cost of acquiring and the cost of maintaining the property. And, since the property is not income-generating, it is not good security for debt. Therefore, most land transactions are made for cash or with only very limited financing. It's simply more difficult to make money on cash transactions than on financed transactions. There are many transaction examples throughout this book that indicate the advantages of favorable financing. But one of the biggest disadvantages of cash transactions is that they limit the number of transactions available. If you have only enough money to buy one business lot, you have only one chance to make a good purchase. But the same amount of cash might make the down payment on several rental houses. With control of a greater amount of property, in different locations, it is more likely that some good investments will be made.

BUILDING AND DEVELOPMENT
A good contractor or developer can make money in any economy and under any economic condition. Poor contractors may make money under favorable market conditions but will probably go out of business during soft markets when construction slumps. I recommend against the construction business for the novice because it involves too many disciplines and skills beyond the capacity of the beginning investor. For example, how much should it

cost to electrically wire a warehouse building? Is it enough to get three bids, or do you need five or ten? Do you even have enough knowledge to ask for a bid? Do you know what you want? If you ask contractors to define the scope of the job, how do you know what is necessary and what isn't?

The lowest bid may not be the best deal. The lowest bid may include substandard materials or may omit necessary items. Once you seal up a wall, it is considerably more expensive to reopen it and redo the project correctly than it would have been to do it correctly in the first place. Are you better off with a time and materials bid, or is this just a method used by the electrician to shift the risk of cost overruns to you? When the electrician submits an invoice, do you know that he or she has done the work being billed? Now ask yourself the same questions for the cement work, the carpentry, the plumbing, the heating and air conditioning systems, the insulation, the roof, even the architecture, the legal status of your title, the reasonableness of your budgets.

The point of this little exercise is to point out that construction or development is an active business. It takes far more than common sense, and it requires substantial experience and training to be conducted successfully. No one can expect to master all the disciplines necessary for construction. Instead, you should master some disciplines or crafts and leave the balance to people you know to be competent in those fields, whether they are your partners, your employees, or subcontractors.

To get started in the construction business, it is necessary to acquire a marketable skill and go to work for someone else. Learn something new and valuable every day. Make contacts with people whose skills complement yours. But keep your goals confidential. Those who are less ambitious than you will be jealous of your goals and will subvert your efforts in ways you could hardly imagine. Also, your employer is not likely to appreciate providing a training ground for a future competitor. When you think you are ready to strike out on your own, talk the matter over with some of your trusted friends and associates. Seek the advice of those whose opinions you respect. Remember, once you have started to inform others of your plans, you are burning your bridges. Your employment situation is jeopardized, and should you change your mind, your work environment would be strained at best and impossible at worst.

Study your situation thoroughly on your own before sharing it with others. Many people have fantasies similar to yours, but never carry them out. I am not sure which reputation is worse—that of a disloyal, calculating employee planning on leaving the firm (and perhaps taking others with him) or the reputation of an unrealistic dreamer who will never realize his or her plans. Either reputation will not serve you well as an employee.

But your plans are not to be an employee any longer. In that, I can only provide encouragement. You must provide the rest. If you are skilled and ambitious, and you have done your homework, you may succeed. But statistics indicate that you will probably fail. Nevertheless, I must encourage you to take the risk. Success is meaningless without effort and the risk of failure. What kind of a life would you have, always wondering what might have been?

FIXER-UPPERS

A very successful traditional method of making money in real estate is to acquire and improve depressed property. In the vernacular of the industry, property in need of repair is frequently referred to as a *fixer-upper*. The profit to be realized from the property's improvement is referred to as *sweat equity*. Both terms are appropriate. A fixer-upper should be a property that may be repaired using primarily the sweat of the owner.

A typical fixer-upper property is a rental house or small apartment building that is dirty. That is, it needs cleaning and painting; it may also need some gardening or window glass repair. Inside, the property may need new floor coverings, kitchen counters, bathroom and kitchen tiles, paint and wallpaper, etc. Avoid property that needs more than cosmetic repairs, unless you have the skill to make those yourself or to evaluate those repairs when made by someone else. It is amazing how much money can be spent inside the walls without adding to the value of the property. Therefore, you should avoid property with material plumbing or electrical problems, problems with the heating system, foundation or roof problems, or significant termite problems. It is safest just to avoid these properties altogether, even though you may find them quite attractive. A property with a significant termite or foundation problem, for example, should sell for a significant discount on what the value of the property would be once the problem is corrected. But, it's a sucker's bet—when is a termite problem really "corrected"? It tends to be a continuing problem for a number of years. The cost of foundation work is frequently prohibitive. Generally, you have to jack up the house, remove old foundation, and pour a completely new one, which is much more difficult than pouring a foundation for new construction.

So, how do you decide what to buy and fix, and what to avoid? As previously indicated, a dirty property, not a dilapidated one, is desirable. Make sure the major "systems" of the property—electrical, plumbing, and heating—are in good working order. Look for evidence of dry rot or insect damage. Look for evidence that the building is settling, like cracks in the basement floors and walls, or cracks in the foundation. Another indication of settling is an uneven roof line. Stand back and take a look at the roof. Does it slope or sag? Sagging isn't good in a horse's back, and it isn't good in an apartment's roof either. You want a property that needs fixing up, not one that needs rebuilding or razing.

Once you have identified a property that is dirty and may be improved by cosmetic repair, prepare a budget of those items that need repair and what it will cost to repair them. Get the best information you can as to the cost of materials and labor. If you are going to do the work yourself, consider the value of your labor to be the same as what it would cost you to hire someone to do the work. Give yourself some cushion in your cost projections. Vandals may force you to repair a window three times before the house is rented or resold, or something worse could happen.

As a rule of thumb, your improvements should increase the value of the property by twice their cost to make the effort worthwhile. This rule will, to a large extent, dictate what improvements are worthwhile and what improvements aren't. For example, adding a swimming pool to a rental house or an owner-occupied house is a highly questionable expenditure. A pool, at a cost of $10,000, may increase the value of the property by $8,000 to $10,000 but probably will not increase the property value by the $20,000 necessary to justify its construction.

When considering improvements, be very pragmatic. Remember that you don't live in the property, so it does not have to meet the standards you require for your own house. The improvements should be good, serviceable, and of general appeal. For example, semigloss off-white latex paint should be used throughout. If you put in custom colors or try to coordinate colors with carpets, they probably will just clash with the prospective tenant's furniture. Improvements made to satisfy the particular taste of one tenant will only have to be redone when that tenant moves in six months.

A classic case of what not to do in the way of improvements involved a friend of mine who purchased custom drapes for her rental house at a cost of $2,000. She could have purchased drapes at K-Mart, at a cost of about $150, that would have been more than adequate. The first tenant to move into the property had several cats that destroyed the drapes in the year during which she occupied the house. The rent on the house was about $400 per month, and as a practical matter the tenant was not liable for the loss of the drapes. Thus, the cost of furnishing drapes to this tenant was over 40 percent of the gross rental income. You can't make money on rental property that way.

The improvements you should make on your fixer-upper property depend largely on what you intend to do with the property. If you intend to use it as rental property for a few years and then sell it, you will most likely want to put in a better quality of carpet than if you intend to sell it immediately. Also, if you intend to sell the property immediately, you may have to realize a greater yield on your improvement dollar than the $2-to-$1 rule of thumb. This is true because, in addition to the cost of the improvements, you will have the transaction costs for the purchase and sale of the property. You don't want the real estate agent to be the only one to benefit from your labors.

Finally, you should note that the availability of fixer-uppers is cyclical. However, because of the natural wear and tear on property, we are constantly generating new ones. When the rental market is strong, you will find very few properties that you can profitably improve. But, when the local factories are laying off employees or closing down, and when people are defaulting on their mortgages and leaving the area, you will find a surplus of fixer-upper properties available at unbelievable terms. Sometimes people will actually pay you to take a problem property off their hands or assume liability for a debt on which they are personably liable. The problem with buying in a soft market is that you must then rent in a soft market. But that is the only time to buy fixer-uppers. If the investment makes sense when the market is soft, you will do very well when the local economy improves, but don't buy negative cash flow. Who knows how long the economy will remain soft before it turns around? Negative cash flow will encourage, and may require you, to sell before it is appropriate to do so.

INCOME PROPERTIES

I am differentiating income properties from fixer-uppers because, while you may reasonably invest in fixer-uppers on the basis of the income you expect them to produce, income properties should be purchased on the basis of the income they are producing currently, adjusted for the cyclicity reflected in the historical numbers for the property. *You should not buy income property on the basis of projected future income.* Reread the previous sentence ten times. Have the sentence printed on the back of your business card and review it before you go to bed at night. Enter the message on a subliminal recorder for your television and play it constantly.

Once you begin to consider the acquisition of income properties, you will be constantly pressured to purchase property on the basis of the income it will generate rather than the income it is currently generating. If you are in a particularly bad mood sometime, you might ask the sellers or their agents why they are selling the property if they are so optimistic about its future. You will find the explanation to be completely inadequate, believable only if you just got off the boat. However, sellers will continue to produce contrived projected data as long as purchasers are willing to use that information as the basis for their investment decision. The quality of information available to real estate investors will be discussed in more detail later. For now, I would just like to say that it is important to base your investment decision on accurate current information.

Income property, like real estate in general, defies characterization in neat little cubbyholes, but I would start with the distinction between residential and nonresidential property which is endorsed by the Internal Revenue Code which recognizes different tax rules for the two kinds of properties. Residential property might be further divided to consider separately houses, apartments, condominiums, cooperatives, and mobile homes. Nonresidential property might be divided to consider retail stores, shopping malls, strip shopping centers, neighborhood shopping centers, office buildings, warehouses, hotels, motels, manufacturing buildings, restaurants, bank buildings, theaters, stadiums, churches, gas stations, parking garages, airports, train stations, bus stations, and the like. Each type of income property has its own advantages and problems of ownership. It is therefore difficult to generalize among them. Yet I believe the similarities outweigh the differences.

For example, all income property is priced based on its income-generating capacity. Different types of property seem to yield different rates of return. Supposedly, the yield is a function of the risks associated with the property. However, the statistics don't support this observation. Supposedly, the yields are greater among the more active forms of ownership, but again there is little statistical support for this observation. I believe the reason that people think the yields vary as indicated is that they should so vary. The truth is that the market is very inefficient. The yields depend not so much on the risk factors as on the quality of the individual deal. The lack of high yields in certain segments of the market is more a function of too many purchasers bidding up the price and down the yields on these investments than it is a lack of risk in these market segments. One obvious example is office space, which has traditionally yielded a much lower rate of return than apartments. But the early 1980s have experienced a substantial surplus of office space. The risk associated with office building construction and ownership is being reconsidered.

The risk in an inefficient market is also its opportunity. Inefficient markets yield a variety in the quality of purchases. You have the opportunity to make outstanding profits at the risk of substantial losses. But there are risks unique to residential versus nonresidential property that merit consideration.

Residential Property

Residential property is that investment property most often purchased by new investors. Frequently, it is not first purchased as investment property, but rather was a young couple's first home or was inherited from an elderly relative. When the couple outgrows the home or the relative dies, the property becomes surplus. If the market for such property is good, the house will probably be sold. If the market is not good, the house will likely become rental property. But, whether the property was first purchased as rental property or evolved as rental property, the novice investors will find that they have become landlords. They will anticipate renting the property for a high enough fee to cover the payments and expenses and putting a little money in the bank each month. They will probably be a little disappointed in the actual results of their rental house business, because they will not anticipate the expenses involved, and they will fail to consider the possibility of vacancy.

Except in very tight markets, or where your rent is substantially below market, you may anticipate that you will lose at least one month's rent per year to vacancy. This is true because tenants tend to move approximately annually, and you will most likely lose one month between tenants when you go in and clean and make the property ready for the new tenants. Most tenants will move on or about the first of the month, so, unless you are able to show the property, rerent it, clean it, and make minor repairs during the last month of occupancy of the prior tenant, you will probably lose one month's rent. If you have a single rental house and it is vacant, your vacancy rate is 100 percent. You must meet the obligations of the property from your own sources unless you have been setting aside a little each month while the property was occupied. As you can see, property ownership requires a certain amount of discipline. It also requires a certain amount of luck. But that luck is not blind. Rather, it is the good fortune that comes about through careful planning. Remember, you are starting a business, and you should go about it in a businesslike manner. From my experience, I have developed the following suggestions for the novice rental property investor.

1. *Join the local property owners' association.* This association will have information of value to the property owner, including local ordinance information for building codes and the like. You might find it surprising to learn that a house that was up to code for your occupancy is not up to code as a rental.

2. *Familiarize yourself with the local laws.* The property owners' association will aid you in this effort. It is important that you know what your rights are and what your tenants' rights are. These laws vary substantially from city to city and from state to state, so assumptions you bring from another area will probably not be correct.

3. *Always use a written lease or rental agreement that is in compliance with local laws.* Use the written agreement even for a month-to-month tenancy. If the tenant is reluctant to sign the rental agreement, find a new tenant.

4. *Always get references from prospective tenants for the previous two places in which they resided.* Contact these references. An amazing number of people get references and don't contact them, apparently satisfied that any references provided will be favorable. This is not always the case. A former apartment manager who had stolen $8,000 from us once used us as a reference on a subsequent employment application. Fortunately, that property owner contacted us. Also, it is important to go beyond the current place of occupancy since the current landlord or property manager may give a positive reference to get rid of a particularly troublesome tenant.

5. *If the tenant should fall behind on rent, immediately initiate eviction procedures.* If the tenant brings the rent current during the procedures, you may choose or be required to honor the original rental agreement. But there are as many excuses as there are creative minds, and if you allow tenants consistently to fall behind on rents, you are never going to collect some of that money.

6. *Consider the tenant to be unsuable.* When legislatures draft landlord-tenant laws, they tend to assume inaccurately that each can use the court system to recover from the other. In reality, it is a one-way street. If you violate a tenant's rights, he or she may sue and recover from you. However, if a tenant moves owing you rent or physically damages your property, it is unlikely that you will ever recover any of your loss. Even should you get a judgment from the tenant, it is unlikely that the tenant will have any assets to pay the judgment. That is not to say that tenants do not have assets, but rather that the assets they have cannot be used to satisfy a judgment. If you sue a tenant, you probably will succeed only in augmenting your losses by the amount of the attorney's fees.

7. *Know your business.* How does your rental unit compare to others in your area? Is your rent competitive? Can your rent be increased and still be competitive? Are you buying your supplies from the best sources available? Is it possible to refinance your property to avoid balloon payments or provide cash for improvements or distribution? Are your tenants maintaining the property or damaging it? Are other profitable rental units available at reasonable prices and terms to expand your business? Can you generate more rent from your property by adding improvements?

8. *Know your environment.* Is the local economy improving or declining? Are the local tenant groups pushing for rent control? Does rent control have a serious chance of passing? If rent control passes, what impact will it have on your profitability and the value of your property? What other legislation affecting your property rights is being considered? What is your liability if you are not in compliance with the local regulations?

Commercial Property

Nonresidential property involves a different set of considerations. While people who own residential property sometimes fail to remember that they are in a business, owners of nonresidential property seldom do. This is true because owners of commercial property tend to have more experience in real property investment and also because the success of their business often is related directly to the success or failure of their tenants. Sometimes the rent paid is a percentage of the receipts of the business. This is very common in retail settings and for restaurants and motels. Other times the rent will not vary with the volume of business of the tenant, but the tenant's success or failure will directly affect his or her ability to pay rent. If you lose a tenant in a commercial building, it may be a long time before you can find a replacement. This is especially true in special-use buildings built to accommodate the needs of a particular tenant. If you own a dinner theater building and your tenant goes out of business, you may find you own a large white elephant. How many closed gas stations and grocery stores have we all seen? An office building may look active and occupied, but an examination of the directory may tell a different story. If none of the businesses have an address on the 32nd through the 35th floor, you might have a large business on the 31st floor occupying the floors above, or you may have four empty floors. If you are considering the acquisition of an office building, whether this highrise or the quaint little two-story building down the block, it is important that you know the health of the business, including the health of your competitors.

There is a large variety in the types of commercial leases available. At one extreme is the full-service lease common in office buildings. In such a lease the landlord provides virtually all of the services necessary to the tenant's occupancy, from heat and lights to janitorial service. At the other extreme is the so-called triple net lease, sometimes called the *NNN lease,* in which the landlord provides virtually none of the services necessary to occupancy. In such a lease the landlord's responsibility will be limited to paying the property taxes, debt service on his or her debt, and sometimes repair to the exterior of the building and common areas. If the building is occupied by a single tenant, that tenant may be responsible for exterior repairs as well.

There is, of course, a continuum of leases between the two extremes. Various methods are used in leases to recover the costs of providing the services. The more services provided by the landlord and partially or totally not recovered from the tenants, the greater the risk associated with the lease. In a long-term lease, the spread between the lease payments and the related costs may get very thin near the end. Most commercial leases for periods of more than one year have inflation clauses tied to some popular index. If you are writing such a lease, make sure the index you are tying to actually exists. For example, if you provide for adjustment of the rate of rent equal to the change in the consumer price index for the city of Spokane, and the consumer price index isn't calculated for Spokane, the court will probably find the inflation clause invalid, but

the balance of the lease will be valid and enforceable. The result
would be a long-term lease with no inflation clause.

Another hazard in renting to businesses is that you may be renting to nonpersons, particularly corporations. If the corporation
finds itself unable to pay its bills, it will likely cease to exist. Depending on the pressure shown by its creditors, it may or may not
file for bankruptcy. At any rate, if you have rented to the corporation, you are done collecting rent from this tenant. And this is true
even if the tenant corporation is six months behind on the rent and
the principals open a new business a week later in the form of a
new corporation with leased space from a new landlord. You can
find some protection from this scenario by insisting on personal
guarantees from the corporate officers whenever you are renting
to a corporation. Then, in the event of a default, you may seek to
recover against the assets of the guarantors as well as those of the
corporation.

THE QUESTION OF QUALITY

The question of quality is a part of a larger question of product
identification. If you are considering entering the real estate investment business, you should do so for one reason and one reason only. You should be entering the business for the purpose of
making money. Whether you make money through the renting of a
luxury condominium or through the renting of a low-rent rooming
house should be of little concern. Yet investors prefer to invest in
"pretty" quality properties rather than average or below-average
rental properties. The result of this preference is that better properties tend to be overpriced, and lower-quality properties tend to
make better investments. This is sometimes referred to as the *pride
of ownership trap*. In other words, if the property is particularly
attractive, it encourages investors to invest in it for the pride of
ownership rather than to earn a good rate of return on their investment. You may have pride in your home; you may have pride
in your car; you may have pride in the accomplishments of your
children. All of this pride will cost you something. If you extend
your need for pride of ownership to your investments, you may
expect it to cost you dearly. The return generated by high-quality
apartments and high-quality office buildings, shopping malls, and
the like is not as high as that realized on investments of a more
modest quality. However, because people tend to value these investments, the resale value will tend to remain high. Some people
associate this maintenance of value with reduction of risk and rationalize the low rate of return. I don't buy it. I don't believe that
high-quality units are any less risky than medium-quality units. I

believe they could be less risky than low-quality units for the reasons detailed below, but again, they are not so much less risky as to justify the return they usually generate.

In the rental business, as in any other business, you must identify your product or service and why the consumer should buy from you rather than from your competitors. Your product is shelter for your tenant's household or business. But it is far more than that, or at least it is far more complex than that, since shelter encompasses the many amenities and attributes that set your building apart from all others. There are qualitative and quantitative elements to the question of product identification. For example, a quantitative analysis would note that you have an 800-square-foot, two-bedroom apartment for rent at $400 per month. It would further note that 800-square-foot, two-bedroom apartments in the area rent in the range of $380 to $430 per month. But no conclusion could be reached as to whether or not the rental is competitively priced until the qualitative considerations are examined.

What does your rental offer besides shelter? Look around. What do you see? Newer wall-to-wall carpets, nice views of the parklike setting, carports, oak kitchen cabinets, newer appliances, fireplaces, small decks—these are the items that the tenant is purchasing. Now, how do your amenities compare with those of the competition?

Also, what is the general feel of the property, its ambience? Does the property feel nice and newer or well maintained, or does it feel run-down and neglected? Would a peer-conscious teenager feel comfortable bringing his or her friends to this apartment?

These questions should be considered prior to your acquisition of the property and also during your ownership so that you can determine whether you are making the best use of the property. This will aid you in remodeling and improvement decisions as well. For example, you might speculate that adding microwave ovens would allow for a $20 per month rent increase that would otherwise not be available. You might further believe that the tenants would be happier with the improved apartments and move less frequently, reducing your vacancy rate from 7 percent to 4 percent. On the basis of this information, you could make the determination as to whether or not the expenditure for microwave ovens appears to make sense.

Before jumping into the purchase, however, you must consider the reliability of your information. Hopefully, your rent estimates and vacancy projections are based on reliable data and not just speculation. Ideally, you would be comparing an identical apartment building to yours. The only difference would be that the comparison property has microwave ovens and yours doesn't. Unfortunately, the ideal is never realized since there are always more differences in the buildings than the difference you wish to consider. The other building might be one block closer to shopping or the bus route, it may have a swimming pool, but yours may have saunas. In addition, the buildings will have different managers, which could make all the difference in rent and occupancy. The differences between the buildings you are analyzing other than the difference you are considering are what the statisticians call *noise* in the samples. It is often difficult to determine if the difference in the rent that you are observing is caused by the difference under consideration or by some other factor (the noise). That is why it is important to know as much as you can about your product on a continuing basis. This should improve the quality of your decisions.

We have noted that quality properties tend to have poor rates of return. It should also be noted that, at the opposite end of the spectrum, poor-quality properties are often not the bargain that they appear to be. This is true for several reasons. First, the poor-quality rental units are "management intensive." Four units renting for $100 each will require much more attention than one unit renting for $400. Also, the tenants tend to be a lower economic class of people who are generally less likely to honor their debts. They usually have some kind of problem which is the reason they live in low-quality rental units. Whether or not they are in a position to correct this problem, few rent these units out of choice. The expenses associated with renting lower-quality units generally constitute a greater percentage of the rent than with better-quality units. In fact, you may reach the point where the building is functionally obsolete. This would happen in situations in which the costs of operating the building exceed the rent that the building can generate. At that point the building has no operating value, and its maximum investment value is its salvage value. Although functional obsolescence is unusual, varying degrees of commercial obsolescence are more common. A building becomes commercially obsolete when it is no longer commercially viable in its current form. Old-fashioned retail space or 1930s-style sleeping rooms no longer satisfy the requirements of modern tenants, regardless of the economic group. The result is a high vacancy rate, with the resulting loss in value for the property. Fluctuations in the economy also can have a major influence on the profitability of this type of rental unit, which tends to be countercyclical. During tough economic times, these units may be quite popular for their low rent, but when the economy improves, you may expect the low-end units to suffer from high vacancy.

Areas of low-grade older units are also subject to shifts in fashionability. From time to time, each community seems to rediscover its older, run-down neighborhoods. The units are rebuilt, and it is fashionable to open a small boutique or gallery in what used to be a mission and still has some of the local color but hopefully none of the smell. It may also be popular to live in these areas where, frequently, fashionable condominiums or cooperatives are built out of older buildings. Some investors who correctly predict such a trend have made a considerable amount of money by renovating older buildings. But you must have great timing and make some great bargain purchases before the area is "discovered." Once the trend toward improvements is obvious, it is too late, as the price of the buildings will reflect their newfound potential.

Even if you do get a bargain in a newly fashionable neighborhood, it is a mistake to hold on to the building for too long. You may expect the rapid appreciation to be short-lived. After all, these are older buildings, with older wiring, older plumbing, older heating systems, and the like. Even if the building is completely rebuilt, the district will not have the parking, highway access, or convenience to better neighborhoods that are characteristics of the newer commercial districts. Eventually, the district is likely to decline somewhat again.

INVESTING FOR APPRECIATION IN VALUE

In addition to cash flow, debt amortization, and tax shelter, profit is made on real estate investments from appreciation in value. That is, the property becomes worth more than it was worth when you purchased it. Why should the property become worth more? As a rule, property value is a function of its current income-generating value and the perception of its future income-generating value.

I previously made the statement that you should not buy income property on the basis of projected future income. You remember I asked you to repeat the statement ten times. Well, now I am going to tell you to buy property for its potential to appreciate in value. Then I am going to try to convince you that I am not being inconsistent. If I succeed in this effort, you may be convinced that I missed my calling and should have gone into politics.

When I said that you should not buy property on the basis of projected future income, the point was that you should not over-pay for property on the basis of optimistic projections. The safest way to do this is to limit the amount you are willing to pay for the property to the value of its current income. Chapter 3 discusses the amount you should be willing to pay. A conservative attitude with respect to the amount you are willing to pay will reduce your risk of loss. But that is not to suggest that you should disregard the possibility of appreciation or discount its importance. Rather, you should limit your investments to those likely to appreciate in value.

Appreciation is where the money is made in real estate, in terms of both the magnitude of the potential profit and its favored tax status. Therefore, such appreciation is what you should strive for. The income to be realized from appreciation will often exceed the income from all other sources put together. As will be seen later, the income from appreciation also will largely receive the favored income tax status of long-term capital gains. Now, many will suggest that the income from appreciation is illusory, since it is caused by inflation and has reduced purchasing power. That is, if your property value increases from $100 to $110, you are no better off if it takes $110 to buy what $100 used to buy. In fact, you are worse off since you will have to pay tax on the $10 gain. This apparent anomaly—taxing someone who is no better off—is part of Congress's justification for preferable (lower) rates for long-term capital gains.

There are two factors that make investment for appreciation particularly advantageous. First, the rate of appreciation may well exceed the rate of inflation. This occurs if, for example, you buy property in growing areas where rent levels are increasing more rapidly than the rate of inflation. This is true even if rent levels are not increasing but investors feel that they will increase and are willing to pay for the higher anticipated rent levels. The main reason that appreciation constitutes such a substantial potential for profit is that you will realize a rate of return through appreciation not only on that property you buy, but also on the percentage of the property you finance. You may buy the property by paying 20 percent down, but regardless of the percentage you pay down, your appreciation will be based on 100 percent of the value of the property. The greater your leverage (the lower your down payment and any negative cash flow or additional cash required), the greater the advantage to be realized from appreciation. The following table assumes a 6 percent compounded rate of appreciation and $100,000 invested at various amounts of leverage.

Description	VALUE OF EQUITY				
	10% down	20% down	30% down	50% down	100% down
Property purchased	1,000,000	500,000	333,333	200,000	100,000
Equity value after:					
1 year	160,000	130,000	120,000	112,000	106,000
2 years	223,600	161,800	141,200	124,720	112,360
3 years	291,016	195,508	163,672	138,203	119,102
5 years	438,226	269,113	212,742	167,645	133,823
7 years	603,630	351,815	267,877	200,726	150,363
10 years	890,847	495,424	363,616	258,170	179,085

This table measures only the value of the equity in the various investments and the change in the value of that equity as a result of a 6 percent compounded rate of inflation. It does not consider any possible operating cash flow from the investment, which is likely to favor the less leveraged investments, or any debt paydown, which is likely to favor the more leveraged investments. As the graph indicates, the rate of return from leveraged investments can be substantial. But, before you go out and buy millions of dollars in nothing-down or substantially leveraged properties, remember that the more leveraged the investment, the greater the risk in general and the greater the suspicion surrounding the investment. Both of these concerns will be explored in more detail in Chapters 4 and 7. For now, consider them in the context of qualifying what the table depicts graphically; namely, that leveraged appreciation offers excellent opportunity for substantial gain.

REAL ESTATE AND INCOME TAX—AN OVERVIEW

Chapter 13 considers the relationship between real estate investment and federal income taxation in more detail, but here I would like to consider the general nature of the relationship.

It is perfectly reasonable not to care why real estate enjoys a preferred tax status but simply to understand what that preferred status is and how to profit from it. However, I believe it is enlightening to consider how the relationship evolved, to understand those relationships, and to consider how they are likely to evolve further in the future.

The first income tax law in the United States was enacted to help support the Civil War. Shortly after the war was over, the federal income tax law was repealed. In 1894, another federal income tax law was enacted, despite question as to its constitutionality. Subsequently, the United States Supreme Court determined that a federal income tax was unconstitutional. This interesting decision indicated that any future federal income tax law would require a constitutional amendment. To the best of my knowledge, no attempt was ever made to return the money collected unconstitutionally. As you can see, pragmatism was alive and well in the 19th century and continues to survive and flourish today.

The constitutional amendment occurred in 1913 and was followed shortly thereafter by a codification of the income tax law. The income tax law was rewritten in 1939 and again in 1953. There have, of course, been many revisions within the structure, judicial interpretations of the law, and Internal Revenue Service rulings and regulations, all of which have caused modifications of the federal income tax law. Thus, the tax law is not static but rather dynamic and constantly changing. Real estate has come to enjoy its favored status as a result of this dynamic change in the tax law.

I believe the favored tax status of real estate investments started out as an accident of accounting. The accident is called *depreciation*. Accountants are in love with depreciation; it is a vital element of the "matching principle." Who can imagine where the world would be without the matching principle? For those few of you unfamiliar with the matching principle, the basic principle is that, when measuring income, you must match revenue as closely as possible with the costs of generating that revenue. It's a totally reasonable and logical principle when you think about it. So, depreciation was originally used to measure income accurately, to match the cost of capital expenditures with the benefit of those expenditures. The intention was to spread the cost of a major purchase among the items that benefited from the purchase and thus to match it with income. For example, if a piece of equipment necessary to manufacture your product costs $5,000 and will be used to produce 50 units before wearing out, you could say that the equipment cost per unit of product is $100 ($5,000 divided by 50). To operate profitably, it is important to recognize expenses such as these in pricing decisions. Therefore, accurately measuring costs is necessary to measure income accurately. Originally, depreciation was allowed as a deduction in an effort to accurately measure income. After all, it is an "income" tax.

However, tax advisors are much less concerned with accurately measuring income than they are with planning deductions to produce as low a tax bill as possible. Thus, a building that might be expected to last 100 years was written off over 30 to 40 years or less. Different accelerated methods were used to write off more of the building over a shorter period. We taxpayers were like children, constantly testing the limits of what the law would allow. Congress and the Internal Revenue Service were like parents trying to administer the law fairly. Guidelines were published to embellish the IRS rule that depreciation methods be "regular and systematic." The estimated useful life of assets was a constant source of controversy. In the context of equipment and personal property, the useful life estimate might actually be an attempt to measure the life of an asset. In buildings, however, the question was not so much "What is the useful life?" as it was "How much writeoff will the Internal Revenue Service allow?" So, it was a game. Accountants and lawyers were constantly "inventing" arguments for writing off property more rapidly, and the IRS, in its effort to be fair, was giving a little here and there. One of the more creative approaches was that of "component depreciation." The theory was that a building was not a single unit, but rather an assemblage of component parts. While the building might be expected to have a "useful life" of 45 years, the electrical system would last 15 years, the carpeting seven years, etc. The way the game was played was that the taxpayer tried to apportion as much of the cost of the building as he could into the short-lived components. The Internal Revenue Service was concerned with the individual apportionment and the weighted average rate at which the building was being written off. Both sides were pretending not to recognize that the sole reason for component depreciation was the more rapid depreciation of the buildings.

Much of the game playing ended in 1981 (at least temporarily) with the legislation that introduced the Accelerated Cost Recovery System (ACRS). Under the ACRS system, the fiction of useful lives was abandoned, and even the concept of depreciation was softened in favor of the concept of cost recovery. Rules were adopted to write off assets over 3, 5, or 15 years, depending on the type of asset. Buildings were written off over 15 years. In 1984, the period was changed to 18 years. Different rules were adopted as to types of depreciation methods allowed for residential versus commercial buildings and the severity of the tax penalty if accelerated methods were used.

The 1981 legislation was enlightened, in that it recognized that depreciation deductions for tax purposes were intended not to measure income more accurately, but rather to recover the cost of assets through deductions. The law also had the effect of greatly increasing the tax advantages of real estate investments and greatly reducing the risks associated with useful life estimation. As I will consider shortly, it may or may not have been wise to increase substantially the tax advantages of real estate investments.

It is interesting to note that old rules and concepts do not die easily. Congress has decreed that the tax law will allow you to write off (or depreciate) assets that are not losing value or becoming functionally obsolete and that may in fact be appreciating in value. But they are still not willing to allow for recovery of the cost of land. Traditionally, land has not been depreciable because it does not get used up; its useful life is infinite. While we have abandoned the concept of useful life with respect to depreciable assets in favor of cost recovery, no one has seen fit to apply the concept of cost recovery to land. Thus, when you buy a building and the land on which it sits as an investment, one of the few remaining arguments you are likely to have with the Internal Revenue Service is the apportionment of the purchase price between the land and the building. You will want to apportion as much as possible to the building, where it is depreciable, and the Internal Revenue Service will want to apportion as much as possible to the land, where it is not. And the beat goes on.

Criticizing the tax advantages in real estate is something like biting the hand that feeds you, but I fear that the trends of the past few years could have long-term detrimental effects on real estate investment and, to a lesser extent, on society at large. What I am concerned about is that real estate may become an investment exclusively of the rich, in much the same way municipal bonds are investments generally limited to the rich. This could become the case if the tax advantages of real estate investment become so substantial as to crowd out considerations like cash flow and appreciation. And, even if these considerations are not crowded out, there is the possibility that they will be priced out of consideration by those most able to do so.

Tax shelters have always been a more worthwhile investment for the rich than for others. For example, if you pay $10 and are able to write off $5 without actually losing value, the rate of return is substantially different for those in the 50 percent tax bracket than it is for those in the 20 percent bracket. Ignoring other considerations, the rate of return is 25 percent for the higher-bracket taxpayer and only 10 percent for the lower-bracket taxpayer since the higher-bracket taxpayer will receive $2.50 in tax savings and the lower-bracket taxpayer will receive only $1 in tax savings. My concern is that high-bracket taxpayers may find this return so attractive that they will bid up the cost and bid down the yield of real estate. For example, if $12.50 was paid for the same $5 write-off, the higher-bracket taxpayer would receive a 20 percent return on investment and the lower-bracket taxpayer an 8 percent return. The higher price would reduce the possibility for cash flow and appreciation. Cash flow and appreciation are important to both the higher- and lower-bracket taxpayers but may be important to the lower-bracket taxpayer, who may need to invest for current cash flow as well as for tax shelter and possible appreciation.

Real estate has long been an investment that provided the vehicle for social mobility. An individual could start from scratch and get rich investing in real estate through hard work, ingenuity, perhaps sweat equity and tenacity. It was a "get rich slowly" scheme that rewarded investors with wealth for a long period of work. As will be discussed later, there are still many opportunities for achieving wealth through real estate investment, especially through creative financing and by using other people's money. But what may be lacking is the training that you get when you make small investments on your own before being entrusted with the money of others. I hope we do not reach the point where real estate no longer offers the opportunity for average people to obtain wealth through their own efforts.

GETTING STARTED $\boxed{2}$

You're reading this book and others like it because you think there is a lot of money to be made in real estate investment, and you would like to get started. The first thing I would suggest is that you reconsider. Why do you want to become a real estate investor? Do you intend to use real estate as a social elevator to lift you out of the middle classes? It may do this, but it isn't as simple a matter as stepping into an elevator and pressing the button. Real estate investing, like any field, involves a lot of work. This is especially true in the early stages. It is not something that you should approach casually. And it will absorb a lot of your time. You should not enter the field, in other than a passive investor context, unless you are prepared to devote the time necessary to make the business a success. That may mean painting the trim on a rental house when you would rather be going to a football game. I have listened to a lot of football games on the radio while working on rental property. It also means taking time away from other activities that you might prefer or that might be worthwhile. For example, now that I have young children at home, I realize that they require considerable time and attention. I want to and need to give them that attention. Now would not be a good time for someone like me to get started in real estate investment.

But, for many, real estate investment in its early stages is like a profitable hobby. It is interesting to shop for investment opportunities and to try your hand at repairs and maintenance. There also is the additional security and perhaps cash flow that are provided by the investment activities. There are certainly worse ways to spend your leisure time. Many people who are otherwise bored with most parts of their life, especially their jobs, find that real estate is a release from that boredom. They are actively working to better themselves. Rather than purchase a lottery ticket and dream of possibly becoming rich, the real estate investor has a plan of action to obtain the desired wealth.

The scope of the dreams varies with the investor. Some would like to have five or ten free and clear rental houses providing retirement income. Others dream of building an empire. It is an interesting phenomenon that in real estate, getting there is half the fun. In other words, it is not so much realizing the goals that is important, but setting the goals in the first place and striving to achieve them. A person without a dream is a sad person. If real estate provides you with the capacity to realize your ambitions, or even just to perceive that they *can* be realized, it has provided you with something of value. That is not to suggest that the opportunities available in real estate are merely illusory. The opportunities are very real. But also very real are the costs in terms of both money and time invested and the exposure to the risk of loss. Do not dismiss the risks when you are considering the opportunities.

CONSIDER THE RISKS

Ask yourself this question: What do I have to lose? If you are young and poor, the answer may be "nothing." Or at least it may appear to be nothing. But consider the alternatives:
- What is your time worth?
- Is there something else that you would rather be doing?
- How are you going to feel ten years from now if your real estate empire is crumbling and you have worked at its construction for the ten-year period?
- Are you going to be bitter and resentful?
- Will you rationalize the good and bad experiences that you have had, or will you honestly be able to say that the experience has been worthwhile and you would not have had it any other way?

Of course, it is not fair to ask or answer these questions in advance. No one knows how he or she will react to the potential adversity until it happens. However, it is important to be true to yourself. Unless you can honestly answer that you feel that you will want the experience regardless of the outcome, you should not start investing in real estate.

Sometimes I find it amusing to hear both rich and less than rich people suggest that wealth is overrated. It is a rationalizing statement. When referring to those who are wealthy, people often comment that, despite all their money, they are not happy. They suggest that it might, in fact, be the money that causes unhappiness. In certain cases, this might well be true. But for the most part, it is better to have money than not to have money. Don't fool yourself. For the most part, rich people are quite happy and content. Money can't buy you happiness, but it can certainly lease some pleasure. And those who are treating themselves well tend to be happy.

The first step necessary in acquiring wealth is to acquire a positive mental attitude. Having considered the risk involved in real estate or in any endeavor, you shouldn't dwell on it or become preoccupied with the negatives. You must believe that you can be successful for the success to come.

Your positive mental attitude must, however, be accompanied by ambition. I know some very capable and intelligent people who will never be rich because they lack ambition. Recently, I was riding in the car with one of these people, and our car was passed by a chauffeur-driven Rolls Royce Silver Shadow. My friend said, "Wow, that sure is nice. I wouldn't mind having one of them." I am generally considered a polite person, and I didn't say anything disparaging to my friend, but I thought to myself that this person would never know such wealth and luxury. It is not enough to wish for things. If you want them, you must devise and execute a plan for their acquisition. This plan may require several years of tenacity and sacrifice, which might make you reconsider whether you want the material possessions that much. On the other hand, you might find that striving to achieve the goal may be more rewarding than the accomplishment.

EVALUATE YOUR STRENGTHS AND WEAKNESSES

In considering the various alternative means of getting started in the real estate investment business, it is important to take a serious look at yourself and determine what kind of person you are. There are opportunities available for nearly every personality type. The important thing is to match your personality with the opportunities. For example, are you a salesperson? Some people seem to be born salespeople. They can sell anybody anything. If you have this talent, you are probably wasting your time with rental houses and small investments acquired to get ownership, repair, and maintenance experience. There are many people who are not salespeople, and you are probably better off hiring them to make your repairs and maintenance. Your skills as a salesperson are better utilized in the capacity of real estate agent or perhaps real estate syndication promoter. You will encounter more success in the latter activity after you have some experience.

While knowing your strengths is important, it is at least equally important to know your weaknesses. You must utilize your strengths to secure your fortune. And you must overcome your weaknesses. It is important not to disregard your shortcomings because it is those items that will tend to be your downfall. We all have a tremendous tendency to deny or discount our human failings. Deep inside, we might know that we have them, but we certainly don't want to admit them to others or even show that we recognize them in ourselves. But nobody is asking you to enter a confessional and tell all. Instead, you are being asked to prioritize your strengths. You might be particularly good at some things, less good at other things, and inexperienced but probably competent at others. On the basis of this prioritization, you should consider where your unique talents are best utilized. Find a position or activity that best utilizes your skills.

It is important to work for personal satisfaction, which is at least as important as compensation. If you work those areas where you are skilled, you will tend to find the personal satisfaction that you seek. You will do better work, and you will be happier. If you are fortunate enough that the areas in which you excel are highly compensated, you may well achieve self-actualization. The other side of that issue is to avoid those activities that do not bring you personal satisfaction. It is important that the work and investment experience bring you the positive experience that you desire. "But," you might say, "sure there are things that I don't like to do, like repairing the plumbing on my rental house, but I can't afford to hire a plumber." I am not talking about these occasional activities that don't please you. What I am talking about is activity that you would consider a significant sacrifice. It is important to limit your sacrifice. Do not live at the poverty level in order to set aside money for real estate investment. You will come to resent the investments if they do not perform up to expectations. Don't take excessive amounts of time away from your family. Your children will be young only once, and if you miss it, you can't ask them to go back and start over. No amount of wealth will restore their youth or yours.

SEIZE THE OPPORTUNITY

If you find that you are unhappy with what you are doing, change what you are doing. That sounds like simple advice, yet many people fail to follow it. There are many traps that people tend to fall into that result in their doing work that doesn't make them happy. One trap is the "blue-collar trap." The blue-collar trap is that experienced by working people. They are earning a reasonably good income and spending more than they earn. They have families to support, and credit is available to them, so they are in a position to obligate themselves beyond their means. They never intended to give their entire working life to the company and always meant to better themselves. But, before too long, their personal and financial obligations have trapped them in their blue-collar jobs. They can't afford to quit, and they will be hurting financially if they are required to go on strike. Their dreams slowly fade as their expectations go unrealized. Before they know it, they are middle-aged and have accepted the fact that they will not accomplish what they had hoped in their youth.

There is a similar white-collar trap. This trap affects workers who are generally better educated than those who are suffering from the blue-collar trap. They have completed their high school and sometimes college educations, and they are employed in a job for which they are skilled. They may be appropriately employed, but they perceive themselves as underemployed. They are dissatisfied with their jobs for some reason. Perhaps they are dead-end jobs with no advancement potential. Perhaps the work is not what they had anticipated, and they are disenchanted. Perhaps the boss or other workers have created an atmosphere that is not conducive to a positive working environment. As with the blue-collar trap, the white-collar workers feel similarly trapped by financial and personal considerations. They are, arguably, in a worse position psychologically than those suffering from the blue-collar trap, in that the white-collar workers have done those things that they are supposed to do, in our society, to achieve happiness and yet still find the situation unsatisfactory. The blue-collar workers feel that they know the way out of their dilemma, regardless of whether they have the tenacity to make the changes. But the white-collar workers may feel trapped and not know the way out.

For these workers, real estate may represent a way out of the trap, or it may be a further element in the trap. They may make the same mistakes in their investments as they have made with the rest of their lives, thus setting up a new trap. The primary element imprisoning these people is procrastination. It is easy to do nothing and perpetuate the situation. It takes a disruption of the pattern that has become so comfortable for these people to get up and do something. When you consider what to do to get yourself out of a rut, consider real estate investment, but also consider other alternatives. Do you have other skills that you can capitalize on or that, although not marketable, bring you personal satisfaction? The important thing is to do something today, not tomorrow or the next day, to improve your life. Now, you might say, "My favorite activity is watching TV and drinking beer." I must unfortunately reconfirm what you already know: that nobody is going to pay you for that. If it makes you happy, continue to do it, but don't complain about the quality of your life, because no one is listening.

GETTING EXPERIENCE

Before you rush out and buy something, you should satisfy yourself that the deal you are getting is as good as you think it is. How do you evaluate it if you don't have practical experience? Unfortunately, experience is a lot like credit. You can't find someone who will give you credit or experience unless you already have some. It's a classic "catch-22" situation.

One way to get the experience you desire is to seek employment in the industry. You might seek a job with a property management company, either as an on-site manager at an apartment complex or in the office. You might seek training as a real estate agent. Or you might work in a career that is real estate–related, like law, accounting, or appraising. The point is to study the market in some capacity before leaping in. If you can find a way to combine your training with a compensating profession, it will seem far less costly.

BUY SOMETHING

There comes a time to stop planning and start acting on the plan. Actually, you can continue planning, as long as you go out and make your first investment purchase. It is difficult to break the ice and make that first purchase. You are nearly certain to have second thoughts after signing the contract. But don't worry. You have done your research. You know that the deal is a good one. So have the courage of your convictions and proceed to purchase the property.

If you are interested in getting into the rental property business, there is no better learning experience than the purchase and management of a rental house. You will do everything. You will survey the market, consider several acquisitions, engage in some unsuccessful negotiations, negotiate the contract, close the acquisition, and take possession of the property. You will advertise for tenants, execute the rental agreement, repair and maintain the property, attempt to collect all the rent that is owed you, attempt to pay all the bills you owe, evict problem tenants, and improve the property. You will keep the books and records, file the tax returns, consider the resale of the property, negotiate the sale, execute the contract for the sale of the property, attempt to collect on the contract obligation, and perhaps foreclose on the contract to get the property back. Best of all, you will acquire this experience with a minimum of cost and financial exposure. You will acquire the experience in your spare time, without giving up your current job. You may pace yourself, acquire a second rental house or duplex if you so choose, or sell the first house and withdraw from the business. To enter the business, you will need the down payment on the first rental house and the capacity to service the debt in the event that the property experiences vacancy or the rent is inadequate to pay the expenses and the mortgage payments. You will also want to bring in a little common sense, some humility, and the capacity to learn from your mistakes.

An alternative to buying a rental house is buying some land. You might buy acreage out in the country or a building lot. The property will be bought for speculation. It may or may not produce income. In general, it will cost you money to own the property. You must pay the property taxes and any interest on the debt on the property. You may correctly speculate on the increase in the property value, or you may guess wrong. The experience to be derived from the ownership of rental property will be superior to that acquired from the speculation on land.

Another alternative to the purchase of a rental house is the improvement of your principal residence. Because of the deferral of tax on the gain from the sale of principal residences, it is possible to build a substantial net worth by buying and improving the house in which you live. After you have improved your first house, you will sell it and reinvest the proceeds in another house in need of repair or improvement. This pattern may be repeated several times without federal income taxes depleting your working capital. To defer gain recognition on the houses you improve, you must get into progressively more expensive houses. Those expensive houses will have the capacity for more gain than less expensive houses. They also have a more limited market and more exposure for speculative loss. Hopefully, the experience you acquire on the smaller houses will give you the background and experience to make a profit on the improvement of more expensive houses.

STARTING WITH NOTHING

There is nothing, and then there is *nothing*. Some people have nothing, and others have *nothing*. Some had to think hard about the price of this book and whether it would be self-indulgent to purchase it. Others *really* have nothing—no money, no experience, and no sense. Fortunately, this need not stop you or anyone else from making a lot of money in real estate. What you lack can be acquired from others. And you need pay nothing for it. Since you have an abundance of nothing, this should prove to be no problem. All that you need to be is a great promoter. As such a promoter, you will be able to acquire partners, and those partners will be able to do for the partnership what you cannot.

FORM A PARTNERSHIP

One question that you might ask yourself is just what you have to contribute to the partnership and just what the partnership will provide you. A strong partnership combines the diverse talents and contributions of the partners in such a way that the whole is greater than the sum of the parts. Therefore, each party benefits from the association with the others.

For example, a partner may be able to provide you with the money you need to launch your investment business. But why would someone give you money to invest? Because you are the promoter. You are the one with the ideas. You have done the work to identify the property and to research its potential. In addition, you will assume the responsibility for the management and maintenance. One way to look at it is that all your partner will put up is the money; you will contribute everything else. Who is really getting the better end of the deal? There are many people who have an investment nest egg, but few who can take that nest egg and multiply it. As a promoter, you are providing something of great value to your partners, provided that the investment is successful. And, even in those instances in which the investment proves to be unsuccessful, you will still be providing something of value if you do your best to make the investment a success and circumstances beyond your control are responsible for your failure.

When you become involved in investments through partnerships, the varying contribution of the partners can be recognized by the partnership agreement and the profit and loss sharing agreement. So, if it is determined that the contribution of the working partner is worth one-third of the equity, and the contribution of the financial partner is worth two-thirds of the equity, the partnership agreement may so provide. Also, the agreement may provide that the financial backer is to receive all of the net cash flow until his or her investment is returned with or without interest, if the parties determine that to be appropriate. The agreement among the partners is reasonably flexible. And, for the most part, it will be recognized by the Internal Revenue Service for tax purposes. The IRS provides that, if the sharing arrangement for the profits and losses of the business is other than in accordance with the money each has contributed, such sharing arrangement must have substantial economic effect. Basically, it must reflect economic as well as tax considerations.

The skills and financial strength of the investment group will dictate the kind of investments the group makes and should also dictate the amount of success that may be expected. It is therefore important to become involved with competent partners. If the partners have construction experience, you may determine that the partnership should enter the construction business. Perhaps you will want to build a new building, or you might wish to take the more conservative approach of remodeling or improving an existing building. Another popular approach is to change the use of a building, as in changing an apartment building into a condominium. But, whatever the activity that you and your partners decide on, it is important that you assemble a group with adequate skills to carry it out successfully.

When to Incorporate

For certain business activities that are more actively than passively investing in rental property, you may wish to incorporate. For example, incorporation is very appropriate in the construction business. In that way the individual investors are shielded to a greater extent than they would have been in the general partnership. But don't get the impression that the corporate shield is absolute. There may be attempts by creditors or other plaintiffs of the corporation to "pierce the corporate veil." They may assert that individual corporate officers or investors should be individually liable for claims against the corporation. Whether or not such a suit would prevail depends on the circumstances involved. For example, in new corporations, creditors will frequently ask for personal guarantees from the principal investors or officers for the advances to the corporation. In such a context, the corporation does little to shield the investors from legal and financial exposure.

Limited versus General Partnership

You may determine that there are two types of individuals involved in your project. There are those who will contribute their effort and others who will contribute their money. In such a situation, it is advisable to consider a limited partnership. The general partnership, or the individual general partners, will be composed of those who will be contributing their efforts and who may or may not contribute any money. The limited partners will be those who are investing only money in the partnership. The general partners will be jointly and severally liable for the debts of the limited partnership. But, provided that the limited partnership has been registered properly, and the limited partners do not actively participate in the business of the limited partnership, the limited partners will be protected from claims against the partnership. Their loss exposure will be limited to the amount they have invested.

The Disadvantages of Partnerships

Joining together with others who have either more money or more experience than you is one good way for beginners to get started in real estate investment. And, it may be an effective way for you to grow, comforted by the company of those who have contributed to your success. However, you should consider the substantial cost of the partnership form of business. You are sharing the opportunity of the investment with others. Equity capital is the most expensive capital. It is also the riskiest from the investor's point of view, and that is why it commands such a high rate of return. But it is important to marshall your resources to make effective use of them. Do not casually enter into a partnership with an unproven partner. Not only will you be sharing the profits from the investment with that partner, but you might also be liable for his or her mistakes. As a general rule, each partner has the capacity to bind the partnership, and each is jointly and severally liable for the debts that the others might incur. Your partnership agreement might restrict the capacity of the partner to bind the partnership, and you might argue that the partner is acting in an individual capacity beyond the scope of the partnership, but it is unlikely that the court will be very sympathetic if the partnership has received any benefit. So, even if the partnership agreement restricts the activity and authority of the partner, if he or she enters into contracts with third parties, purporting to act on behalf of the partnership, you may find that the other partners are liable.

In addition to giving up the financial opportunity of the investment to your partners, and bearing the risk of your partners causing you liability exposure, another disadvantage in the partnership form of business is that you give up control. The decisions that you could have made without consulting the opinion of others now require some kind of consensus. You must convince your partners that your ideas should be implemented. This does have a positive side, in that you should consider the input of those whose opinions you respect. But now you are required to consider their input, and should you disagree with the majority of your partners, it is likely that your decisions will not be implemented.

A partnership is both the best and the worst way to do business. In a good partnership, the skills of the partners complement each other, or the partners contribute the money so that the working partner can realize his or her ambitions. In a bad partnership, the partners are dissatisfied with the contributions of their fellow partners. They question their partner's judgment, they are apprehensive about their partner's capacity to legally bind the partnership. Frequently, people make the mistake of going into partnership with friends and relatives. While such a partnership usually has the advantages of trustworthy and friendly partners, it has the disadvantage that the partners have been chosen because they are friends, not because of the skills they can contribute. It is also difficult to maintain a business relationship with a friend or relative. If you go into business with your son, and he screws up, what are you going to do, fire him? Or will you dissolve the partnership with him? Also, what is the strain of the business relationship going to do to your personal relationship? Don't jeopardize your personal relationships over business concerns. It is simply not worth the cost.

People also have a tendency to go into partnership with those who are very similar to themselves. Sometimes this makes sense. A group of lawyers would be expected to form a law partnership. They can perform better as a group by complementing each other's specialty. In fact, it may be necessary for them to work in a partnership in order to have the capacity to specialize. But frequently, it is a mistake to go into partnership with your clone. If your partner is very similar to you, what will he or she contribute that you couldn't have contributed? Instead of finding someone who is similar to you, it is better to find partners who have skills that complement yours.

Some overlap is fine, but split the responsibilities of the partnership so that each partner has clearly defined responsibilities. Do the best job you can in your area and try to avoid second-guessing the work of your partners. Make major decisions, like those affecting acquisitions and dispositions of the property, at the partnership level by achieving a consensus of the partners. But leave the day-to-day decisions about the operations of the business to those who are responsible for them. Try to obtain a proper balance between the rigidity of rules necessary to maintain control over the activity of your partners and the flexibility of authority necessary for them to perform their functions.

GET STARTED

Whether or not you have money, whether or not you have experience, the important thing is to get started—not tomorrow, or after you finish this book. Get started today. Actually, I would like to think that reading this book is a good method of getting started by learning from the experience and mistakes of others. Hopefully, you will avoid some of the same mistakes. If you do, the mistakes will be much less costly than they were to me or my acquaintances. But a lot of people read books and don't put their knowledge into action. This is worse than not seeking the knowledge. The effort represented by this book is intended to provide practical assistance. It is not intended as a philosophical thesis that you should read for its innate value. Obviously, it falls short of the scholarly thesis. The book is valuable; the knowledge is valuable only if put to practical use.

You may not feel ready to take the plunge. You may be nervous and insecure. You know that you will make mistakes and that those mistakes will be costly. What difference does it make? Yes, you will make mistakes. Yes, you will do things that in retrospect seem incredibly stupid. But you will also do things right. You may or may not get rich from the effort, but you will have done something that many do not do. You will have lived. You will no longer approach life as a spectator sport. Instead, you will experience the exhilaration that comes from participation. And if you fail, you will start over—older but wiser from the experience.

Start today. Tomorrow you will be a day older. This doesn't mean, however, that you will ever be too old. In the absence of Alzheimer's disease, there is nothing in age that should disqualify or dissuade you from making real estate investments. Your age is just another factor to take into consideration. As you get older, you may wish to avoid investments that would require you to expend a substantial amount of physical effort on repairs and maintenance. On the other hand, you might use your gray hair as a "money magnet." Since you appear more mature, investors may be inclined to place greater trust in your judgment. You are also never too young. As a minor, you may not have the legal capacity to enter into contracts, but even that is a situation that can be overcome. You will need the cooperation of adults—whether your parents, your guardian, or the family attorney—but you *can* get started. It is very easy to put off starting to invest until you lose the motivation. Don't allow yourself to become trapped by your own procrastination.

LOCATING REAL ESTATE INVESTMENTS | 3

I am reminded of the story of the man who, while walking down the street one night, encounters another man crawling around on his hands and knees. The first man asks what the second is doing and is informed that he is looking for a lost contact lens. The first man begins helping the second in his search and, after an hour of futile effort, asks where the contact lens was lost.

"Oh, I lost it over there by the alley," said the second man, pointing to an area some distance from where the two were searching.

"Then why are we searching here?" asked the frustrated first man.

"Because the light is better" was the matter-of-fact response.

Many times in real estate investment, the potential investors look where it is more convenient to look for investments, rather than where good investments are likely to be found. It is natural to want to find that nice, well-kept rental house at a bargain price in the nicest neighborhood in town, but you won't find it there. One of the things that makes the nicest neighborhood the nicest is that all the homes are well kept and owner-occupied. Rental houses tend to be less well kept than owner-occupied houses, if for no other reason than the tenant's lack of substantial financial commitment to the property and the usually shorter duration of the occupancy.

49

So, you will tend to find rental houses in neighborhoods of other rental houses, with perhaps some smaller owner-occupied houses. This would have the natural tendency to occur, even it it were not for the various zoning laws that tend to define neighborhoods and make the construction therein more homogeneous.

BEGINNING THE SEARCH

DEFINE YOUR OBJECTIVES

When you are looking for real estate investments, it is important to define both your long-term and your short-term objectives. Your long-term objective might be to make an early retirement living from the rental property income. Your short-term objectives should be designed to segment your long-term objective into various attainable and measurable goals. For example, your immediate short-term objective might be the location and acquisition of your first rental house.

FINDING FIXER-UPPERS

Once you have defined your objectives, you can begin your search. If your objective is to acquire a depressed fixer-upper property, your search will be much different from that of a person seeking to acquire a small apartment building. In looking for a fixer-upper property, one strategy you can employ is simply to drive around town, looking for boarded-up houses. Other indications of depressed properties are uncut grass, broken windows, old and tattered For Sale signs, and a generally dirty appearance. You may find the owners of these properties by talking with the occupants and visiting the public records library in the county office building. Fixer-upper properties are sometimes advertised in the classified section of the newspaper, but if they are so advertised, the seller perceives the potential for increased value, and you are less likely to negotiate a superior purchase.

I once acquired a rental house that was advertised in the classified section of the local newspaper under the classification of building lots for sale. The house was an old, run-down, two-bedroom house on a lot that merited much better. The lot sat on the side of a hill and had an excellent view of a lake and a mountain range beyond. The property was owned by the estate of the deceased previous owner, and the heirs lived out of the area. The family attorney was interested in liquidating the estate and distributing whatever cash could be generated. He did not have a high opinion of the property, as evidenced by its advertising classification, and actually considered the house a detriment to the value of the lot. The purchase price we negotiated was lower than the value of the lot without the house. Actually, the valuation would have been appropriate if my intention had been to raze the existing house to build a superior structure on the property. The value of the lot should have been reduced for the cost and inconvenience of removing the old house. But it was not my intention to destroy the old house. Instead, we followed a two-stage improvement plan.

The first stage involved improving the house for rental. This involved painting and making minor cosmetic repairs, as well as installing new carpeting and linoleum. The cost of these improvements was about $1,000. We rented the house for five years with only minor additional repairs. Then it was time to do something more substantial with the property. But rather than tear down the old house, we determined that remodeling was more appropriate. We put $26,000 into improvements that included finishing the basement, remodeling the kitchen, installing thermal windows and doors, laying carpeting throughout, and adding view decks and a swimming pool. Then we moved in. Shortly thereafter, we obtained a mortgage on the property for investment purposes. The appraised value of the property for the purpose of the new financing was about $100,000, and we borrowed $55,000. The price of the original lot and house? We purchased it in the mid-1970s for $8,000.

We found this particular investment property because we were looking for it. It is amazing what you can find when you know how and where to look. But the deals will not come looking for you. You need to get out and find the values.

LOOKING CLOSE TO HOME

It is better to start looking close to home. You are familiar with the property in your area. You can distinguish the better neighborhoods from the less desirable areas. You know where development is occurring and where it is being considered. Also, after you purchase the property, you will have to perform whatever management or other activities are required of the owner. It is more convenient to manage property that is close to your home. However, some investors have a tendency to carry this to an extreme. It is not uncommon to see investors buy up the other houses in the block on which they live. There are some advantages, of course, in living so close to your investments. It is relatively easy to keep your eye on property that you can see from your kitchen window. But there are also disadvantages. Your tenants will probably consider you available for repairs and maintenance anytime your car is in the driveway, and it may not be good business to become too friendly and socially active with your tenants.

The biggest disadvantage is the tendency to pay too much for the property. You might find it peculiar that I would suggest that you would be unaware of the value of property on the same block as your own house. After all, the proposed rental house is probably very similar to the house you own, being of a similar age, size, construction, etc. Surely, an astute investor, living in the same area, should know the value. But, regardless of whether or not you know the value or should know the value, there are several reasons that you are likely to pay too much for the property. First, you are valuing the property as an owner-occupant. You are likely to place a higher value on the property as an owner-occupant than you would objectively place on the property as an investor. Second, you are not in a position to consider the value objectively since you probably have a positive image of your own property and your previous decision to buy the family's home. If the asking price is too high, you are less likely to question it since a high value implies positive things about the property that you don't wish to question.

Finally, there is the human tendency to become a victim of what I refer to as the "monopoly syndrome." Ever since we climbed down out of the trees and wandered out onto the plains, we have been insecure about our territories. We have the desire to be lord and master of all we survey. Also, we feel that it is desirable to build an empire of some sort, to put together something of significance. And buying up all the property on our block would be a significant accomplishment. When we were young, we all played the board game Monopoly. In that game, you are encouraged to buy property in close proximity so that you can trade in your houses for a hotel. Some people seem to think that real life works this way and that it is more desirable to buy the house next door than the one a mile down the road. But unless the neighborhood is changing in character, as is the case when an older neighborhood is giving way to a commercial district, you are simply not going to be able to trade in your houses for a hotel. And you should be willing to pay no more for the house next door than you are willing to pay for a comparable house a mile away.

Still, you shouldn't stray too far from home. You are less likely to make investment mistakes in a familiar area. Eventually, your ambition and/or resources will encourage you to look beyond your local community for real estate investments.

If you do much traveling around the country or around the world, you will find a wide range of property values on investments. You may also find a wide range in construction quality and local regulations governing both construction and the landlord-tenant relationship. These are just some of the many factors that vary among markets and are among the reasons why real estate must be evaluated in terms of the local market.

THE LOCAL MARKET

It is often said that real estate is bought and sold in a "local" market. This statement might seem strange when you read about a Denver apartment bought by a California syndication from a Chicago joint venture firm. However, this transaction, like all others in real estate, is reflective of the local market. What does this mean, and why is it so?

Well, one reason that real estate is bought and sold in a local market is because it is stuck there; you can't move it. And the importance of location in real estate should not be underestimated. According to the old saying, three things are important in real estate investment: location, location, and location. In our complex modern world, other considerations certainly are also very important, but location remains prime among the considerations affecting value and appreciation. Why is this so, and how much effect does location have? How important is a particular corner to a retailer, a view office to a law firm, a particular neighborhood to a resident? The relative importance of these items is reflected in the relative value of the property, but it goes beyond that. If a property is in a prime location, it is more likely to have a quality building on it. This quality building will enhance the property value of surrounding property as well. The surrounding property may then also merit the construction of quality buildings. Each new building will enhance the value of the property on which it sits and the value of surrounding property. New construction will upgrade the area, and a business district will evolve.

THE BUSINESS DISTRICT
The business district is worth examining in more detail:

- How is it defined?
- What are its boundaries?
- What is the relative value of the property within the district?
- Is the district growing, or is it shrinking?
- Are property values within the district appreciating, or is the district becoming run-down?
- What is the likelihood of urban renewal?

As you can see from these questions, a business district is a dynamic thing. It has a gestation period, it is born, it grows, it matures, it declines, and eventually it dies. A new business district may then be born on the ashes of the old.

It is important to recognize the life cycle of a business district when you are considering investing. Life cycle is part of the business district's "definition." Another part of that definition is the center of the business district. The center may be the tallest building, perhaps the newest building, or the center of office space. It may be defined otherwise. The center will command the highest rents; it will have the highest occupancy, perhaps with a waiting list. The center has that certain ambience associated with leadership and success. Many businesses want to or need to convey an image of success, and nothing conveys the image of success like prestige offices in the high-rent district. Conversely, the farther removed from the center of the business district, the lower the rent and prestige. Property value, of course, is a function of the rent it generates and the income it produces. The highest value is at the center of the district, with property getting progressively less valuable the farther it is from the center of the business district.

Another part of the definition of the business district is its boundaries. Frequently, a business district's boundaries will be defined by the topography, both natural and man-made. Water—in the form of a river, lake, sea, or ocean—will generally stop building and form a boundary. Steep hills are not as effective a barrier to development as water, but they often stop or slow down growth in the business district or channel it in other directions. Among man-made obstacles are railroads, highways, and incompatible buildings such as warehouses and hospitals. Man-made obstacles pose more of a psychological than a physical barrier, but that barrier is no less real. It is more than a cliché that a building can be located on "the wrong side of the tracks"; it is an actual economic and physical detriment. Investors are often tempted by what appears to be a bargain on "adjacent" property. This is similar to the theory of buying property in the path of progress. The theory is that the property will increase in value as the business district grows and its desirability as a building site increases. The theory is valid and has been employed profitably by many investors, provided that the property is not separated from the business district by a barrier. The key is to be realistic about the barrier; ignoring it will not make it go away.

Occasionally, development will jump a barrier, as when a business district expands beyond a highway. However, the bet that a development will be successful on the other side of a barrier is a long shot. If the potential rewards are worth the risk, perhaps the investment will be worthwhile, but generally the risk should be avoided. Development is far more likely to follow a path of less resistance.

So, if you are considering investing in real estate within a business district, whether in an office building, a retail building, or land, consider the definition of the district. Position yourself on a nearby hill or similar vantage point and map the area. Walk and drive around the district and consider the ambience. Consider the direction and magnitude of growth. The quantitative factors involved in the profitability of the property will be of paramount importance in the investment decision. These factors will be addressed shortly. What is important here is not to disregard the qualitative factors. These factors are important to the current profitability of the property and will be very important to the appreciation of the property.

A CYCLICAL MARKET

In considering the local market, so far we have addressed the microeconomics of the business district. There are, of course, similar microeconomic considerations involved in residential neighborhoods, retail districts, and other real estate investments. But, in considering the local nature of the real estate market, macroeconomic considerations are of greater importance. Macroeconomics focuses on the overall economic condition of the local market. Economists would object to this definition. When they consider macroeconomics, they are studying the national economy and such things as the money supply, gross national product, and the rate of inflation. When I consider the macroeconomics of a local market, I am also considering inflation, productivity, and the like, but I am recognizing the variability in these factors from one local market to another. Also, the local real estate market tends to exaggerate the cyclical nature of the market economy.

It is the local variation in real estate values and performance that is the most surprising element of the business to novice investors. You simply cannot carry assumptions from one market to another. There is no substitute for researching the market conditions in the particular market in which you are considering investing.

At first, the inconsistencies among markets will appear baffling. Why, for example, does office space rent for twice as much in location A than in location B, while apartments rent for 10 percent more in location B? Why do building standards and expenses vary so much among locations? If you ask questions about these matters, you will get answers, but you may not arrive at the truth. It is important to consider the source of your information and whether that source has something to gain by not being truthful.

The veracity of those in the business and the reliability of the information given to you will be considered in detail later. At this point, it is important to note that these differences exist and that there are logical reasons for the differences. Also, if you understand the reasons for the market conditions better than others in the market, you have the opportunity to realize unusually good profits.

Property values are a function of the rents generated by the property and the net income the property yields. Values are also a function of the perception of what rents and profitability will be in the future. This is true because property tends to be a long-term investment. You buy property not only for the income it generates currently, but also for the income it will generate five years and ten years hence. Like everything else in a free economy, rents are a function of supply and demand. However, because of several factors, a simple measurement of supply and demand is inadequate. In fact, it would be more accurate to say that rents are a function of supply and demand over time, as affected by government regulation and political pressure.

Time is an element in the value of rents because rent is the sale of time. More precisely, it is the sale of the use of property for a period of time. In addition, leases will set rents over a period of time. Even if the rent level is not fixed and static for that period of time, but rather is tied to an inflation index or is otherwise variable, the negotiations will reflect the supply and demand for the rental property at the time of the lease and the perceived supply and demand for property over the term of the lease.

Another time factor is that rents tend to be inelastic and fixed for a period of time, at least for several months. Except where there are peculiar government regulations or unusual lease provisions, rents simply don't go up and down each month. There are generally legal restrictions and notice requirements for rent increases, and there is a reluctance on the part of property owners to lower rents. The result of these various time factors is a time lag in rent adjustments. Thus, in periods of high inflation, rent increases will lag behind other increases. When inflation slows, rent increases may not, and in a deflationary environment property owners will attempt to maintain rent levels. The time lags also mean that the best clue as to what rents will be in the future can be found by looking at the rent levels in the past. Thus, the financial and other history of the property is very relevant.

One of the effects of the time lag that you should be aware of is the attempt of property owners to catch up when a rent increase is implemented. The pattern is a period of relatively flat rents followed by a period of rapid rent increases, followed by another period of relatively flat rent levels. In addition, the periods of rapid rent increase encourage new construction. Either the rent levels may get up to the point where new construction is justified by the rate of return or, more likely, builders will see the rapidly increasing rent levels, forecast continued increases, and build in anticipation of those increased rent levels. The problem is that in building they are adding to the supply of the rental property and decreasing the likelihood that the rent levels necessary to justify the construction will be realized.

All of these factors make for a cyclical real estate market. There will be periods of high occupancy and rent increases, periods of great construction booms, and periods of excess capacity, high vacancy, and falling rents. These periods will vary among local markets, so you may have a prosperous periods in one market and a depressed period simultaneously in another market. Generally, however, tenants are not able to take advantage of the variation in markets. If you work in San Francisco, it is not practical to live in Houston, even though you might like to do so since the rents are so much lower. Similarly, if you are a Washington, DC, attorney, it is not possible to have your office in Detroit. Thus, the San Francisco, Houston, Washington, and Detroit markets will all have their own local characteristics. And those characteristics will have very little to do with the market conditions in the other markets. That is why it is often said that real estate is bought and sold in the "local" market.

REAL ESTATE ADVERTISING

When you are looking for your first investment property, you will inevitably encounter advertisements. The vest majority of real estate advertising occurs in the classified section of newspapers, and the vast majority of those ads are placed by real estate agents. Like any other profession, real estate has its own language, and since real estate advertising is expensive, a shorthand has evolved so that an inexpensive advertisement can contain a lot of information. The combination of the unique language plus the shorthand limits the audience that can decipher the ads. The following list contains come of the commonly used terms, arranged according to the frequency of their use.

GRM refers to the property's gross rent multiplier. This is a figure that compares the asking price on the property to the annual scheduled rent (the annual rent the property is supposed to generate if it is operated the whole year without any vacancy). For example, if a ten-unit apartment has units that rent for $300 a month, the monthly rent is $3,000, and the annual rent is scheduled at $36,000. If the seller is asking $200,000 for the property, its gross rent multiplier is $200,000 divided by $36,000, or approximately 5.55. Since apartment buildings generally sell for gross rent multipliers ranging from about 6.5 to about 9, this would appear to be a bargain purchase. However, considering the gross rent multiplier is only the beginning of the analysis.

Cap rate or **net cap rate** refers to the net capitalization rate of the property. This is a more complex calculation than gross rent multiplier, and it is also more meaningful. The calculation is a comparison of the asking price with the net annual profit of the property before depreciation, debt service, and income taxes. It is calculated by deducting from the income of the property all the expenses of the property except depreciation, debt service, and income taxes and comparing this figure to the price of the property. The rate is expressed as a percentage of the asking price. Thus, a net cap rate of 13 percent on a property means that the property generates a rate of return of 13 percent (before the excluded expenses) on the asking price. Why are certain expenses omitted? Depreciation is a noncash expense, and unless the property is owned until it is functionally obsolete, the expense tends to be an accounting and tax fiction. Debt service payments are omitted because the calculation is an attempt to measure the income the property will generate to service the debt and generate a return to the property owner. In effect, debt service is eliminated to avoid distorting the measurement because of the financing; the measurement is the real return on the property before tax considerations if the property was purchased for cash. Income taxes are not considered because the amount of tax benefit or cost the property will produce depends on the income tax bracket of the owner. The calculation is an attempt to measure the profitability of the property without income tax considerations.

The net cap rate is a sophisticated calculation. It recognizes that the net income from the property is what should be considered rather than the gross receipts. It takes into consideration the fact that expenses that materially affect those values vary among properties, and it disregards those expenses that are usually irrelevant or that depend on the individual owner's situation. It also makes possible the comparison of vastly different properties on a common scale. The only caution I wish to offer is that the measurement is often inaccurate since it relies on faulty data. It is necessary to verify the data carefully and not rely on the information given.

Closing costs down means that the property can be purchased with maximum leverage. You need pay only the closing costs to purchase the property. Presumably, the balance of the purchase price will be financed by the seller or through the assumption of the underlying debt. The terminology indicates that the seller wants to sell the property so much that he or she doesn't propose to realize any cash on the sale but simply wants to avoid paying to sell the property. Therefore, if you pay the transaction costs, you may purchase the property. The prudent investor should beware of properties that the current owner wants to dispose of so eagerly. It may in fact be a good deal, or there may be problems with the property that the current owner may attempt to conceal or at least refrain from volunteering. Also, beware of the fact that the term *closing costs down* is among the most misused in the industry. It implies a minimum down payment, but frequently it includes such costs as real estate commissions, various taxes, loan assumption fees, and a multitude of other costs that may make the acquisition not very leveraged at all.

Cash on cash is the measurement of the cash return of the cash investment in the property. It too is calculated on an annual basis. It varies from the net cap rate in that, while depreciation and income taxes are still not considered, the debt service cost on the property is included as an expenditure, and the rate of return is calculated as a percentage of the cash down payment required for the property rather than the total purchase price.

Split or **split down payment** means that a portion of the down payment will be paid at a date later than the closing date. In an effort to improve the salability of the property and enable those otherwise unable to purchase property to acquire it, the seller is agreeing to defer receipt of some of his or her equity until a later date or dates. This may materially improve the rate of return on the property, since future installments may be paid from the tax savings generated for the owner by the property. However, as with any deferred payment, it will eventually come due, and provision must be made for its payment, if the property is not to be forfeited in conjunction with the due date of the installment.

Balloon payment is a large payment due at some specific future date. The reason for balloon payments is that lenders want to retire their loans within the parameters they consider prudent or necessary. The lender may be a bank that simply has a policy of limiting the period of its loans, presumably to reduce its risk. Or it may be the seller, who is willing to provide financing for the purchaser for awhile but eventually wants to cash out his or her interest in the property. As a purchaser you should avoid balloon payments if possible. Unfortunately, they are becoming more and more a fact of life in real estate investments. The balloon payment due date will arrive, and if you haven't prepared in advance for it, it will arrive much sooner than you realize. Frequently the balloon payment will mean that preferable financing must be replaced with more expensive debt. Sometimes refinancing proceeds will not be available, and the balloon payment may result in the loss of the property. That's why balloon financing is sometimes called *bullet* financing, and the gun is pointed right at your head.

Tax shelter is a curious element to include in a real estate advertisement since real estate is generally a tax shelter. Why advertise a common characteristic? You might as well advertise that the apartment building has a roof. Frequently, if tax shelter is advertised, that is code for an investment that is of questionable economic value. In other words, the seller wants too much for the property for it to make sense as an economic investment, but by paying too much, you will be buying an excellent tax shelter. *Don't do it.* If you are that determined to buy an uneconomic investment, you are unlikely to have an income tax problem for long.

Scheduled income is one of a variety of terms used to indicate the level of income the property is supposed to generate. It is the posted rent times the number of units for the year without consideration of any vacancy or any discounting on the posted rent. Frequently, the term is misused. Often it is wishful thinking at best and outright fraud at worst. The scheduled rent may be presented at $400 per unit per month when the actual rent is $340 per unit per month, and the building is averaging 10 percent vacancy. What kind of recourse do you have against such misrepresentation? Generally, you have none. In presenting such information, a real estate agent usually will include a disclaimer as to its reliability, and unfortunately, the legal doctrine of caveat emptor, or "let the buyer beware," is still alive and well in real estate transactions. It is up to you to verify the financial information you receive (see Chapter 5 for more information on this subject).

Terms are often advertised. Sometimes the specific terms the seller is offering are advertised, as in "Terms: 10% down 20 years 12%." Other times the advertiser will simply say "terms." This may mean that the seller is flexible and is willing to negotiate with the purchaser to arrive at mutually acceptable terms, or it may mean that the seller has specific terms in mind, but has simply not chosen to detail those terms in the advertisement. Terms are very important in real estate transactions and will frequently make the difference between a mediocre and a superior investment.

Fixer means a property that is in need of repair. It is a term used to describe a wide variety of properties in various conditions, from dilapidated shacks to superior properties in need of trim paint. You are supposedly getting a superior purchase since you are willing to assume the responsibility for improving the property and making the necessary repairs. What is being advertised is opportunity. The problems of the seller, reflected in the condition of the property, create opportunity for the person able to correct the problems. Buying fixer properties, improving them, and either operating them profitably or selling them at a profit has been a popular vehicle through which many small investors have become rich. This was explored in Chapter 1. Remember that opportunity and risk go hand in hand. When viewing someone's problem as your opportunity, you may tend to disregard the possibility that the seller's problem could quite easily become your problem.

Diamond in the rough is the name often given to a unique type of fixer property. The real estate agent is representing that the property has unusually good unrealized potential. Also, like a diamond, it takes an experienced eye to identify the potential of the property. A subtle, seductive kind of flattery exists in this type of promotion. The agent intimates that you are particularly knowledgeable in being able to identify the potential that others are missing. Just be careful that the rough is not too rough and the diamond is not glass.

Conversion candidate refers to a property that is currently a rental property but has the potential for conversion to individual unit ownership in the form of condominium or co-op apartments or condominium office or retail ownership. It is implied that the property is of such superior quality and appeal that a homeowner would consider the purchase of a unit. It is also suggested that there are no legal restrictions preventing or significantly impeding conversion. As to the latter matter, please note that the real estate agent is not a lawyer and is not expressing a legal opinion as to the convertibility of the property. Such professional advice must be sought elsewhere. As to the former consideration, it is apparent that the seller or agent has a high opinion of the property, which may make it difficult to negotiate an acceptable purchase price. It is far better for you to determine that the property has conversion potential than to have that potential represented by the seller.

A rule of thumb is: Do not pay for the conversion potential. As with most rules, this is hard to practice since the seller will attempt to realize the potential in the sale. The acquisition should make economic sense as a rental property independent of its conversion potential. If it does, you have breathing room. It isn't necessary to convert the property immediately to avoid feeding the property. Thus, you will have the flexibility to sell the units now or wait for a more favorable market, depending on the economic conditions. As a practical matter, you will have to pay some premium to buy a quality property with conversion potential. Just make sure you avoid paying too much for that potential.

Problem ownership is a feature that is seldom directly advertised but is often intimated. For example, the ad might indicate that the seller is from "out of town" or is "flexible" or "anxious." All of these terms indicate that the current ownership is having problems with the property. Real estate professionals are firmly convinced that there are no problem properties, only problem ownerships. They are convinced of this not only because they have seen problem situations turned around, but also because for business purposes they cannot afford to recognize the possibility that some property is simply problem property. Problem ownership provides unique potential; problem properties present a deadly trap. The ability to differentiate between the two is a skill acquired with experience.

OTHER ABBREVIATIONS

In addition to the previously listed abbreviations you will find that real estate advertisements contain many abbreviations for common features of investment property:

Ba. Bath, usually used to advertise multiple baths.

¾ Ba. A bathroom with a shower rather than a bathtub.

½ Ba. A bathroom with neither bath nor shower, but toilet and basin only, usually advertising extra facilities, as in 2½ baths.

BR. Bedroom. *8 1BR, 16 2BR* indicates a 24-unit apartment composed of eight one-bedroom units and 16 two-bedroom units.

CP. Carport. A structure built to provide shelter for an automobile, with a roof and paved floor but without walls.

Gar. Garage. A carport with walls and doors.

D/W. Dishwasher. Indicates that there are dishwashers in some or all of the units. Do not assume that all the units are so equipped.

Disp. Garbage disposal. Again, do not assume that all the units have garbage disposals.

F/P. Fireplace. Some or all of the units are equipped with fireplaces.

A/C. Air conditioning.

K. $1,000, apparently a derivative of *kilo* in metric measurement. Most often it is used in the context of terms, as in "200K down."

NNN or **net net net.** Refers to a so-called triple net lease, in which the tenant is responsible for all or nearly all of the costs associated with the occupancy of the property. The provision is common in commercial leases but is very rare in residential leases.

Studio. For some reason, this term has very different meanings in various parts of the county. In most places, *studio* refers to an apartment without a separate bedroom, also sometimes called an *efficiency.* However, some places use the term *studio* to refer to an apartment with two or more floors that has the bedrooms at a higher level. In most places, this type of an apartment is referred to as a *townhouse* (see below). Also, in nearly all locations *studio apartment* refers to an apartment in a multi-use building in which professionals conduct business and also reside. Common businesses in such buildings include music and art instruction and everything from collection and detective agencies to law and medical offices.

½BR. Half bedroom refers to a large closet or small room usually adjoining another bedroom with the only access being through the other bedroom. It's incorrect to call the space a *bedroom;* however, it is convenient for housing small children or babies that the parents wish to monitor during the night. The space may also be used as a small office, sewing room, or for storage.

T/H. Townhouse apartment. A large multi-floored apartment with the bedrooms upstairs and the main living areas downstairs. Frequently considered prime candidates for condominium conversion.

W/W. Wall-to-wall carpeting. Since this feature has become so common, it is frequently omitted from advertising.

There are, of course, as many abbreviations as there are people trying to save money on classified advertising costs. The above list is by no means complete. Usually the abbreviations can be interpreted from the context in which they are found. For example, "near U, hosps, prkg" means that the building is located near the university and hospitals and has parking either on the property or nearby. Another example, "1st last dep," means that in order to move in you must pay the first and last month's rent and damage or cleaning or other deposit. If you don't understand what an abbreviation means, ask questions. After all, advertisements are suppose to communicate information, not cause confusion.

OTHER ADVERTISING FORMS

In addition to classified advertising, there are other real estate publications published locally and nationally by real estate exchange clubs and others. These represent a small but growing segment of the market. Also, many homes and condos are sold through open houses, with or without classified advertising support. Sometimes the only advertising for the property is the street signs during the open house.

FORECLOSURE SALES

Another source of information on property for sale is the posting of tax and foreclosure sheriff's sales at the local county courthouse. The property listed on the bulletin board at the courthouse or within the official postings will be offered for sale at a public auction for cash to the highest bidder. The property being sold at the foreclosure sale may be free and clear of all encumbrances if it is being foreclosed by the first mortgage holder, or it may be sold subject to the first mortgage and any other prior debt if being foreclosed by a junior lienholder.

Property being sold though foreclosure sales is obviously depressed. All attempts to bring the property current have met with failure, and the foreclosure sale represents the last recourse of the lender to recover the amount of the debt short of any deficiency proceedings. A foreclosure sale is a terrible way to realize the value of the property. The sale is for cash, generally with at least a 10 percent deposit at the time of the sale and all of the cash due within 30 days. In addition to the lack of financing, the sales are not very well advertised and are not very well attended. Most often the lienholder and perhaps the debtor will be the only interested parties in attendance.

Because of the general lack of interest in this market, foreclosure sales represent an opportunity to realize substantial bargains. However, you must have the cash to make the purchase. Regardless of the relationship you think you have with your banker, do not assume that you can put together a loan to complete the purchase within the 30-day period that the local law generally allows. If you can't bring the necessary cash to the sale to complete the purchase, you have no business bidding. Also, beware of the rights of the debtor and other lienholders. Local laws may provide them with the right to redeem the foreclosed property within a specified period of time. Redemption rights are another reason that sheriff's sales or foreclosure sales tend to yield depressed selling prices.

Whether you locate property through classified advertising, other advertising, exchange clubs, government or private foreclosures, street signs, word-of-mouth or other sources, your next consideration is the value of the property. In order to evaluate the quality of your investment, you must first determine the value you place on the property and compare that value to the price and terms being asked for it. Chapter 4 considers these questions.

VALUING REAL ESTATE: 4
WHAT IS IT WORTH?

APPRAISALS

When you consider the value of anything, you are conducting an appraisal. When you evaluate the value of a property you are considering buying, that is an appraisal. The formality of the procedure you employ may or may not improve the results of your effort. Most real estate agents who have completed a three-hour appraisal course, and all who have had no such course, feel competent to provide you with a market value appraisal of the property you are considering. Most will offer to do so free of charge. And the appraisal is worth exactly what you pay for it.

Some of you, especially real estate agents, may think I am being unduly harsh in my assessment of the value of real estate appraisals. I am not. If anything, I am being generous in suggesting that they have no value, rather than that they have negative value. Unfortunately, in many instances their value is negative. And what is worse is that the appraisals are of highly questionable value regardless of the supposed professional capability of the appraiser. In fact, the situation is so bad that many of us tell appraisal jokes. For example, the MAI appraisals are the most respected in the industry, but they are so bad that a friend of mine suggested that the MAI (Member, Appraisal institute) stands for "made as instructed." In addition, I have heard it said that someone was seeing an appraiser to request an appraisal on his $2,000,000 building.

The two jokes illustrate the disrepute with which I hold the profession. Many others would concur. However, probably few will admit to it or be so blunt. Why is my assessment so negative? Why is the quality of appraisals so poor? And, aside from in deepest confidence, why won't others tell you about the sad state of the profession?

My assessment comes from reading hundreds of appraisals. I have found that, in general, appraisals significantly overstate the value of the property. However, there is little consistency in this. Sometimes the appraisal is close to the actual value, and still other times the appraisal is actually low. In many ways it would be better if the appraisals consistently overstated the value. That way you might discount the value, say, 20 percent from the appraisal and arrive at a realistic value. Unfortunately, this is not possible.

ADVOCACY VERSUS ACCURACY

I believe the reason that appraisals are so poor is that they are seldom ordered in an honest attempt to arrive at the actual value of the property. Instead, they are ordered because the purchaser intends to use them for other purposes. It may be a requirement for a loan secured on the property, or it may be used as a negotiating ploy. There are many other reasons why an appraisal may be ordered, but seldom is it because the purchaser really wants an independent assessment of the value of the property. In fact, the purchaser doesn't want an accurate appraisal, instead, he or she wants the appraisal slanted or exaggerated to suit his or her purposes. For example, if the property owner intends to use the appraisal for a negotiating ploy, it is important to him or her that the value be overstated. If the building is reasonably worth $1,000,000, the owner will want it to be appraised for substantially more; say $1,400,000. Then, on the basis of this appraisal, the owner will advertise that he or she wants $1,200,000 for the property, *a full $200,000 below appraisal*. It makes a nice advertisement since it appears that the owner is substantially discounting the property from its fair value in order to sell. In fact, the owner is still asking $200,000 more than he or she is willing to settle for. However, by indicating that he or she has already discounted the property substantially, the owner is hoping to secure a higher offer than would otherwise be made. The appearance that the seller has already discounted the property will impose an inhibiting factor on the purchaser's otherwise natural inclination to offer less than the asking price. Thus, a $1,400,000 appraisal for a $1,000,000 building is valuable to the purchaser of the appraisal (the seller of the property).

What is the value of an accurate $1,000,000 appraisal? Well, for negotiation purposes it has no value. The seller could suggest that he or she just wants to sell the property for what it is worth. But the purchaser wants a bargain and wants to pay less then the property is worth. Thus, if you obtain an appraisal for $1,000,000 and use it in negotiations, it will decrease the likelihood that you will receive an offer of $1,000,000 for the property.

Appraisals are also commonly used by lenders to support a loan and occasionally by purchasers as a negotiating ploy. In all these instances, the appraisal is obtained for advocacy, not accuracy. But appraisals can only be misused so significantly if the profession is willing to cooperate. For example, auditors are under similar pressure to misstate financial statements, and yet the accounting profession has a very favorable reputation for veracity. Appraisers, on the other hand, not only accept influence by the client, but most often solicit input from the client as to the purpose of the appraisal and the value that the client is seeking. I don't mean to suggest that the client can obtain any appraised value desired; however, through various mechanisms the client can exert substantial influence on the value obtained. If you understand what an appraisal is, how it is compiled, and why, you will be in a position to consider whether or not the appraised value is reasonable and in what areas the value has been unduly influenced.

THE APPRAISAL PROCEDURE

In its most basic and elementary form, an appraisal is an estimate by a real estate agent of the market value of the property. The agent will prepare the estimate at your request because you have told him or her that you might be interested in selling the property. The appraisal may be oral, or the real estate agent might put the estimate in a brief one-page letter. What the agent purports to provide is a free market analysis. It is, of course, not free since to obtain it you must endure a sales pitch while the agent seeks your listing of the property for sale. The extent of the work the agent does will not be obvious from anything you receive. At the low extreme, the agent may do nothing at all other than receive your description of the property and respond with an estimate of what the property would sell for. Indeed, he or she may not even look at the property. However, the agent will probably at least go to the effort of going out and walking through the property. Then, he or she will estimate the market value of the property. How the agent goes about making this estimate depends largely on how responsible the agent is.

Using Comparable Property

The best method is to compare the property with comparable property that has recently been sold. If the comparison property is truly comparable, and the transaction was made at arm's length between two unrelated parties, neither of which sold or purchased under duress, the comparable sale may shed light on what the two parties to that transaction consider the value of what appears to be a comparable property. If one comparable sale is good, two or more comparable sales must be better. And a responsible appraiser will seek several comparable sales so that the measurement is not distorted by peculiar differences among the properties. Usually, the appraiser will represent that he or she has considered several comparable properties in arriving at the estimate. However, the appraiser will decline to provide you with the addresses of the comparables since he or she has not obtained the permission of the property owners to use their properties for comparison purposes. If this has been represented, you really have no way of ascertaining whether the agent has really done the work represented. You may wish to obtain a second opinion or even a third or fourth.

THE LISTING AGENT'S APPRAISAL

When a real estate agent gives you a market value appraisal, what the agent is really doing is estimating what he or she thinks the property will sell for. The agent is seeking a listing from you to sell the property for a commission. The listing is a legal document in which the agent agrees to expend his or her best efforts to sell the property, and you agree that, if the agent presents an acceptable purchaser at the price and terms agreed to, you will pay the commission. Let's assume, for a minute, that you wish to sell a house, and you have called three real estate agents for market appraisals. Each has come out to the property and looked around. Each has taken notes, gone back to the office, and written you a letter containing a value estimate. Also, each has suggested that you ask about 10 percent more than the estimate because "you can always come down, you know," and to arrive at the price indicated you should ask more and negotiate down. The problem is that the estimates are $105,500, $107,000, and $115,000. You wish to hire one of the agents, and this is all the information available to you. Which one of the agents do you hire? Well, perhaps the one estimating $105,500 is the most realistic and will sell the house more quickly and with less inconvenience than the others. Perhaps the one estimating $107,000 is realistic but is more ambitious than the one estimating $105,500. Maybe the one estimating $115,000 is the most ambitious of all three.

If you are typical, you will list with the agent who claims to be able to sell the property for the most money. After all, what do you have to lose? You won't owe the agent a commission unless the agent actually produces a buyer at the asking price. However, you may be giving up the services of one of the other agents that would have resulted in the property's sale, in the hope of getting a price for the property that is unrealistically high. At least two agents think a price of about $106,000 is realistic. You should consider the possibility that the third agent is engaging in the common and disreputable practice of "buying" the listing. This agent may know that the property will sell for about $106,000, but he or she also knows that you want to be told that the property is worth more. By telling you that it is worth $115,000, the agent will get the commission. When the agent brings you offers of $102,000 and encourages you to counter at $106,000, he or she will recognize your disappointment and express sympathy. You will rationalize that it appears that the other agents were right, but at least the property is being sold. However, if the agent gets listings by engaging in this practice on a regular basis, how much time will the agent have to devote to the sale of your property? Do you wish to do business with someone who exhibits this kind of business ethics?

Agents who buy listings do more damage to the real estate market than is apparent on the surface. They give sellers an unrealistic assessment of the value of the property and impede transactions that would come together more easily if the parties were more realistic. Also, disreputable agents make it more difficult for reputable agents to remain that way and earn a living. If one agent regularly buys listings, before long the practice will become prevalent in the market. Unfortunately, the practice of buying listings is common in most markets in the United States.

MAI APPRAISALS

While the less formal real estate agent appraisals are probably the most numerous, those considered the most valuable are prepared by professionally trained and educated appraisers. There are several organizations licensing appraisers of professional quality, but the most predominant and respected appraiser is the MAI appraiser. What sets the MAI and other professional appraisers apart from the masses of amateur appraisers is the methodology, not necessarily the results. Appraisers are called upon to express an opinion as to the value of the property. They are, in effect, asked to render an opinion as to the value based on their superior knowledge, training, and experience. How does a professional organization license good judgment? It can't. Therefore, the MAI does the next best thing, which is to train its members to use a methodology that eliminates most of the subjectivity from the appraisal. If the discipline is established and followed, the result may not be accurate, but at least it will be supportable. The problem with eliminating subjectivity is twofold. First, you really can't eliminate subjectivity. As will be seen below, there are many areas in the appraisal process where subjective judgment is required. Second, the appraisers are in the habit of relying on the methodology rather than resorting to that rare, uniquely human characteristic of common sense. When the appraisal procedure results in a value estimate far removed from what the property is worth, or what anyone is willing to pay for it, the undaunted appraiser proceeds to issue his or her appraisal anyway. This is because the appraiser can rely on the methodology to escape professional liability. The appraisal contains his or her assumptions and disclaimers and notes that the appraisal is merely an opinion as to the value at a particular point in time. The appraiser does not render an opinion as to the value one week prior to or one week subsequent to the date on the appraisal report or at any other time. These disclaimers have resulted in the remarkable ability of appraisers to avoid litigation and liability. They are simply not held responsible for errors in their estimates, even though investors rely on the information to their detriment, provided that the appraiser strictly adheres to the methodology.

So, appraisers, pressured by the client to arrive at a certain value, have virtually no legal restrictions preventing them from giving in to the client's request. The only real constraint is that of personal reputation. If the appraiser wants to be in the business of providing appraisals for banks, he or she must develop a reputation for reliability and conservative judgment rather than exaggeration. This constraint is real but reasonably pliable. Since banks will loan to only a fixed percentage of the building's appraised value, say 75 percent, the appraiser can make a substantial error before the bank would lose any money. Also, there are enough less reputable people in the profession who do enough work for buyers and sellers of property rather than banks to assure that the appraisal purchaser will always be able to buy pretty much what he or she wants.

MAI appraisers use a three-pronged approach to valuing property. They consider the income approach, the replacement cost approach, and the market value approach in appraising improved property. Usually, the replacement cost approach is not considered in appraising land.

The Income Approach

The income approach focuses on the income that the property will generate. Then it considers what a reasonable rate of return is on an investment of this type and derives the value. For example, if the property is thought to generate a return of $100,000, and the appraiser determines that a 13 percent return is reasonable on a property of this type, he or she will determine that the value of the property is $100,000 divided by .13, or about $770,000 using the income approach.

The problems with the income approach lie in the accuracy of the income and expense information provided and the subjectivity of the rate of return. The appraiser is not an auditor and will generally rely on income and expense information provided by the property owner in determining the income from the property. While gross misrepresentations will not get past the appraiser, the owner can substantially influence the appraised value by inflating income and shaving expenses here and there. The appraiser will note the source of information and disclaim responsibility for its accuracy. As to the question of the rate of return, this is a very subjective determination that will materially affect the value derived. For example, if the appraiser chose a return 1 percent higher or 1 percent lower than the 13 percent chosen, the value would vary from about $715,000 (at 14 percent) to about $833,000 (at 12 percent). So, why was the 13 percent figure chosen? Supposedly the appraiser considers the various factors involved in determining the reasonable rate of return for this investment and, using his or her judgment, derives a rate. Among the factors that should be considered are the risk and illiquidity of the investment, the tax benefits from the sheltered cash flow and write-offs that the building will generate, and the appreciation potential of the property, given its age, upkeep, and the like. However, I think it is unlikely that much consideration goes into the determination of this rate of return. I would suggest that usually it is a seat-of-the-pants estimate of what the appraiser considers reasonable. Worse, I think the rate often is derived from the result that the appraiser wishes to obtain. In our example, if the appraiser wants to obtain a value of $833,000, a rate of 12 percent will be used. If the appraiser wants to obtain a value of $715,000, a rate of 14 percent will be used. Each factor is unique, and there are enough other factors to consider that the rate is supportable if the appraiser is at all creative.

The Replacement Cost Approach

The replacement cost approach is less subjective but is also considerably less relevant. The approach is to consider the cost of replacing the property with new construction. The value of the land and that of the improvements are considered separately, and generally the personal property is disregarded or included only at its depreciated value. Real estate is supposedly bought and sold on the basis of the income it will generate now and over its useful life. What it would cost to replace that property has little to do with the value except as it imposes a constraint on the income that the property will generate.

Usually, property sells for less than its replacement cost. This is true for several reasons, including the substantial inflation in construction costs and the fact that the used property is not as attractive as new construction. The attractiveness of the property will influence the amount of rent it will generate and the appeal it will have to a new owner. So, under normal circumstances, the replacement cost of property will impose an upper limit on the value of existing property. However, under unusual circumstances, property may actually sell above its replacement cost. For this situation to occur, the property must be generating abnormally high income, and there must be something preventing new construction. These elements are related in that the income may be high because new construction can't compete. The supply of replacement property is limited. What would cause a restriction on new construction? Well, high interest rates prevent a lot of construction by making it economically infeasible.

Location also may be very important here. If there is a limited amount of good space on which to build, which is always the case to some extent, the existing buildings will have an advantage. Zoning and construction restraints will also have an impact. For example, many well-meaning bureaucrats will get restrictions enacted that require such things as the inclusion of a certain amount of low-income housing in a development plan. This requirement will reduce the viability and attractiveness of new construction and may well restrict its supply. Also, when laws change that would affect new construction, there is usually what is referred to as a *grandfather clause*, which allows existing buildings a variance from the new restrictions. Grandfather clauses can make existing buildings unique, and restrict the competition from new construction. In that circumstance, their value may well exceed the cost of new construction. Sometimes the value of new construction would be completely irrelevant since new construction is not permitted. One example that comes to mind is a shoreline management act with which I am familiar. The act recognizes that the general public has an interest in the construction on the shoreline lands, whether those lands are private or public. The act imposes permit requirements for new construction within a certain number of feet of the shoreline and disallows the construction of residential apartments, condominiums, or houses on piers over the water or tidal lands. However, as with nearly all legislation of this type, there was a grandfather clause that allowed for the maintenance of property of this type, constructed before the effective date of the legislation. So the existing pier apartments became unique and therefore not subject to the competition of new construction. Before too long, their value appreciated to well in excess of their replacement cost, and the rents they commanded reflected the limited supply of these unique units.

But the circumstances in which the replacement cost is exceeded by the market value of property are unusual. Generally speaking, if the market value is approaching the replacement cost, the buyer will construct new buildings rather than buy an older building. Therefore, as a rule of thumb, I would suggest that, if you are considering the purchase of a building that is more than five years old, your purchase price should not exceed 75 percent of the replacement cost. This figure should be more than the original cost of the building, reflecting appreciation of the prior owner, but from your point of view, the rule will provide you with some margin of comfort from competition from new construction. This is because the sale's price should reflect the market and the income that the property will produce, and if that income yields a price that is 25 percent below the cost of new construction, it follows that the general rent level for units like the ones you are considering would have to increase by 25 percent before the new construction is justified. If rents go up, you will, of course, benefit. If they go up so much that new construction makes economic sense, your rents should more than offset the vacancy that the new construction is likely to cause. However, you can't be certain that new construction won't be built, even though it is uneconomic. New projects may 'be built in anticipation of higher rent. But your 25 percent "discount" on the price of new construction makes new construction unlikely. And in the event that it is constructed, you have the capacity, because of your reduced costs, to be more competitive.

The Market Value Approach

The market value approach is the best, most relevant measure of value available. It is less subjective than the income approach since the appraiser doesn't have to speculate as to what rate of return is appropriate. It is also more relevant to the sale of existing property than is the replacement cost approach. According to this method, the property is compared with a number of similar properties that have recently been sold to arrive at an estimate of the worth of this property as reflected in those prior sales.

As with the other approaches, the value of this estimate depends on the quality of the data being considered. Here, the primary concern is with the comparable properties being considered. Since all properties are unique to some degree, the first question is whether the comparable properties are truly similar enough to be considered comparable. The nearer the comparable properties are to the subject property, the better in terms of both physical location and physical characteristics such as the number of units, their age, configuration, amenities, and construction. Sometimes, when the property is large or unusual, as in a single-purpose building, it is necessary to obtain a comparable property from a different economic area. This should be avoided, if at all possible, because of the local nature of the real estate marketplace. However, if you are considering the value of a large shopping mall in a metropolitan area, it would be better to get a comparable from another metropolitan area than it would be to compare the property to a strip center or neighborhood grocery store that just happens to be located nearby. The point is to obtain the property that is the most comparable to the subject, recognizing that no two properties are exactly the same. In reading the appraisal, pay close attention to the comparables to consider how similar they are to the subject property.

The next question is: How accurate is your information about the comparables? As I indicated previously, it is difficult enough to get reliable information about the property you are considering. How do you expect to get reliable information about properties that you only wish to use as comparables? I feel that appraisers are far too inclined to assume that this information is accurate. They face quite a dilemma. The client wants an appraisal for the lowest possible cost. He or she intends to use the appraisal for the various purposes considered previously and would like to have it done yesterday. The client may or may not care about the quality of the work performed but definitely wants it to look professional. However, the client is probably not willing to pay to have the books and records of the subject property audited, and he or she is certainly not willing to have the books and records of the comparable properties audited. The appraiser is caught in the middle between what is necessary to do a good job and what the client is willing to pay for. Therefore, the appraiser is constantly using information of questionable quality.

Producing the Final Value

After considering the various measurements of value, the appraiser is put to the subjective test of considering which is the best measurement of value and to what extent the other measurements should be taken into consideration. For homes, the replacement cost and market value approaches are most important; for land, the market value approach; and generally for income property, the income and market value approaches.

The net result of the effort is a single dollar value estimate of the value of the property at a single point in time. The appraisal itself will be many pages long, but all of the information contained in the report is support for the estimated value. It is evidence that the appraiser has done the work claimed and that the methodology is supportable. It looks professional.

In reality, the appraisal looks better than it really is. I have indicated those areas where the procedure is lacking or subject to undue influence from those with an interest in the outcome. But, in addition to the other problems, there is a fundamental problem with the concept of appraised value. That problem is that it is naive to suggest that the value of the property can be stated at a single value. Instead, the value varies depending on the quality of the financing. For years, the appraisers ignored the financing on the property. Now, the appraisal states that the value is for a cash purchase and assumes average financing. If the financing on the property is particularly attractive, the appraiser might adjust the value to reflect the value of the favorable financing. But generally, appraisers disregard the financing. How can they do that? How can they disregard such an important element in value determination as the financing on the property? And why don't they recognize the variability in value that would result from interest rate and financing variables? Well, it is important for appraisers to arrive at a specific value. They think that the client is looking for a specific value and would regard a range of value or anything different from a specific value as a cop-out.

The appraisers are probably correct in their preception that the general public, including their clients and the users of appraisals, are looking for a specific value of the property. However, at least part of the reason that clients are looking for a specific value is that they have come to expect it from the historic practice of the industry. If the industry reflected the greater sophistication to which I believe we are entitled, the clients would come to appreciate the improved work product. And I feel that there is no excuse for not considering the relative value of the financing when considering the value of the property. It is simply too important to the consideration of value to be disregarded. In many cases, the financing will be unspectacular, reflecting the current market conditions of variable rates and short-term balloons. In those cases, the financing will not augment the value of the property and may in fact diminish its value. However, in those instances where the financing existing on the property or offered by the seller is substantially superior to that of the marketplace, it should be considered in the determination of value.

In summary, I feel that the current state of appraisals at all levels is very poor. I believe that they are more often misused than used for legitimate purposes or at least more often influenced than used to obtain an accurate unbiased estimate of the value of the property. The users of appraisals are responsible for the abuse, but the appraisal profession has contributed to the sorry state of affairs by failing to prohibit the kind of abuse common to the industry. Also, the appraisal profession is not very sophisticated either in considering elements affecting value beyond the scope of its methodology or in recognizing inadequacies in applying the methodology.

Unfortunately, you can't expect the profession to change. Too many people have an interest in maintaining the status quo. Unless the real estate, banking, and insurance industries demand a better-quality product and better-quality analysis, without client influence, the industry will remain the same.

VALUING REAL ESTATE BEYOND APPRAISALS

Now, after spending several pages telling you that appraisals are not worth the paper they are printed on, I am going to tell you to use them. Don't use them naively. Recognize their limitations and inaccuracies, but if an appraisal is available, use it as a starting point in determining the value of the property. Also, use the appraisal technique. Consider the market value, income approach, and replacement cost of the property. Do a better job than the appraiser would of verifying data and confirming the reliability of the comparables.

The important step is to carry the analysis beyond the scope of the appraisal. Appraisals are designed to estimate the value of the property as of a single point in time. They do not consider the appreciation potential of the property except tangentially as it might affect the market value of the comparables. Otherwise, the appraisal considers only how the property is performing and is valued currently. The income approach is for the current period. The replacement cost is that currently in existence. Even the comparables are of property that has sold in the recent past. However, these sales should reflect expectations for the property in the future.

As I stated earlier, you should not buy property on the basis of future expectations, but rather on current financial strength as supported by the financial history of the property. The current income from the property should place a limitation on the amount you are willing to pay. But you should buy only property that has excellent appreciation potential. So, consider the economic environment of the property and its likelihood for appreciation.

THE CYCLICAL MARKET

Also consider the risk that the property will depreciate in value. In doing this, you should consider the cyclicity of the market, as well as the general economic trend for the area. I recently considered buying and syndicating a large apartment complex in Houston, Texas. The complex appeared to be running efficiently under adequate management, with a vacancy rate of about 4 percent. It would produce a positive cash flow on a relatively low down payment of around 10 percent split over two years. The property would continue to produce a positive cash flow as long as the expenses remained relatively stable and the vacancy rate remained under 10 percent. Physically, the property was impressive, with well-maintained brick buildings in a garden court configuration. It appeared to be an excellent purchase. However, when I checked the census data, as provided by the local apartment owners' association, I found that in this particular census area the vacancy rate had climbed to in excess of 20 percent twice during the preceding five-year period. The market was very cyclical. Rents appeared to be moving up rather constantly, and property values appeared to be increasing, but the cyclical market imposed too big a risk, so we didn't make the purchase. Sure enough, within nine months the vacancy for the area exceeded 30 percent. Had we completed the purchase, we would have had significant negative cash flow, which we would have had to service (pay) to avoid losing the property. Similar properties were selling for substantially less money nine months later because expectations for the area had changed significantly. On the basis of those sales, it would have appeared that we would have had no equity in the property nine months after our purchase.

So, am I telling you to avoid cyclical markets? No. A lot of money can be made in cyclical markets if you buy and sell at the right time. What I am telling you to do is to consider the cyclical nature of the real estate market and to use the old stock market technique of buying low and selling high. This is, of course, much more easily said than done. It involves contrary thinking and is not without risk, but the rewards may be substantial. You will find that the market has a very short memory. When times are good, vacancies are down, and rents are up, the participants will forget the bad old days of high vacancy and low rents. They will price their property as though the good times will last forever. On the other hand, when the market is hurting, those who have not jumped off their delinquent buildings will literally give them away to end the pain. Nothing-down deals will proliferate in such a market, where the seller is just trying to find someone to assume the negative cash flow.

In an extreme example of a soft market deal, a former acquaintance of mine was actually paid $50,000 to purchase a large apartment complex from a group of dentists. The dentists were personally liable for the debt, and they needed someone with a strong financial statement to satisfy the bank and relieve them of their liability. In addition to the debt relief, the $50,000 paid to the purchaser reflected the fact that the buildings, operating as they were, would not support the debt and were not worth the amount of the underlying debt. The purchaser was buying a complex that was "a bridge too far" removed from the economic area in which the tenants might work. The apartment complex was on the fringe of development, and a stalled local economy made the units surplus. Nicer, more convenient apartments could be rented for less. The dentists were stuck with a financially debilitating white elephant. But the purchaser proceeded to paint it gray.

When he purchased the complex, the occupancy was about 20 percent. Most of those tenants were new to the area and unfamiliar with the local market. Their occupancy was short-term as they found a better deal and moved. The apartments were new and very nice, but the rent was overpriced. The purchaser immediately reduced the rents 30 percent in an effort to reduce turnover. The immediate effect of this was that a bad situation was made much worse because of a reduction in receipts. But the rent reduction was a calculated risk designed to increase the occupancy. The purchaser could break even at lower rents with approximately an 85 percent occupancy. The overall vacancy rate for apartments ten miles closer in was about 10 percent. What he had to do was to find a way to "move" the complex ten miles closer to the industrial area that was some 20 miles removed. What he did was to lease two 12-passenger vans and to offer tenants free transportation to and from the factories. With three shifts, the two vans were able to transport 66 tenants to and from work. The service made the apartments more popular than those closer to the factories. It was not provided without cost and inconvenience to the property owner but the effect was worth it. The 104-unit apartment complex became profitable within six months of the purchase. And the purchaser never did put any of his own money into the property. As he would tell it, "the cash flow zeroed out and became positive just about the time the $50,000 ran out." His goal had been to turn the property around without having to dip into his own pocket, and that was accomplished.

THE STABLE MARKET
Opportunities are also available in more stable markets. The risk is reduced, and usually so is the expected rate of return. For many people, however, a lower return without the risk is a better deal. Not everyone has the personality to live in an environment of substantial risk. Fortunately, there are markets that are considerably more stable than those just described. Every market has a degree of cyclicity, but some are much less cyclical than others. What is important to realize is that, in even the most stable of markets, you should beware of buying at the top of the market. A softening in rents and occupancy of even a few percentage points can materially affect the value of your investment.

The difficulty in buying low and selling high lies not in buying low but in selling high. It is easy to identify depressed markets in which bargain purchases may be made, but real estate is a long-term, illiquid investment, and it may take some time to sell it for what you feel it is worth. If you must sell it in a hurry, you will almost certainly have to discount the price. Therefore, you should allow yourself some lead time in the sale. If you offer the property for sale when you see the market peaking, you have waited too long. By the time you can complete negotiations for the sale, the market will be declining, and the price will have to reflect the reduced expectations.

Seasonal factors are also relevant. Property generally looks best in the late spring—after the snow melts but before the grass turns brown. It should be cleaned up, touched up, and generally made more presentable for the prospective purchaser. Leave nothing with which a prospect can find fault. Make the property look as if it is worth the asking price, but don't get upset when a prospective purchaser offers substantially less. It is not an insult to offer less than the property is worth; it is just part of negotiations. For further information on preparing a property for sale and negotiating the sale, see Chapter 9.

The best way to assure yourself an adequate price on the sale of the property is to start with a bargain purchase. The next step is superior management and the realization of the potential of the property, followed by aggressive but realistic expectations for the sale. In going through the time and effort of analyzing the property, your goal should be to obtain a bargain purchase. Do not strive for mediocrity. Anyone can make an average purchase. Your effort should be aimed at the realization of instant equity as the result of obtaining a property that is worth more than you are paying for it. But beware of being a pig. Remember that pigs are the ones that get slaughtered. If the deal seems too good to be true, it probably is.

THE VALUE OF THE PROPERTY TO YOU

Up to now, we have considered the value of the property to the marketplace. That is, we have considered the value that the market puts on the property. But the value that the market places on the property may or may not be the value that you place on the property. In general, the appraised market value of the property should be thought of as an upper limit on the possible value of the property to you. If you feel that the value of the property is in excess of that indicated in a good appraisal of the property, you should still refrain from offering more than the appraised value for the property. You should consider the possibility that you have an inflated impression of the value of the property. The value of the property is probably less than its appraised value and almost certainly doesn't exceed the appraised value.

In considering the value of the property to you, consider your net worth and what the property does for you. The deductions from depreciation on the property shelter your other income and result in a lowering of your tax bill. Compare your income tax bill with and without a proposed investment, and you will be able to quantify this advantage. If you compare this advantage to your investment in the property, you will be able to express this advantage as a percentage return on investment. The other advantages of property ownership can be quantified similarly and the overall rate of return on the property calculated.

The next question that you must answer for yourself is whether or not the calculated rate of return on the property is enough. You have other uses for the money, both in terms of other investments and for consumption, and you have to determine if it is worth forgoing these alternatives uses for this investment. Now, you may calculate that the rate of return on this investment is expected to be 30 percent, and you might determine that alternative investments of comparable risk and illiquidity do not produce as good a yield, but you still should refrain from making the investment if your need for current consumption requires that your investments remain liquid or that you forgo any kind of risk.

After you calculate the rate of return you expect from the property at the price and terms you are considering, you must consider whether or not it is adequate. If not, you must find a way to increase the yield. Conversely, if the rate that you determine exceeds your minimum investment threshold, consider whether or not it might be necessary to adjust your offer in a subsequent round of the negotiations and where you might be able to give a little. But never adjust the price and terms of your offer unless it is necessary. Get the best deal that you can and never indicate to the seller that you were willing to pay more. Show the seller the courtesy of maintaining his or her illusion of getting the most possible out of the investment. This little courtesy costs you nothing.

NEGOTIATIONS 5

Real estate is bought and sold through negotiations of the principals, usually assisted (or hindered) by agents. The procedure is little different from the purchase of clothing at a Latin American market. Sellers start out asking far more than they expect to get, and purchasers offer far less than they are willing to pay. With each offer and counteroffer, the parties get closer and closer together until either they arrive at a price and terms acceptable to both parties or the negotiations break off.

This analogy illustrates an important element in negotiations that is usually overlooked by the novice; namely, negotiations are not something you win or lose. Instead, negotiation is the art of skillful compromise. You must satisfy the needs of the other side at the least cost and inconvenience to you. If you are determined to "win" the negotiations, you will focus on only your needs and objectives, disregarding those of the other side. As a result, you severely limit the possibility that you will negotiate an acceptable deal. And worse, whether or not you negotiate a deal, you will cost yourself money. It is expensive to negotiate deals that aren't completed, and there are much better uses for your time. If you have disregarded the needs of the other party but still manage to put together a deal, it probably won't be the optimum deal for you. By focusing on your needs only, you will probably offer more than the other side needs, in either the price or the terms. If, instead, you train yourself to listen to the needs and objectives of the other side, you may find a way to accommodate those needs and objectives. At the very least, you may save yourself a lot of time by realizing that you and the seller are not likely to compromise on your competing needs and objectives. In either event, it pays to listen to the other side.

THE BUYER'S POSITION

Unless you inherit or are otherwise given something to sell, you will enter your first negotiations as a buyer. Initially, you will be at a disadvantage because you will have less skill and experience than the seller. However, you also have a significant advantage that you might well overlook. That advantage is that you have many possible properties to buy, while the seller has only a limited number of properties to sell. You may shop around and consider the best deal, while the seller is a merchant with one product on the shelf. The seller must make that one product competitive. If he or she is unwilling to do so, you should let him or her sell the property to someone else.

As a buyer, your objectives will vary, depending on your intentions for the property. If you intend to turn the property around quickly, the financing on the property may be less relevant to you than if you intend to hold the property for a longer period. However, remember that real estate is usually a long-term investment. The transaction costs are significant, dictating a long-term holding period. In addition, the illiquidity makes for a long sales period, and the tax advantages require a longer-term holding period.

"But," you say, "I am going to hold this property for only a short period. I know the property is worth at least $1,500,000, and its cost to me is $1,200,000. I want to realize my profit. I don't care about the tax consequences, and I don't care that my transaction costs will be approximately $100,000. I want to sell the property and realize my profit of at least $200,000. Why should I care that the financing has a balloon payment due in three years? There is no way that I am going to own the property for more than 18 months."

The problem is that your purchaser's objective will probably be a longer-term holding period. When buying property, you should always consider the fact that eventually you are going to want to sell, and your purchaser is going to want to get a good deal too. You should do everything you can in the purchase to set up the eventual sale. For example, obtaining long-term assumable financing in the acquisition will aid your efforts when it is time to sell.

THE SELLER'S POSITION

As the seller, you are looking forward to cashing in your investment. Ideally, someone will come along and offer you more money for the property than you ever imagined it would be worth. Also ideally, that buyer will offer you cash. However, the ideal is not often realized. Instead, you will probably compromise on both the price and the terms in order to make the sale.

Most likely, you will have held the property long enough to obtain tax advantages on the sale (see Chapter 13), and you are about to be rewarded for the quality of your purchase, management, and improvement of the property. The reward may be little more than the bailout of a problem situation, or it could be a very substantial gain. In fact, with today's leveraged investments of meager cash flow and substantial tax shelter, it is likely that you will realize more gain on the sale than your total profit from operations of the property, regardless of how long you held the property and your tax situation.

There may be some tax reasons why you would want to defer collection of the cash on your sale, but usually you will want to receive as much cash as you can, as soon as possible. Traditionally, part of a sale was the obtaining of new financing. Either the seller or the purchaser would obtain the financing necessary to supplement the purchaser's available cash and cash out the interest of the seller. But more recently, the interest rate and financing situation has created an environment in which acceptable financing is often simply not available from third parties. Owners who wish to sell property in such an environment must provide the financing. The nature of that financing will be considered in more detail in Chapter 11. For now, it is sufficient to note that the financing that the seller provides means that he or she has not cashed out his or her interest, and therefore it has fallen short of the ideal.

SETTING THE STAGE FOR THE NEGOTIATIONS

Real estate negotiations usually start with the seller indicating a willingness to sell. This may come in the form of signing a listing agreement with a real estate agent, it may be initiated with a less formal conversation with the agent and/or the signing of a less formal letter or letter of intent. Another possibility is that the seller might place a for-sale-by-owner advertisement in the newspaper or simply put a For Sale sign on the property.

THE PURCHASER APPROACHES THE SELLER

Sometimes the prospective purchaser will initiate the negotiations for the property. This occurs when the purchaser is interested in a particular piece of property and contacts the owner to inquire as to whether the owner is interested in selling the property. This is an unusual situation, because generally the purchaser has income or speculation interests that are fairly interchangeable among properties. The purchaser also recognizes that, if negotiating with an owner who hasn't expressed an interest in selling, it is unlikely that they will reach an agreement.

The purchaser who initiates the negotiations may do so for a variety of reasons, but two predominate. The first possibility is that the purchaser has a particular use for the particular property. It may adjoin other property that he or she owns, be an excellent location for the purchaser's new store, or whatever. To a property owner and seller, the existence of such a potential purchaser is a gift from heaven, because the purchaser's need for that particular property makes it worth more to him or her than just about anyone else. If you as seller hold out just long enough, you will negotiate a better deal than you would have thought possible.

The second possibility is that the potential purchaser hails from a much different venue. There are people in the business who prey upon unsophisticated sellers who are unaware of the value of the property that they own. They will research the property records to locate the owners and contact a large number in the hope of locating a few who are unaware of the effect appreciation has had on their property value. A common situation is one in which an elderly widow is the owner of her house, which was bought 50 years ago for $10,000. She knows that inflation has affected the value of everything and that her house is worth far more than $10,000. However, her husband handled business matters, and she is unprepared to deal with them. When that nice Mr. X offered her $50,000 cash for the property, she could hardly believe his generosity. He explained that it might be a little too much but that she reminded him of his mother. What would her opinion be of Mr. X if she found out that the actual market value of her house was in excess of $150,000? To varying degrees, transactions of this type are made every day. Education and sophistication are valuable assets, and few would deny that in our society it is acceptable to use your superior knowledge to generate a profit. However, few would suggest that the illustration above is a legitimate use of such knowledge.

BUYERS' AND SELLERS' PERCEPTIONS

Under normal circumstances, of course, the disparity in knowledge between buyer and seller is not so great; in fact, a disparity in perceived values is necessary to the maintenance of the market economy. Both the seller and the purchaser must perceive that they are getting a good deal, perhaps the better of the deal. When that is the case, the transaction is facilitated. The buyer is more optimistic about the present and future value of the property than is the seller. In fact, the value might actually be different for the two. The buyer might make better use of the tax advantages than the seller. Specifically, the buyer can depreciate the property under the current accelerated rules over a short period (see Chapter 13) on the basis of the current purchase price. The seller probably has used the majority of the tax advantages that he or she could realize. The seller may have less advantageous depreciation rules and probably has a lower depreciable basis. In addition, the buyer probably perceives him- or herself as a superior owner in that he or she will provide better management for the property. At least half the time, such buyers are fooling themselves in this perception. But the accuracy of this perception is not necessary; only its perceived accuracy is necessary.

As to the perception of the future, buyers are by their nature an optimistic lot. Investors in general have to be optimistic, and investors in long-term illiquid investments have to be especially so. Sellers are not necessarily pessimistic. They may be cashing in on one investment in order to make others. But frequently the seller is selling because he or she feels the time is right and is more than a little concerned about the future. The seller might not perceive a declining market, but at least he or she feels that continuing to hold the property is not worthwhile.

As a purchaser, you should be asking yourself what the seller knows that you don't know. Perhaps the answer is "nothing." But be aware of the fact that the seller may be in a superior position to the buyer to obtain inside information affecting the value of the property. The seller has owned the property for some time and may be privy to information on such things as plant closings and the like. Generally, the seller will not be required to reveal this information to you, even if you request disclosure of all the information the seller has about the local economy that might affect the value of the property. The general rule in latin is caveat emptor; in English, "let the buyer beware."

An owner of property who indicates a willingness to sell always has a figure in mind when deciding what the property is worth. The real estate agent will push the seller to reveal such expectations because the agent needs this information to serve the interests of the seller. The agent may then decide that the seller has to adjust those expectations. Obviously, in many cases the seller's high expectations may have to be lowered to result in a sale of the property. On the other hand, agents who are really doing their job might well adjust the asking price of the property upward. It is the agent's responsibility to facilitate a transaction, and agents regard themselves as market makers. Because it is their job to further the best interests of their clients, an agent who represented the widow in the example above would not allow such a rip-off to take place. However, minor rip-offs are common. The agent does not get paid if the deal does not go together. The agent's commission is a percentage of the sales price in most instances, so it is in the agent's best interest to get the best price reasonably possible for the seller. Still, agents are often motivated to obtain mediocre performance because a smaller commission is better than none at all.

So, the property is on the market. The owner has indicated what price and terms on the property would be acceptable but probably hasn't indicated a willingness to give anything away. He or she must, however, indicate that he or she is reasonable and interested in selling the property. The listing price and terms will probably not be realized, but setting the asking price is a delicate balancing act. If the price is too high, potential purchasers will be put off; if the price is too low, the seller has limited his or her options in negotiations and has given up on the possibility of a higher selling price. Once the property is listed, the seller can do little more than maintain the property and wait.

STARTING THE NEGOTIATIONS

As the purchaser, you first become aware of the property through advertising, whether you have responded to an advertisement for this particular property or responded to the agent's advertisement of a different property and were referred to this property as well. The agent will have prepared a brief, one-page summary on the property, which is distributed to potential purchasers. The summary is very cryptic. It will indicate the number and type of units, as well as the asking price and terms, and it may contain some financial information on the property. This is all the information that prospective purchasers have on which to determine if they might have some interest in buying the property.

Usually, a prospective purchaser's next step is to set up an appointment to be shown the property. This physical inspection will tell you a lot more about the property. However, it will be a sampling only. It will involve an inspection of a few of the individual units and a cursory walk-through examination of the overall property and grounds. The seller will represent orally that the sample units are representative of the property, and you will be pushed to make an offer.

The offer that you make will probably be contingent, which means the offer is conditional. It is intended to do two things: (1) establish a dialogue between the buyer and seller as they attempt to make a deal; (2) establish the parameters within which the negotiations will proceed. In this latter respect, you are faced with a similar balancing dilemma as the seller when the seller established the asking price. You will want to demonstrate serious interest in the property, while at the same time offering as little as possible.

The offer is conditional for several reasons. The primary reason is that you do not have enough accurate information to make an intelligent offer. The offer will be conditioned on verifying the accuracy of the information received and the assumptions being relied on. The offer is also intended to measure the reaction of the seller. If a low and "safe" offer is accepted too quickly, you are likely to be scared into thinking that something is wrong with the property. At the opposite extreme, if the seller fails to adjust significantly the asking price and terms in the counteroffer, he or she is sending a clear signal that the asking price and terms are reasonably firm. The signals communicated in the initial offers indicate whether or not a deal is likely to be completed. The conditional offer "entitles" you to ask more from the seller. Sellers are generally unwilling to make their financial records open to the general public. The information is personal and confidential, like a business trade secret. However, if the seller accepts your contingent offer, or counters it, by accepting the contingency, he or she has agreed to open up his or her records to your inspection. You as the prospective purchaser, have certain obligations as well. You have agreed to review the information within a certain time period and either remove the contingency or remove the contingency and adjust the offer.

It is during this offer-counteroffer contingency period that the negotiations are most likely to reach an impasse and break off. The reason for the failure to complete the deal is one of human failings. And the principal human failing is the seemingly endless capacity of human beings to misrepresent facts to suit their purposes.

WHO HAS THE INFORMATION, AND WHY CAN'T YOU GET IT?

As briefly eluded to earlier, a curious factor in real estate negotiations is the fact that the prospective purchaser is expected to make an offer on the property before obtaining the necessary information to make an intelligent one. Sometimes the initial offer will be made before you have looked at the property or at any of the actual financial information on the property. Under these circumstances, only a fool would make an offer from which he or she would not withdraw if the information turned out to be inaccurate. That is the principal reason for the evolution of the contingent offer. You would like to buy the property and would like to be able to rely on the information presented by the seller. Unfortunately, that information is not always reliable.

You or your accountant should review the actual books and records of the property. You should examine the general ledger, the checkbook, the invoices, and other so-called source documents. You should contact the utility companies, major suppliers, the insurance company, and the state taxing authority. You should also insist on reviewing the property's tax return. The property itself will not have a tax return, but the owning entity will. The information should be specific enough to identify it with the property. For example, if the property is owned by a partnership, the partnership tax return should be examined. If the property is owned by an individual, you should examine those portions of the individual tax return that apply to the property. If the seller refuses or neglects to provide this information for your inspection, you should withdraw from negotiations and refuse to continue with the purchase. There is simply no real reason for the seller's failure to provide you with the necessary information. You can assume that, if you aren't being given the information necessary for your verification, the information is materially false. And, even if you think you trust the seller, you will find property available where this blind faith is unnecessary.

Another peculiarity in information verification is that, for some reason, sellers do not recognize the need to adjust the offer when the information they have provided is materially false or in error. However, the purchaser must adjust the offer in order to preserve the quality of the negotiated deal. The seller has no right to expect the purchaser to honor an agreement that was engineered on the basis of false information, unless the purchaser has failed to review the information or make the offer appropriately contingent.

WORDS TO BE AWARE OF

While you should be wary of all the information you receive, there is some information that is practically labeled as fraudulent. There are certain words that, when used in association with financial statements, label those statements as false. Among the words to be aware of are:

Expense factor
Pro forma
Projected
Scheduled or budgeted
Stabilized (income or expenses)
Normalized (income or expenses)
Stated rents or expenses
Street rents

Also, be especially attentive to the disclaimers as to the reliability of the financial information that often accompany the statements. Find out who prepared the financial information and how reliable it is. The words listed above and other similar words mean that the information contained in the document does not reflect the actual history of the property, but rather reflects what the preparer feels the property should yield. Although the results are essentially the same, the different words reflect different methods of misrepresentation. My definitions for the suspect words are as follows.

Expense factor means that the expenses indicated for the property are not the actual expenses for the property. The expense factor is usually a percentage of the rent figure (which may also be incorrect) that the preparer feels is reasonable. Supposedly, the preparer is drawing upon experience and expertise to indicate what the expenses should be. Almost certainly, the property's actual expenses are much higher than the expense factor indicated. The excess expenses will be attributed to poor management, accounting methods, and/or other aberrations. In fact, you should be more interested in what the actual expenses are for the property. Yes, you may be able to improve on the expenses shown by the current management. However, you should consider the possibility that the current management is quite efficient and professional and that the property is simply expensive to own and operate.

In some parts of the country, it is common to estimate expenses for the property based on costs per square foot. This is just as illegitimate as estimating costs as a percentage of rent. The important thing is not to use expense factors. Use actual expenses, and you will more accurately evaluate the property.

Also, beware of expense factors being buried within a series of actual expenses. Round numbers are suspicious. They mean either that the actual expense information wasn't available to the preparer or that the actual information was discouraging enough that the preparer felt the need to "adjust" the figures.

Pro forma financial statements and **projected** statements are very similar. Both profess to project the income and expenses into the future. The extent to which the statements reflect or depart from reality varies among statements. Sometimes the statements reflect the current expense and revenue amounts and merely adjust the future to reflect a "budgeted" rate of inflation. More often, the projected or pro forma numbers combine income the property has never generated with expenses below those it has experienced and project those figures into the future at a rate of inflation higher than the economy is currently experiencing.

Scheduled or budgeted income and expenses also are misleading. Generally, you schedule income and budget expenses. Here, reality imposes its ugly presence and puts reins on creativity. However, the reins are held very loosely. Scheduled rents are supposed to reflect the income the property could generate if only...well, fill in the blank. Each property seems to lack something that prevents it from realizing its potential. Management problems are the favorite because they are correctable problems. Another favorite is a poor economic condition that has since improved. But, regardless of the reason that the scheduled rents and budgeted expenses are not being realized, it will be implied that a new owner could realize the schedule and budget, if the property is operated the way it should be. In reality, realizing the budget will probably not be impossible, but it will be very difficult.

Stabilized (income or expenses) reflect a different kind of problem for the property. For some reason, the property in question has a checkered past. On occasion, it has performed reasonably well, but on other occasions, the property has experienced problems. The financial statement preparer has a very selective memory, remembering the good history and disregarding the poor performance. An attempt will be made to explain away the poor history. Then the superior history will be assumed to continue into the future, with perhaps further adjustments for inflation. The problems of the past will be assumed to be corrected. Each property has the capacity for a range of performance. No property demonstrates this more clearly than the property on which the financial statement preparer feels the need to present a stabilized statement. It is more than a little conceited and naive to assume that you will duplicate what your predecessor did correctly and avoid his mistakes and that you won't make different mistakes or experience different adverse economic conditions.

Stabilized income reflects a dream world, a world of accomplishments in which adversity does not exist. Even if you should achieve this performance for a while, you cannot expect it to last indefinitely.

Normalized (income or expenses) is a synonym for *stabilized income and expenses;* however, it is more often used in situations where the overall economy, instead of the individual property being considered, has experienced inconsistency. Don't rely on this. Either or both of the economy and the property could have been inconsistent. You must inquire of the preparer to determine which is the case. Then you should discount the statement against the actual history of the property.

Stated rents or expenses are just that: stated. They are not real. They are invented, perhaps out of thin air. Sometimes they reflect the best history of the project or the history of competitors' properties. Other times the figures are pure fiction.

Street rents are the highest individual rents being realized or scheduled to be realized on the property. They do not reflect any promotional discounts or market discounts. For example, the street rents on the property for an apartment might be $400 per unit. But most of the units are actually rented for $360, and it is common to discount the rents still further for six-month leases. Once again, you can't rely on the figures you have been given. It is necessary to determine where the truth is being hidden and why.

WHAT ARE YOU OBLIGATED TO BUY?

When you are negotiating for the possible purchase of real estate, you are dealing with the very serious matter of signed legal documents. Be very careful of what you are signing and what it obligates you to do. If you are unfamiliar with the field (and often even if you are experienced), it may be advisable to contact your attorney before signing anything. Be careful of the wording of your contingencies and the wording of the contingencies in the counteroffer you receive from the other party. Do not assume that the seller has duplicated your wording in the counteroffer. It is more likely that he or she has substantially altered the wording to the effect that you may obligated to purchase the property when you think your offer is still conditional.

A common inspection contingency may be worded as follows: "This offer is contingent upon purchaser's inspection and written approval of the property and its books and records within 15 days of seller's acceptance."

With this wording, if you do not provide written approval, there is probably no obligation on the part of either party to honor the deal. But what if the contingency does not provide for written approval, and you make no effort to inspect the records? What obligation is there on the seller to supply the needed financial information for your inspection within the contingency period? It is important for these obligations not to be ambiguous because ambiguous obligations lead to lawsuits. In this type of lawsuit, the only winners are the attorneys. Even if you win the suit, your victory will not be without legal and emotional costs. In fact, as you become worth suing—that is, financially strong enough to make a suit worthwhile—you may find yourself being sued simply for the harassment value. Your attorney or insurance company will encourage you to settle even the most frivolous of suits to avoid the exposure, however insignificant, to possible loss. This attitude, of course, encourages the proliferation of frivolous suits. Attorneys have a vested interest in the legal process and the maintenance of suits, regardless of their merit. Insurance companies are very pragmatic and care only that they minimize their loss on a case-by-case basis. But insurance companies' tunnel vision in settling suits probably results in more and greater losses by encouraging such suits. In fact, I have often heard it expressed by attorney acquaintances of mine that the existence of an insurance company in the claim makes a suit much more likely, both because the existence of insurance makes the defendant more suable and because of the insurance company's propensity to settle.

In the context of offers to purchase property, it is important that your inaction not bind you. It is acceptable to word your contingencies so that overt action on your part will obligate you to make the purchase. Indeed, this is what you intend. But make sure you are not obligated to perform until the financial or other information is verified. If someone is pushing you to buy a property on the basis of ambiguity in the offer and hasn't provided you with actual financial information, it is likely that the property is not as represented. You have no choice but to resist the suit and attempt to settle the matter at as low a cost as possible.

It is important that your wording be clear, unambiguous, and nonbinding until such time as the contingency is removed. The wording for such a contingency depends on individual circumstances. This book does not purport to offer legal advice; however, I would suggest an inspection of the property and records contingency that is as specific and unambiguous as the following:

This offer is contingent upon purchaser's inspection and written approval of the property and books and records of the property within 21 days of seller's acceptance of this offer. This contingency is solely for the benefit of the purchaser, and in the event that the purchaser fails to remove the contingency in writing within the contingency period, the offer shall be null and void. Seller shall make available for purchaser's inspection, within seven days of seller's acceptance of this offer, the following documents:

1. All financial records for the property, including but not limited to the checkbook, general ledger, rent rolls, expense records, income statement, balance sheet, and statement of changes in financial position, for the prior three years.
2. Any appraisals on the property written within the prior three-year period, whether prepared by an independent appraiser or an employee of the owner.
3. Any insurance policies currently in force on the property or in force within the prior three-year period.
4. The real and personal property tax statements and related documents for the property, for the prior three years.
5. The federal and state income tax returns for the ownership entity for the prior three years.
6. Any other financial documents prepared for the property or its owners within the past three years.
7. Any structural or soil engineering studies prepared for the property in the seller's possession or ordered for his benefit or prepared for the prior owners. If the seller is aware of such a study not in his possession, he agrees to assist the purchaser in securing the study.

In the event that the seller fails to provide the documents within seven days of his acceptance of this offer, the offer shall be null and void.

Seller agrees to make the property available to the physical inspection of the purchaser and his authorized agents, including his accountant, structural engineer, real estate agent, lawyer, and any other representative or representatives that the purchaser shall choose. Purchaser agrees to coordinate his inspection or inspections with the property managers to avoid disturbing or inconveniencing the tenants.

You might think it odd that you would have to go to such lengths to protect yourself from the illegitimate claim that you should be required to complete the purchase of property or be held responsible for the seller's damages. Well, it is better to take the precautions indicated than risk a lawsuit. However, as this is being written, I am being sued on a contract for the purchase of a small apartment building. The offer was contingent on my inspection of the property and its books and records. When the offer was accepted by the seller, the books and records were requested. However, all that was provided was a very unrealistic pro forma financial statement. The property was located halfway across the country from my office, so we were not going to inspect the property until the financial information was verified. The contingency period expired without the contingency being removed, so the deal should have lapsed. However, suit was commenced on the theory that we should have been required to inspect the property, that we should be responsible for the seller's damages as measured by his subsequent sale for $10,000 less than our contingent offer, and finally, that we should be required to pay the seller punitive damages in the amount of $25,000 to dissuade the kind of business practice we demonstrated. We did not make it specific that the contingency must be removed in writing. Nor did we make it specific which financial documents we would be requesting. I believe that the suit is totally without merit and that eventually we will prevail; however, to date we have already spent more than $2,000 in legal fees to defend the suit (we will spend in excess of $5,000 in costs by the time the suit is completed), which we will probably not be able to recover from the plaintiff. We have also spent many hours answering interrogatories and depositions and providing documents for the inspection of the plaintiff. So, regardless of the outcome of the suit, its harassment value should be apparent. We could choose the easy compromise and settle the suit for a dollar amount that would almost surely be less than our legal costs in the suit. But doing so would encourage this kind of frivolous suit. Therefore, we will defend rather than compromise this suit, and we will attempt to counterclaim for our damages and costs, even though we will probably not be awarded our damages.

No amount of precautions can totally insulate you from the possibility of lawsuit, but taking prudent precautions can substantially reduce your exposure.

ENTER THE PHANTOM BUYER

As you negotiate for the purchase of a piece of real estate, you will find that it is not a smooth and regular process. Instead, it will proceed in fits and spurts, sometimes looking as though a deal is coming together and other times looking as though an irreconcilable impasse will cause the negotiations to break off. It is during one of these impasse periods that you are likely to encounter a character peculiar to real estate investment, but who has cousins in other unique major purchase contexts. The character of whom I speak is the notorious phantom buyer.

As I indicated previously, the buyer has a negotiating advantage over the seller in that the buyer can buy any number of properties while the seller has only the property in question to sell. When the negotiations begin to break off, the buyer can always consider the purchase of a different property. The seller will have to await the arrival of a new prospective purchaser, unless the seller can revive interest in the deal.

In an effort to revive interest in a property when negotiations have broken off, the real estate business invented the phantom buyer. Supposedly, someone else is very interested in the property, so you are urged to make an offer or remove contingencies or otherwise proceed to a commitment as soon as possible. The existence of another buyer is also represented to indicate that the value of the property is significant. Therefore, the phantom buyer is even used to indicate why the seller is reluctant to negotiate.

There is only one response to phantom buyers, and that is to disregard them. Treat them as though they don't exist—in all likelihood, they don't. Even if other parties are interested in the property, you don't want to get into a bidding war with them. When the seller's agent suggests that someone has indicated a willingness to pay more for the property than you have offered, tell the seller to go ahead. You aren't interested in matching the offer or exceeding it, and you are particularly interested in avoiding a competitive bidding situation. If others are more interested in the property than you are, they deserve it, and you shouldn't be interested.

What you are doing is calling the bluff. More often than not, the phantom buyer will fail to purchase the property, and when it is reoffered to you, your bargaining position will have improved substantially. If you don't get carried away with the bargaining advantage, you might strike the deal you seek.

I wish that the phantom buyer would die an inglorious death. As I have indicated, the existence or lack of another interested party should not affect the value you place on the property or have any effect on your willingness to negotiate for it. If the seller and the seller's agent can be made to see that the phantom buyer is irrelevant, perhaps the negotiating ploy will no longer be used. As it is, the ploy is more of a detraction from negotiations than it is an aid to the negotiation.

TERMS, TERMS, TERMS

It has been suggested by more than one popular author that the three important elements in buying real estate, which were once said to be location, location, and location, should be changed to terms, terms, and terms. I can't overemphasize the importance of terms. The selling price of the property is only one element in considering the quality of the deal. The terms for payment of that selling price are the measure of the quality of the deal. This is true because, in measuring the rate of return, you must consider the return on the amount you have invested in the property. The smaller the denominator (the amount you have invested), the higher the rate of return. Thus, the less money you have invested in the down payment and the costs of carrying the property, the higher the likely rate of return.

Another reason that leveraged investments tend to yield higher rates of return is that, with the investments adjusted in value to reflect the rate of inflation and with the cash flow growing from the property, the amount of the purchase price that can be deferred will, in many instances, be paid by the property through operations or refinance, rather than by the purchaser. In other words, the purchaser benefits in that the property "buys itself."

KEEPING THE NOTHING-DOWN PROPERTY

The flip side of the advantages of leverage is the risk. In negotiating the best terms for the acquisition of the property, remember that, to maintain the ownership of the property, you must service the debt you place on the property. It is no trick to buy property for little or no money down; the trick lies in keeping the property that is so purchased. If the seller is so disenchanted with the property as to be willing to sell it with no money down, he or she is not likely to be making money on it and instead is probably feeding the property every month.

How much property can you afford to feed? Well, perhaps you will find it worthwhile to feed a small amount of property for a limited period of time. In fact, the tax advantages might well mean that after tax the property is costing you far less to carry or may actually be producing a net after-tax cash flow. But feeding property gets very old very quickly. A negative cash flow property is no fun to own. Until you turn it around and start generating positive cash flow, your rate of return declines with each month of ownership and with each contribution of capital.

Therefore, I suggest avoiding negative cash flow properties. So, now you should simply be able to resolve not to buy any negative cash flow properties and go about your business. Oh, how I wish it were that simple. Unfortunately, in the initial years of ownership, when the debt on the property is a high percentage of the price, and the related debt service is a high percentage of the gross rents, it is very difficult to avoid negative cash flow. Generally, after you have held the property for a period of time and have experienced the usual appreciation in rent, it will be easier to carry the property and the cash flow will become positive. Indeed, it used to be common to say that there are no bad investments in real estate. If the seller can hold on long enough, inflation will make the bad investment look good. Inflation has definitely been a cure for mediocre real estate investments. But bad investments are still bad. If the expenses of operating your property exceed its income, and inflation increases both revenue and expenses by the same percentage, the property will get more and more negative each month. Furthermore, recent economic history has shown that you can't even count on something that seemed as basic to our economic system as inflation.

How do you avoid negative cash flow property? Start out avoiding any properties that are scheduled to produce break-even or negative cash flow. With the capacity for misrepresentation that exists in this business, if the best the seller can suggest is that the property is going to break even, it is likely that the property will have to be fed. Also, you should know that there is no such thing as a break-even property. Either the property is making money or it isn't; it doesn't just break even. One of my favorite expressions used by real estate agents is *essentially break-even*. In English, that means that the property is showing or scheduled to show a small amount of negative cash flow. If the property is scheduled to show a small amount of positive cash flow, it is not "essentially break-even" property but is instead positive cash flow property. After eliminating the obvious negative cash flow and marginal properties, the next step is to consider carefully the financial information presented on the remaining property you are considering. Beware of those words that indicate that the statements are false and seek verification, through tax returns and the like, of financial information purported to be actual and correct. It is also advisable, especially if you are just starting out, to allow yourself a comfort margin. That is, assume that initially you are not going to do as well as the current owners and limit your purchases to those that have positive cash flow after deducting for the comfort margin.

Still, nothing-down property is a tremendous temptation. You may have the opportunity to own or control a substantial amount of property with a small amount of your own cash. You may rationalize that the negative cash flow is nothing more than a deferred down payment. Or you may consider the tax benefits and determine how little it really costs you to carry the property.

Negative cash flow does limit your options. Generally, adequate refinancing will not be available, and the negative cash flow places a limit on how long you can reasonably carry the property. You must turn the property around within the time frame indicated or reduce the negative cash flow and extend the period during which you must eliminate the negative cash flow. You also must remember that the property you wish to turn around is subject to cyclical fluctuations. It is important to be realistic and pragmatic. Ask yourself these questions and answer them honestly.

- How long can you carry the property if it continues to produce the current amount of negative cash flow?
- How likely is it that the cash flow might get even worse, and what would this do to your budgeted turn-around period?
- What can you do now and in the near future to improve the cash flow situation?
- What will it cost in terms of improvement and promotion to turn the property around?
- Finally, do you have the personality to assume the risk involved in owning substantial property subject to a large amount of debt? Will you be able to sleep at night? Is the return worth the financial and emotional costs involved?

Once you have considered these matters and found yourself suitable and able to make such investments, you are ready to proceed through negotiations to an acquisition.

REASONS NEGOTIATIONS FAIL

There is no end to the list of potential reasons for failed negotiations and property that fails to close. Some negotiations are doomed from the start. The seller and purchaser are so far apart that you begin to wonder if they are talking about the same property. In this context, the negotiations will result in nothing more than frustration and wasted time for the participants. Why the parties continue to negotiate when they are so far removed from each other is beyond my comprehension. Even in those instances when protracted negotiations finally result in an agreement, both sides are going to feel as though they lost the negotiations since they had to compromise so much.

Limit your negotiations to properties that appear to meet your investment criteria and are offered at a price that appears close to acceptable. The negotiations still might fail, but your chances for success are improved. Unfortunately, many negotiations fail even though the parties could have agreed on an acceptable price and terms. In this context, the parties are within the range of reasonable compromise, but it is the negotiation process and the parties that have failed. In my experience, the following is a representative list of the reasons that negotiations fail and property fails to close.

FAILURE OF COMMUNICATIONS

The negotiations process is one of strained communications between adversarial parties. It is not surprising, therefore, that my list includes several problems with communications. The first is a general failure of communications. This occurs when, for some reason, negotiations break off. The purchaser may make an offer for which he or she receives no response. Similarly, the seller might make a counteroffer to which the purchaser does not respond. There is no objection there is simply no communication. The other party will consider the lack of communication as an indication of a lack of interest in the property by the party that fails to communicate. It might well be that the party is very much interested in the property and the deal that the parties are approaching, and the communication of lack of interest may be quite accidental and unintentional. Sometimes, like body language, the party is unaware of what saying nothing actually communicates.

EXCESSIVE COMMUNICATIONS

At the other extreme are negotiations that get bogged down by too much communication. The parties engage in excessive communications, both formally through the process of offer and counteroffer and informally in writing and orally. They are so concerned with the many petty details of the transaction that they lose sight of the overall objective of arriving at an acceptable bargain and closing the transaction. The negotiations will break down when all the details can't be resolved satisfactorily.

MISREPRESENTATIONS

The seller might misrepresent the condition of the property or the financial information. The purchaser might misrepresent his or her capacity to raise the money to close the deal. If the truth had been known, the parties might have been able to arrive at an agreement. Perhaps the financial information or condition of the property is not unacceptable to the purchaser, or perhaps the purchaser could close the property if given an additional 30 days or a slightly restructured deal. But when one party discovers that the other side has lied to further the negotiations, the reaction is likely to kill any chance of making a deal.

UNEXPECTED COMMUNICATION

What happens when you make a nice, "safe," conservative and very contingent offer, and give the seller a week to accept, and the seller accepts it the same afternoon? This unexpected behavior on the part of the seller is likely to scare you into questioning the deal. It is important to recognize that you communicate in many ways that you might not intend. Always consider how the other side is going to react to what you say and do.

EXPIRATION OF TIME

Sometimes the negotiations are under a time constraint. Frequently, the time constraint is imposed by the tax law, where the purchaser may need to close by a certain date for depreciation purposes or for the identification of property for a like-kind exchange (under the new rules). Other times, for any number of reasons, one or both of the parties will place a time constraint on the negotiations. If a deal is not negotiated within the constraints, the negotiations will cease.

AGENT FAILURE

It is important to know what the agent is doing for you and to the negotiations. A poor agent can kill more deals than a good agent can construct. It is important to recognize that it is the agents that will do the actual communicating between buyer and seller. Consider who your representatives are and what that says about your business judgment.

OVERREACHING

There is a tendency in negotiations to overplay the situation and ask for more than the other side is prepared to give. This usually comes about when it appears that a deal is coming together and the parties are approaching a compromise. Then, suddenly one of the parties alters the terms in such a way as to constitute a major change. The other party is unprepared for this change and views it as an indication that the first party is not serious about negotiations or the property.

NEED TO WIN

Those who need to "win" negotiations will seldom succeed and will acquire few properties. That is not to say that you shouldn't strive to get the best deal possible. Instead, you should recognize that the other side doesn't have to lose in order for you to win. You may be able to take advantage of the unfortunate circumstances affecting the other party in some situations, as for example in the case of a foreclosure. But you will find far more frequently that you can succeed in negotiations if you don't need to "win" at the expense of the other party.

FRUSTRATION

Negotiations can be a frustrating process. When the counteroffer of the other party makes it clear that you haven't adequately communicated your position, or that the other party won't accommodate your needs, there is a tremendous temptation to throw up your hands and seek your opportunities in a field that requires less creativity and patience. This is especially true if you have had a series of unsuccessful negotiations. Frustration is something that we must all deal with individually, and how you deal with it is up to you. It is important that you find your own way of living with and learning from frustrating experiences.

BUYER'S AND/OR SELLER'S REMORSE

After the deal is struck, there is almost always some self-doubt on the part of the participants. Both parties wonder if the deal is the best that could have been structured. If there is an opportunity to do so, many will seek to restructure the transaction or to withdraw. This is unfortunate in the majority of situations, where the parties are seeing ghosts manifested by their insecurity. The deal may not be as good as they thought, but it is probably not as bad as they now imagine.

Negotiations will succeed when both the seller and the purchaser are committed to their success. The parties must maneuver through a mine-field of potential problems that could kill the negotiations in order to arrive at an acceptable compromise. When the negotiations have been successful, the parties are ready to proceed to our next issue: the closing of the acquisition.

THE ACQUISITION | 6

After you have reviewed a number of properties, considered the market, and negotiated for several without success, you will finally arrive at a purchase price and terms agreement with the seller of your first investment property. Hopefully, you will have carefully reviewed the financial and other information for the property before removing the contingencies. Also, before obligating yourself to complete the acquisition, you should be sure that you will be able to raise the money necessary to close the property and, if there is a negative cash flow, to cover that cost for at least one year. Don't assume that you can raise the money either from a bank or from equity partners unless you either have a firm commitment for such funding or have enough experience in such activities that you can conservatively budget the raising of enough money to complete the acquisition.

CLOSING COSTS

In addition to the down payment that you have negotiated with the seller, you will also have to pay the purchaser's portion of the closing costs when you close the property. It is important to budget adequately to cover these costs. And when you buy your first few properties, or when you buy properties in other states, you may be surprised at the nature and magnitude of the costs. Some of the common costs that you may be required to pay all or part of include the following.

TITLE INSURANCE
In most cases, title insurance costs will be charged to the seller. However, the parties may agree contractually to apportion these costs differently.

ESCROW COSTS
Usually, the escrow costs are split equally between the buyer and the seller. The cost may vary substantially among escrow companies, and it may pay to shop around. Your concern should be with the competence and independence of the escrow company. It is common for the purchaser to offer to use the escrow company of the seller's choosing, subject only to the purchaser's verification of independence. But since the purchaser is going to have to pay half the costs of the escrow, I think it is only fair that he or she have some input into the selection of that company. As a practical matter, if the purchaser indicates a choice of escrow company, the seller is unlikely to object to the purchaser's choice. That assumes, of course, that the purchaser's choice is not unreasonable.

INSURANCE
It will be necessary for the purchaser to purchase insurance commencing with the date of the closing and to provide proof of that insurance at the closing. If the property is free of debt, the amount and nature of the insurance will be at the discretion of the purchaser. However, if the property is financed, the lender will impose insurance standards and requirements on the property. It is important to make sure the insurance you purchase is in compliance with the requirements of the lender.

PRORATED EXPENSES
The closing date will establish the date at which the responsibility for the operating expenses of the property shifts from the seller to the purchaser. Some expenses, the most material of which are usually real estate taxes, are paid substantially in advance, and the seller is entitled to be reimbursed for those expenses on closing.

LOAN ASSUMPTION FEES
These days, it is common for real estate loans written by financial institutions, and in some cases even those written by individuals, to include clauses that entitle the lender to loan assumption

fees. Supposedly, the fees are intended to compensate the lender for the costs associated with allowing the assumption and to compensate for the additional risk associated with a new and unproven borrower. In reality, the fees are being charged because the lender is in a position to prevent the transaction from taking place, and with that kind of leverage the fees will generally be charged. The fees are the responsibility of the purchaser since it is that party who is assuming the loan.

LOAN PREPAYMENT PENALTIES

Even if you are paying cash, there may be some loan fees to pay. These are prepayment penalties on the underlying loan that the seller had and the purchaser won't be assuming. Who should pay these costs? The seller will feel that the purchaser should pay the costs, because if the purchaser hadn't chosen to pay off the loan, the costs wouldn't have been incurred. The purchaser thinks the seller should pay the costs because all the purchaser wants is a cash purchase. It isn't the purchaser's fault that the seller or a previous owner was foolish enough to encumber the property with a loan that has a prepayment penalty clause. I don't believe there is any standard practice dictating which party pays the cost, so in this case more than in the others, it will depend on the agreement between the parties. As to who should pay the costs, I would lean toward the seller—unless, of course, the seller happens to be me.

LOAN COSTS

If new financing is necessary in the acquisition, there will be various loan costs to pay. Generally, the conventional lender will have loan fees of about 2 percent of the proceeds and various other costs, including appraisals, title reports, filing fees, legal fees, document preparation fees, etc. These costs also vary substantially among lenders. VA lenders and other nonconventional lenders generally have higher fees, which may be paid by the buyer or seller depending on regulations and the agreement between the parties. I have seen the total loan costs vary from about 1 percent of the proceeds to as high as 10 percent of the loan proceeds (on small loans).

SYNDICATION AND OTHER COSTS

If you intend to raise the equity to buy the property through the formation of a group of investors in a partnership or limited partnership, be aware that substantial costs will be associated with that endeavor. It is not uncommon for such costs to exceed 20 percent of the proceeds so raised.

APPRAISALS, SURVEYS, AND LEGAL COSTS

Even in the absence of new financing, you may find it desirable or necessary to contact an appraiser, a structural engineer, a lawyer, or an accountant for professional advice on the acquisition. The costs of these services depend largely on the amount of service you purchase. Basically, the services are sold on a time and expenses basis, with the professional charging you for the amount of time you use. Don't assume that the meter is not running; it nearly always is. To make efficient use of the professional's time, come as prepared and organized as you can. Don't be unfriendly with these professionals, but avoid wasting their time and your money by discussing unrelated matters with them. If you want to chew the fat with someone, go get a haircut.

REAL ESTATE COMMISSIONS

The general rule is that real estate commissions are the expense of the seller. The agent works for the seller and is compensated by him or her. This arrangement may be modified by agreement of the parties or the purchaser might choose to hire and compensate his own agent, however the general rule is that the expense is that of the seller. Whether or not this is really the seller's expense as a practical matter is discussed in more detail in Chapter 12.

INTEREST RATE ADJUSTMENTS

Although these are not specifically closing costs, beware of interest rate adjustment clauses in the loan you intend to assume. These clauses vary substantially, but the thrust of the provision is to allow the bank to adjust the interest rate on the loan to a new borrower. When banks talk about adjusting rates, they mean *increasing* rates. It is important for you to consider how much the bank will increase the rate to you and how much this affects the value of the property. The adjustment may be restricted by the loan agreement—for example, no more than 2 percent—or the bank may be able to adjust the rate at its discretion. Sometimes loan interest rate adjustment clauses will kill a deal or make refinancing necessary.

OTHER COSTS

This list is by no means complete. There are many other costs, both insignificant and substantial, that sometimes find their way onto closing statements. To prepare adequately for these costs and avoid them when possible, I would suggest contacting an escrow company or title insurance company in the state where the property is located to discuss the expected costs and the possibility of escrowing the transaction with them. The meeting will be promotional for the escrow company, so for the cost of a lunch (if you can't figure out a way to get the company to pick up the check) you should be able to get a handle on the likely closing costs involved in your transaction. If you keep in contact with these knowledgeable people and aren't reluctant to discuss costs with the other party to the transaction, you will avoid nasty surprises at the closing.

As an illustration of what can happen, consider the following example of a closing that I attended in my younger and more foolish days.

The property was a large, 218-unit apartment complex. The purchaser was a limited partnership, formed by my partner and me for the sole purpose of making this acquisition. We syndicated the partnership to limited partners to raise the necessary cash. The property was located in Oregon and was our first acquisition in that state. We knew that Oregon's real estate taxes were very high, and this was confirmed by the financial information that we reviewed. Also, a review of the underlying loan revealed that the lender had the option of raising the interest rate on the transfer of the property by 2 percent and had the right to charge an assumption fee equal to 2 percent of the original loan value, which had been $2,000,000 for a potential fee of $40,000.

I suggested to the real estate agent that the bank was being excessively greedy in claiming both the interest rate adjustment and the assumption fee. After all, because of the interest rate adjustment, it was in the bank's best interest that the transaction be completed, and I didn't think the fee was reasonable. I told the agent that we would pay the additional interest but that we wanted the bank to waive the assumption fee. Later, he advised me that the bank had agreed to waive that fee. The annual taxes on the property were $80,000. However, we were closing the property on November 30, so we reasoned that our prorated expense would be $80,000 times 32 days divided by 365 days or approximately $7,000.

When I went to the closing, I was met with some very unpleasant surprises. First, it appears that the real estate agent had never contacted the bank, and the bank had no intention of waiving the loan assumption fee. Second, it seems that in Oregon the taxes are paid on a fiscal year basis through June of the following year, so about $40,000 more taxes than I had calculated were to be paid at closing. The total difference in fees and closing costs between what I had budgeted and what was being assessed was about $80,000.

Well, I didn't have the $80,000, and I was unable to close the property as planned. Instead, the various parties went about attempting to salvage the transaction. The first choice was to approach the bank about waiving the assumption fee. But at this point our bargaining position was very much reduced. We had raised over $500,000 for the transaction's closing with further obligations for a like amount in future installments, and we had incurred substantial costs in that effort. We wanted to buy the property. We had a lot of time and money invested in its acquisition, and the bank knew if it held out for its fee it would probably be paid. The next choice was to hold the real estate agent responsible for the costs incurred as a result of his negligence. Unfortunately having a legal right and a practical remedy are two different things. Part of the agent's commission was deferred, and he wouldn't be collecting $40,000 in closing. Furthermore, he argued that the fees would have been charged in any event, and he should not be held 100 percent responsible. I didn't agree. I felt that, if the question of waiver of the fee had been considered before we had spent a lot of time and effort on the transaction, the bank would have reduced or eliminated the fee in exchange for the interest rate adjustment.

The net result of this mess was an adjustment by all the parties involved (except the bank). We raised the additional funds for the taxes. We, the seller, and the two agents involved absorbed the cost of the loan assumption fee. The proration of that fee was not equal, but I am sure all parties paid more than they thought were their fair shares. Finally, rather than the customary one hour, this particular closing took two weeks for me to complete.

THE ESCROW

The escrow company is an independent third party, paid by the principals in the transaction to receive the money and legal documents and to ease the transfer of ownership. The escrow agent will generally record the contract and sale of the property after determining that the purchaser is in compliance with the terms of the contract with respect to the closing. Then he or she will release the purchaser's funds to the seller. The escrow agent does not render a legal opinion on the marketability of the title or on the value of the property. The agent's function is quasilegal in that he or she considers whether or not the purchaser is in compliance with the terms of the contract before recording the transfer. However, in most states escrow agents need not be attorneys and need not have one working for them.

In the event of a conflict, the escrow agent will usually try to resolve the dispute between the parties. But the escrow agent doesn't want to get in the middle in the event of a legal conflict. Therefore, in the event that the parties appear to be in conflict and unable to resolve their differences, the escrow agent will seek to extricate him- or herself. First the agent will attempt to determine if there is agreement as to the disposition of the earnest money. Perhaps both parties agree that the money is refundable to the purchaser since the contingencies are not resolved. Or both may agree that the money is to be forfeited to the seller because the purchaser has failed to perform his or her obligations. If the parties are in disagreement as to who is entitled to the earnest money, the escrow agent will deposit the funds with the local court of competent jurisdiction and interplead the parties. In so doing, the escrow agent is recognizing that he or she does not have the capacity to resolve the conflict and is leaving it up to the court and the parties to resolve.

The escrow agent is like a person who is paid to hold a bet. The agent has no interest in the outcome of the wager and agrees only to hold the funds for the relatively small fee involved. The last thing the escrow agent needs is to become embroiled in a conflict between the parties; the fee is simply not worth the problem. Therefore, you will find that many escrow agents will simply refuse to continue with the transaction when conflicts between the parties arise.

TITLE INSURANCE AND
LAWYER'S ABSTRACTS OF TITLE

Title insurance does not insure that the title to the property in question is clear of all encumbrances. In fact, the term *title insurance* is something of a misnomer. Title insurance actually is research into the legal status of the title of the property and publication of a report on the status of the title. The exceptions of record on the property should be detailed on the report. The insurance element of the title insurance is simply the company's guarantee of the accuracy of its work. If you experience a loss as a result of the title insurance company's failure to record a defect of record on the property, the company will generally make good your loss. The fee will depend on the price of the property since this determines the company's exposure. If you are acquiring a property in a state where title insurance companies are licensed to do business, consider yourself lucky. If the state law requires that only lawyers are allowed to research the title of property, you will find that essentially the same service costs you considerably more. There is also an insurance element in the lawyer's abstract of title in that, if the lawyer's negligence results in failure to record a defect in the title resulting in damage to the client, the attorney's errors and omissions (malpractice) insurance should cover the loss.

Read the preliminary title report and question anything unusual that appears on it. Perfected liens—that is, liens that have a judgment attesting to their legitimacy within the statutory period—must be paid on the transfer of the property. You are entitled to receive a clear and unencumbered property except for those items, like the underlying financing, that you have agreed to accept.

The title insurance policy is for the purchase price of the property. If the company fails to detect a mechanic's or materialman's lien for, say, $10,000 on a property that sold for $200,000, the policy will reimburse you for your costs in paying that debt. A problem with the value of the property limitation could occur in that very rare circumstance where the title insurance company fails to detect that the property was previously sold and that your seller is not the owner. This could be especially burdensome if the error went undetected for a number of years and the property appreciated in value during that period. If, under your astute management and generally favorable market conditions, your $200,000 building appreciates to $400,000 in value, and then you discover that the seller was not entitled to sell the building to you and someone else claims ownership, the title insurance company will reimburse you for only the original purchase price of $200,000.

LAWYERS

Chapter 12 considers the use of professionals in detail, but here I will consider the use of lawyers in the context of the acquisition and the closing. You should obtain professional help in any context where you lack the skill to protect your interests adequately. How do you know if you will need the professional help? Well, if you have to ask that question, you probably need help. If you are attending the closing of a property for the first time, it is advisable to bring along a competent attorney who is familiar with real estate transactions. You may not need one, but you might bring one along for counsel as a precautionary measure. Unfortunately, most people don't contact attorneys until after they are in trouble. They make mistakes because of their lack of experience or poor judgment, and then they seek legal advice to get them out of the situation or to correct the problem. At that point, the lawyer can only assist in mitigating the damages. If the client had called for help earlier in the transaction, many of the problems might have been avoided or reduced.

It is sometimes suggested that lawyers are deal killers. Real estate agents generally feel that lawyers will kill a deal more often than not, and they visibly cringe when the client informs them that an attorney will review the deal. There is some truth to this reputation in that most attorneys feel that they are being employed to find fault with the transaction or, at least, that they are being paid to point out the problems in the transaction. In that context, they frequently point out problems that will result in the termination of the deal. If an attorney advises you of a defect in the title, unfavorable clauses in the loan documents, or other legal problems with the transaction, and those problems kill the deal, you are better off with it dead.

Lawyers are a peculiar lot. They somehow feel that their legal training makes them competent to advise you on financial matters as well as legal matters. This should seem strange to you. After all, your plumber does not feel that a plumbing background makes him or her competent to advise you about your wiring. In the case of lawyers, sometimes they are competent to advise you on financial matters; frequently they are not, because law schools offer remarkably little financial education. You might assume that all lawyers are of superior intelligence and that they will therefore offer better advice than your brother-in-law. But, while law schools are difficult to get into, and the students do have to have good grades and test results, this is not necessarily indicative of superior intelligence. Perhaps the lawyer is of average intelligence and did well in school only because he or she was too physically lazy to become a carpenter. Furthermore, even superior intelligence doesn't mean that a lawyer has the financial training or experience to give you reliable advice. Still, lawyers will almost always give you financial advice, and that advice will almost always be conservative or negative, partly because that is what you expect and partly because the attorney has less to lose if the advice turns out to be bad. You are not going to be disappointed if the property does better than expected, but if it does not do well, and the attorney failed to caution you, you will feel that the advice you received was poor.

In the context of acquiring property and closing the acquisition, you should seek legal advice if there is anything about the transaction that you don't understand or that exposes you to loss. You may or may not wish to seek the attorney's input into the financial aspects of the transaction, but if you do so, make sure your decision is based on the lawyer's having other financial education or experience.

THE CLOSING

If you are the kind of person who works well under pressure, you will love real estate closings. The closing is the time when the seller and the purchaser sign the legal documents for the transfer of the property. Aside from the earnest money, it is also the time when the purchaser is required to deposit the down payment. If the purchaser does not have the down payment at the time of closing, he or she will forfeit the earnest money and will in all likelihood lose the property. Similarly, if the seller hasn't provided for the cure of the defects in the title, he or she will release the purchaser from the obligation to perform and may be subject to suit for misrepresentation for the damages caused to the prospective purchaser.

SETTING THE DATE

Thus, the closing date represents a deadline for performance. It is also the date at which legal rights and responsibilities shift from the seller to the purchaser. When considering an appropriate date, you must consider many factors. First of all, the seller and purchaser will want to complete the deal as soon as possible. The longer the transaction remains open, the more chance there is that something could go wrong. Also, both parties are subject to a psychological phenomenon known as *seller's or buyer's remorse*. It is also sometimes called *cold feet*. Both parties begin to wonder if perhaps they could have gotten a better deal. The seller may be concerned with the purchaser's capacity to perform, and the purchaser will become concerned with a variety of factors affecting ownership, ranging from the physical condition of the property to concerns about the economy and international affairs. The shorter the period between acceptance of the deal and the closing, the less likely it is that the deal will disintegrate because of nagging self-doubts.

However, as the purchaser, you will want to allow yourself plenty of time to satisfy your obligations with respect to the transaction. If you estimate that it will take four to six weeks to raise the down payment required for the transaction, the closing should be scheduled no sooner than 60 to 90 days. Remember, it always take longer than you think it should to accomplish these things.

So, close as soon as practicable, but allow yourself enough time to perform. One recourse you have is to set a flexible closing date. You could provide for the closing within 60 days if you feel that you can perform within that period and provide for an extension of 30 to 60 days at the purchaser's option. The seller will probably be inclined to go along with a provision of this type since it is in the seller's interest to facilitate the purchaser's capacity to perform. In such a case, however, the seller is likely to request additional earnest money for the extension. If you have reached the point where an extension of time is necessary for the closing, carefully consider your capacity to perform within the extended period. Consider your performance within the initial period as indicative of your performance during the extension and don't pay additional earnest money if you are not going to be able to perform. It is better to lose your initial earnest money than to lose a larger amount a month or two later.

Other factors will also influence your choice of a closing date. Two of them are the tax law and your obligation on the financing. Under the current tax law, you are encouraged to close property near the end of the month. That's because, under the depreciation tables prescribed by the IRS you are allowed to depreciate the property for a full half-month in the month of acquisition if you owned the property for any part of the month. To construct the tables, the IRS now uses mid-month convention that assumes that property acquired any time during the month was actually acquired mid-month. And if you close the property on the last day of the month, you will have very little income from the property for that month to offset your depreciation-produced loss. End-of-the-month closings are especially important near the end of the year. For example, a property closed on November 30 will have roughly three times the first year depreciation of a property closed on December 1 (one and a half months instead of one half month, though the rounding in the tables distorts this slightly).

As to the question of your payment obligations, you will want to schedule the closing so that you can collect as much money as possible before making the first payment. If you structure it right, you will be able to collect the majority of two months' rent on the property before having to make your first payment. For example, if your payment is due on the fifth of the month, you may want to schedule the closing on the sixth. You would own the property for 25 days, and the seller would own the property for five days in the month of closing (assuming a 30-day month). So, you would be entitled to five-sixths of the rent for that month. If the rent had already been collected by the seller, you would receive credit for the collection in closing, thus reducing the cash necessary for closing. Also, it is likely that you would collect a majority of the following month's rent before the payment was due. Thus, by scheduling the closing on the sixth, you are enabling yourself to collect nearly two months' rent before making a payment.

Actually, it isn't necessary to contrive to schedule the closing on the date following the payment obligation to obtain this benefit. Interest is paid in arrears. So, if you closed the property on the first of the month, and a payment was due on the fifth, you would be responsible for five days' interest, and the seller would be responsible for the balance. It is likely that the escrow agent would collect one month's payment from the parties in this context by withholding the appropriate amount of interest from the seller and charging the purchaser for his or her percentage of the obligation. This arrangement is not necessary, but many people consider it prudent. At the very least, the seller must be charged for his or her interest obligation through the closing date. If you can talk the escrow agent and the seller out of charging the following payment to you in closing, you will significantly reduce your closing costs. You will, however, have to deposit your percentage of the payment with the lender, perhaps through the escrow agent, when it is due.

As you can see, the tax law encourages a closing date near the end of the month, while normal financing arrangements encourage a closing date shortly after or around the first of the month. You may have to choose between the two conflicting motivations, or you may be able to structure the date to get the best of both worlds. If the seller is carrying the financing, you may be able to structure the closing for the last day of the month, with payments due on the final day of each month, but not delinquent or subject to any penalty for a grace period of, say, ten days. For example, you close on November 30. You receive credit for one day's rent and are charged for one day's expenses in the closing. You take one and a half months depreciation on the property for the year of acquisition. You collect all the rents for the month of December and pay all the related costs. Your next payment is due on December 31; however, it is not delinquent until January 10. In effect, your payment is due on January 10. Therefore, you should be able to collect the rents for January before having to make the payment. Finally, if you are lucky enough to have December 31 fall on a Friday or Saturday, you may be able to write a check and mail it on December 31 and not have it clear the bank until at least after the legal holiday on the following Tuesday. If your tenants pay promptly, you may be able to cover the check with January's collections while deducting the interest expenses for tax purposes in the preceding year.

In a leveraged investment, setting the closing date and payment obligation can have a significant impact on the return on investment. And in any transaction, it is worthwhile doing what you can to minimize the benefits of the available cash and tax advantages generated by the property.

THE CLOSING PROCEDURE

The closing itself is a meeting between the parties at the office of the attorney or escrow company during which the papers are signed and acknowledged. As purchaser, you will usually bring a certified check for the amount necessary to close the transaction and deposit it with the escrow agent. The check need not be certified unless the parties have so stipulated, but it will unravel the nerves of everyone in the room when you pull out your checkbook and start writing out a personal check to close the transaction. In fact, I have done this a few times, for the entertainment value of the reaction of the other parties to the transaction and because of the inconvenience of obtaining certified checks.

Most of the formality and symbolism that once dominated the closing has now been eliminated. The seller no longer hands the purchaser a clod of dirt in exchange for a peppercorn to symbolize the transfer of ownership of the land. The modern version is the transfer of keys that sometimes takes place at the closing. However, with larger properties managed by professional management companies, the owner may never see the keys to the property. In fact, it is becoming more and more common for the seller and purchaser to meet with the escrow agent separately and not come in contact. In fact, for many properties that I have purchased, I have never met the seller and have no idea what he or she looks like. Many attorneys and escrow agents would prefer to avoid having the seller and purchaser meet because their meeting is likely to cause conflict. This is especially true where the negotiations have been long and difficult.

Typically in attendance at the closing will be the seller, the seller's real estate agent, perhaps the seller's lawyer and other advisors, the buyer, the buyer's real estate agent, the buyer's lawyer and other advisors, and the representative of the escrow company. Each party in attendance has a separate and distinct business interest that is served by such attendance. The interests of the buyer and seller are fairly obvious. However, the interests of the professionals in attendance and how those interests vary from those of the principals they supposedly represent are often overlooked. For example, in larger property transactions, at least two real estate agents are usually involved. This is because of the increasing tendency among real estate agents to specialize as either a seller's representative (the listing agent) or a buyer's representative (the selling agent). Neither agent gets paid unless the deal is completed. Therefore, it is not uncommon for the buyer's agent to push the buyer into completing the transaction, even though an unfortunate turn of events would justify the buyer's withdrawl. The lawyers are the hired guns, the bodyguards of the respective clients. They are there to protect their clients in the event that trouble breaks out. The attorneys are there for a fee, and they have no real interest whether or not the deal is completed. The escrow agent runs the show and makes sure that everyone performs his or her obligations.

CLOSING DOCUMENTS

There are also many documents involved in a typical closing, usually including the deed to the property, the real estate contract that details the agreement between the parties, and the documents relating to the financing. There are the leases for the long-term tenants and the leases for the property if any of the property is on leased land or if the interest being transferred is a lease. Frequently, a rent roll is provided that lists the current tenants and their status and rent level. Often an inventory of personal property is provided. There is usually the title insurance policy and report or a lawyer's abstract of title. The purchaser will receive the purchaser's closing statement, which details how much money the purchaser is being charged and for what it is being used. The seller will receive the seller's closing statement, which shows how much (or little) the seller will receive of the purchaser's money after paying his or her portion of the transfer costs and fees.

It is important to review each document carefully. In the event of ambiguity, have them rewritten to clarify the understanding and agreement of the parties. It is remarkable how a seemingly innocent document can cause you so many problems later if it is not carefully analyzed and clarified. One example of this was a property that we purchased for a limited partnership. Among the documents we received at closing was a personal property inventory. The property consisted of over 190 apartments and over seven acres of grounds. Listed on the personal property inventory were the simple words "lawn mower." When we inspected the property, we noted the recent-model, tractor-type, riding lawn mower that was used on the property. We were also pleased to note that the lawn mower was equipped with a snow blade which would come in handy in the local climate. The value of the lawn mower was about $4,000 to $5,000. Naturally, we assumed that the lawn mower we would receive was the one that had been used on the property. In fact, our offer was to purchase all the real and personal property used in the apartment complex. When we took possession, however, we found that the tractor riding lawn mower had been removed and in its place was left a push mower—an old push mower, without even an engine, for seven acres of grass! This was only one of several problems we had with the seller in this transaction. It is important to head off this type of problem by being as careful as possible to define specifically all the terms used in the transaction. We should not have accepted a personal property inventory with a description as ambiguous as "lawn mower." Instead, we should have insisted on a specific description, such as "Kenmore model 1600 riding lawn mower with snow blade, ID #618456-9." If you insist on such a specific definition, the seller may think that you are being petty and demanding, and maybe you are, but you won't be cheated out of a $5,000 lawn mower.

So, where are we now? You have reviewed the market, negotiated the acquisition and closed the property. You are now a property owner, and are about to get rich, right? No! Your problems have just begun, because regardless of the quality of your performance in the analysis, negotiation and closing, you will have to perform well in ownership and management of the property in order to make money on your investments. So, take a deep breath, relax for a minute, and then proceed to Chapter 7.

MANAGEMENT AND OPERATING COSTS | 7

The importance of good management is not adequately emphasized by most real estate investment books. Management tends to be treated as a given condition, with very little discussion of what must be done to establish, develop, and motivate good management. The fact is that management does not come together by itself. Instead, a considerable amount of time and effort must be devoted to establishing and developing good management. Now that you have acquired your first investment property, management should be one of your primary concerns.

TO MANAGE OR NOT TO MANAGE?

In considering the difficulties associated with management, you must consider the possibility of avoiding the many problems by hiring a management company to manage your property. The desirability of hiring a management company depends on the needs and capabilities of the owner, balanced against the competence of the management company and the additional costs of professional management.

For many property owners, professional management is either a necessary evil or a reasonable alternative to the drudgery of personal management. But professional property management is not without disadvantages.

The first disadvantage of hired professional management is that it isn't free. The cost can be quite substantial. Usually, the management company will charge you 5 to 10 percent of the gross rents and other income collected. This fee covers the office functions of management only, and you will also be charged for the cost of on-site management, including the property manager's salary. Frequently, the management company will provide maintenance and repair of the property at its cost. But, again, this is not always the case. Sometimes the maintenance will be charged at an hourly rate calculated to pay the costs and absorb some of the management company's overhead, and sometimes the management company will charge for its maintenance services at a rate schedule to produce a profit.

Another disadvantage of using professional management companies is the quality of services offered. Management companies range from excellent to abysmal, from experienced and competent to inexperienced and incompetent, from trustworthy to thieving. Hiring of management companies is considered in Chapter 12. Here, it should be noted that the quality of management companies is, overall, mediocre. I believe this performance should be expected (although not tolerated) since the management company cannot be expected to have the same kind of interest in the property as the owner.

Finally, when you transfer management of your property to a management company, you are transferring control of the property. You are releasing control of your property, subject to the contract provisions of the management contract. It is difficult to give up something as important to the cash flow and the appreciation of the property as management control. Therefore, in most cases, I would recommend that you manage the property yourself or hire the personnel to manage the property as employees rather than hire a professional management company.

Initially, you will probably manage your investment property yourself. You will also perform all the necessary maintenance functions, including writing your own rental advertisements, showing the property, collecting the rent, cleaning the property between tenants, and making minor repairs. As a small property owner, you will tend to view these functions as just part of owning the property. If you think about them at all, you probably will label them as the overall function of management—work that needs to be done, which the property at least initially could probably not afford to pay someone else to do.

After managing your investments for a period of time, however, it's not uncommon to lose sight of the value of and take for granted the services you provide to the property. For example, if someone responds to your ad and wants to see the rental at ten o'clock in the evening, you go out and show the property.

When you do hire management employees, one of the first shocking realities that will confront you is that those employees simply will not show the same kind of dedication as you do. They may or may not answer the ten o'clock phone call, but, even if they do, the best you can expect is for them to make an appointment to show the property the following day.

Thus, we introduce the primary management dilemma, the motivation of underpaid employees. Management pays at a low level since it is generally nonunion labor and is popular employment for retirees, young people, or otherwise marginal employees. Motivation starts with hiring people who are capable of being motivated.

HIRING MANAGEMENT EMPLOYEES

The usual prudence that you are expected to exercise in all management decisions applies especially to hiring management personnel. Always get multiple references and always contact the references given by the applicant. A lukewarm endorsement should be considered as negative, a positive endorsement as neutral, and a glowing endorsement as positive, but no more. Remember that, these days, an employer can be sued by former employees for slander if he or she gives a negative reference. Consider the tone of the endorsements and attempt to read between the lines to determine what the reference is really saying.

Bond your employees or insure yourself against employee theft. Then do everything within your power to eliminate the temptation to steal. Just as it is the employee's duty to perform their responsibilities and not steal from their employer, it is the employer's responsibility to reduce or eliminate the opportunity to steal.

Match the employee with the job. Hire people who not only are competent and ambitious but also are going to be happy with the job and the pay level. If possible, hire people for whom the job is particularly attractive. For example, many a retired couple applies for the job of resident manager. The husband is a good handyman, and the wife feels competent at keeping the books. They will get a free apartment, and the salary will supplement their social security. The work keeps them busy while not occupying 100 percent of their time. In summary, it appears to be a good match.

The Right Attitude

In finding a good match between manager and property, you must find employees who have the right attitude. The fact that the apartment manager is a salesperson is frequently disregarded. When applying for the job, prospective managers will emphasize how handy they are, and how responsible and competent they are in handling books and records. They will seldom mention that they are good salespeople and that they feel competent that they can sell the product. Yet, it is important that they have good sales skills since this, ultimately as much as anything else, will determine their level of success.

A good salesperson starts out by recognizing the fact that he or she *is* a salesperson. This sounds peculiar because, if you work in a shoestore or an auto dealership as a salesperson, your capacity is obvious and not subject to any real question. However, everyone who comes into contact with the public or with customers or clients is to some extent involved in sales. Thus, the attitude of the maid in your motel room will have some influence on whether you choose to stay at the motel on your next visit. And no amount of advertising and promotion can overcome the bad will created when a customer is treated improperly. But, in the context of managing apartments, most employees don't really consider the fact that they are involved in a sales capacity. This is a mistake, and the mistake is costing the property owner money.

The second thing a good salesperson does is to familiarize him- or herself with the product. He or she will know the attributes of the product and be familiar with its shortcomings. The salesperson will know the product's actual market; namely, those who know the product represents a good purchase. He or she will also know the potential market: those who don't fully realize the advantages of this product over the competition.

The third thing a good salesperson does is to promote the product and make a sale. He or she will point out the product's attributes, which might otherwise be overlooked. The salesperson will probably let the customer discover the shortcoming on his or her own. The salesperson will listen very carefully to what the customer says and what the customer really means and attempt to show how the product satisfies the customer's needs.

Finally, a good salesperson utilizes the feedback he or she receives from the customers and communicates that information to those who should receive it. If a particular product is not selling well because of a design defect, the salesperson is likely to be the first person in the organization to become aware of the problem. If there is communication between the salespeople and those in a position to correct the problem, it may be corrected more quickly and at reduced cost to the organization.

A sales-oriented attitude is what I like to describe as "the right attitude" for the apartment manager. It is the manager's job to sell apartments. They will not sell themselves, and a shy, withdrawn person should not be in the business. When showing an apartment, the manager should not just simply open the door and step back, allowing the prospective tenant to wander around the apartment unattended. Instead, the apartment manager should lead the prospective tenant through the apartment, pointing out the attributes and answering the tenant's questions in as upbeat a manner as possible. The manager must point out the amenities of the property. Does it have a swimming pool and/or recreation building? What about laundry facilities? Is it close to shopping, schools, a bus route? If the manager "sells" the apartment, occupancy will be much better than if the manager just "shows" it.

My favorite example of the benefits of "the right attitude" involved red carpeting. A short time ago, we bought a large apartment complex that was well maintained and very attractive except that some of the apartments had red carpets in the bedrooms. A few even had red carpets throughout the apartment. The first resident manager we hired was convinced that the red carpets were a significant problem for the property. He was negative and apologetic about them, noting that there was a problem in that they did not coordinate well with the tenants' furniture. Not too surprisingly, few of the units with red carpet were rented. This, of course, reinforced the first manager's perception that the red carpet made the units unrentable. Now, we recognized that the color was not stylish, and it probably did clash with tenants' furniture, but the carpeting was practically new, and it just didn't make sense to replace it. So, we decided to replace the manager instead. We were particularly careful to get someone with the right attitude who would promote the attributes of the property, rather than dwell on the negatives. The next manager was much more successful in renting the units with the red carpeting. In fact, it was something of a challenge for him, and, shortly thereafter, the occupancy in the units with red carpeting was higher than that of the apartment complex as a whole. Of course, the overall occupancy was greatly improved. The manager promoted the units with red carpeting by suggesting that these units provided the opportunity for an exotic decor or that they were our "Mediterranean design" units. I don't know if anyone stopped to consider whether there was anything synonymous about the Mediterranean region and the color red, but the sales methods were very successful.

In suggesting that you refrain from pointing out the negative characteristics of the property, I am not suggesting that you defraud anyone. I am simply emphasizing the importance of promoting the positive. And, while you should not conceal defects, remember that overweight people do not wear form-hugging clothing. Minor deceptions are a part of our lives; they are almost expected. Prospective tenants do not expect managers to point out the defects, but they do expect them to be truthful when they discover defects on their own.

MOTIVATING MANAGEMENT EMPLOYEES

As mentioned above, the task of motivating management employees is difficult because of the pay level. Unless you have been very selective in your hiring, or you have more than the usual amount to offer them, the people you hire will probably be marginal employees. The larger the complex, the higher the quality of the employees you can expect to hire. For example, a larger complex with a full-time manager, an assistant manager, and maintenance people is easier to manage because it has the capacity to make more efficient use of personnel, and it offers the employee more career development opportunities. The salary level will still not be very good, but the increased efficiency will provide the opportunity for marginally better compensation.

Money, of course, is an excellent source of motivation. This is particularly true among people who don't make much of it. People for whom $20 is a considerable sum will be more motivated by the incentive of that amount than people for whom $20 is trivial. The key in using money as an incentive is to tie the compensation to the desired behavior. And, in measuring whether or not the desired behavior is being realized, it is important to measure those characteristics over which the particular employee has control. So you would want to tie the compensation of the apartment manager to the revenue from the project and the compensation of the maintenance person to achievement of the maintenance budget. This assumes that it is the manager's job to rent apartment units and maximize revenue and the maintenance man's job to use discretion in purchasing supplies and hiring labor to maintain the project.

At some of our apartment complexes, the manager is responsible for renting units but has no input into the rent level. In that context, we compensate the manager not on the basis of gross collections, but rather on the basis of units rented. Thus, the manager might receive his or her own unit, and, say, $10 for each unit rented. In a 50-unit complex, this would result in a maximum compensation of a free apartment unit and $490 per month (the manager isn't paid for renting the unit he or she lives in). On a nicer, newer, 50-unit complex, the management and ordinary maintenance task is approximately equivalent to a half-time job for a single employee. If the apartment would normally rent for $300 per month, the employee is being compensated at a rate of $790 per month, or $9,480 per year, which isn't bad for half-time work. In addition, under the federal income tax law, if the employee is required to occupy the property for the benefit of the landlord (which is always the case for resident apartment managers), the compensation of the free apartment is a nontaxable fringe benefit. Finally, there is the convenience factor. How valuable is it to the employee not to have to commute to work? In addition, the manager seldom has any specialized clothing or uniforms to purchase and to some extent has some flexibility in setting work hours, priorities, and activities. It is generally a comfortable, low-pressure job.

In establishing the method of compensation and other methods of motivation, you should beware of encouraging suboptimal behavior. Suboptimization occurs when the employee optimizes his or her particular function at the expense of the overall operations. Consider the following illustrations.

1. The apartment manager is paid on the basis of the number of units rented with no consideration given to any qualitative factors. To maximize the number of units rented, the manager agrees to rent a one-bedroom apartment to a family of six. The space is not adequate for the family's needs, and they spend several uncomfortable months in the apartment before moving away. When they leave, the evidence of being cramped is obvious from the condition of the apartment they left behind. The walls are marred, the carpets ruined, and the drapes stained and torn. The cost of repairing this apartment for a new tenant will exceed the rent that had been paid by the previous short-term tenant. But the maintenance costs come out of another budget, for which the manager is not responsible and that has no bearing on the amount of the manager's compensation. The apartment manager is considering renting the refurbished apartment to another large family.

2. The maintenance person receives a bonus if the repairs and maintenance are accomplished within the amount budgeted for those expenses. The maintenance person has determined that the budget is inadequate for the building and that the only way to maintain the building within the budget is to cut corners and do less than the optimal work wherever possible. The result is short-term cost savings at the expense of the long-term objectives of the property. There is a slow and at first imperceptible decline in the property. Eventually, it will cost considerably more to make the repairs than if the work had been done right in the first place.

There are of course, many other examples of suboptimization. To avoid it, consider qualitative as well as quantitative indices of performance. It is very difficult to tie compensation to qualitative factors. Employees tend to be more satisfied with quantitative measures of their performance because there are less subjective, less at the discretion or judgment of someone else. Since employees are more receptive to quantitative measure, they will be more likely to perform in the desired manner. There is positive reinforcement since the employee knows immediately that his or her efforts will be appropriately rewarded. The important thing is to recognize the capacity for suboptimization and not to disregard qualitative factors. Set standards to ensure compliance with the qualitative factors. For example, you might have a rule that no more than two tenants occupy a one-bedroom apartment. All tenants may be required to fill out a credit application and give references. If properly applied, these measures will provide assurances that both the quality and the quantity of the tenants is being considered.

In the context of maintenance, it is more difficult to set standards of general applicability. Sometimes a broken appliance can be repaired economically, and other times it is better to replace it. Also, you can only patch a roof so many times before it has to be replaced. The problem is that each situation is unique. So, since the function does not lend itself to handy rules of thumb, you must instead rely on your own judgment or the recommendations of those you know to be competent.

THE OBLIGATIONS OF THE EMPLOYER

Whether you're hiring managers or maintenance people or both, you assume many legal and moral obligations as an employer. The legal obligations are easier to address because they are better defined. There are many things you must not do. For example, you must not discriminate in your employment on the basis of age, sex, race, religion, or ethnic background. You must not fire employees without just grounds. You must not slander or libel your present or former employees (or anyone else, for that matter). There are also many things that you must do. You must withhold income taxes and social security taxes from the employee's check and deposit the taxes with the government. You must provide a safe place of employment. You must provide certain statutory fringe benefits, like workers' compensation insurance. These days, your legal obligations are quite substantial.

Your moral obligations are also substantial, though harder to define. You are responsible for the livelihood of your employees, and, to some extent, you are responsible for their future expectations. You have a moral obligation to act responsibly in this capacity, which entails more than merely satisfying your legal obligations. It includes such things as promoting based on merit and promoting from within the organization whenever possible. Listening to you employees is also very important. They will tell you what they wish to gain from the employment relationship in addition to their paycheck, and they will tell you what they are willing to contribute to the success of the organization. You may be surprised to hear what your employees have to say. Many would trade away a wage increase for improved working conditions; and frequently fringe benefits, like group medical insurance, are considered more valuable than cash.

When I first considered investing in real estate, I failed to consider the significance of my role as an employer. I considered how much property I intended to buy, how much money I intended to raise, and what the property would be worth after a period of time. This was a mechanical process of calculating appreciation, and I felt confident in my ability to realize the projected return. I knew the importance of negotiating a good purchase, of improving the property and holding it long enough so that all the appreciation wasn't used to pay the transaction costs. I suppose that I considered the fact that the property would not run itself and that I would have neither the time nor the desire to perform all of the management functions myself. But I really didn't fully appreciate the importance of good management or the importance of my responsibility as an employer until I was invited into the homes of some of my managers, and I met their spouses and children. When I heard them talk about their goals and ambitions, it struck me that I was important to them, and my reliability and responsibility would impact their ability to realize their dreams. This is a heavy responsibility to recognize, but unless you are prepared to accept it, you shouldn't be in the property management business.

OPERATING COSTS

Underemphasized as much as the importance of management in the popular literature is the significance of operating expenses. This can be a substantial oversight for the novice investor. In fact, I have often heard the novice investor considering an acquisition either completely disregard the operating expenses or discount their magnitude. The novice considers the purchase of a four-unit apartment building with total rents of $300 per unit, or $1,200 per month, and thinks he or she will make $100 per month since the payment is "only" $1,100. It is more likely that the property will cost $200 per month or more in negative cash flow to maintain ownership. That estimate also assumes that the owner performs most of the management and maintenance functions and doesn't consider the cost of those contributed services in measuring the cash flow.

Why does it cost so much to operate the property? There simply are many expenses in the operation of the property that tend to be overlooked by the novice. Each one of these expenses may not amount to much, but, when considered in total, they represent a significant percentage of the rent of the property.

How big a percentage of the rent should you expect the expenses to take up? This is a very difficult question to answer since expense factors vary substantially among properties. The expenses vary with the area of the country, the magnitude of the property taxes, the services provided for the particular property, and the rent levels against which the expenses will be calculated. For example, if the expenses of operating a particular property are $100 per month, the expense factor will be 50 percent if the rent on the units is $200 per month, but only 25 percent if the rent is $400 per month. There is very little direct relation between the expenses of operating a property and the amount of rent the market will bear. However, there is *some* relationship since, if the yield from the property after expenses is inadequate to support new construction, there will be a limitation on the supply of apartments, which will tend to cause an increase in the rent level. So, there is some correlation to be seen between high expenses and high rent. The result is that expense factors for an area tend to be similar, and a significant departure from the average experience of the area will be regarded with appropriate suspicion. I live in a community where a 40 percent expense factor is typical for newer properties, where the tenants pay heat and electric costs, and an expense factor of under 35 percent is unlikely to be accurate. Older buildings will require additional maintenance costs and have a higher expense factor, as will buildings where the landlord pays the cost of providing the heat, air conditioning, and electricity.

If you insist on a rule-of-thumb expense factor, I would suggest that it not be less than 35 percent of rents, and it is frequently higher. In Oregon, for example, where the property taxes are quite high and the rents are relatively low (at this writing), it is unlikely that the expenses will be less than 40 percent. In California, it is harder to generalize since the state's markets are so diverse and the various rent control schemes tend to distort comparisons. Each other state and local market will have unique expense characteristics. Some will have high utility expenses, others high taxes.

But, as I have indicated, when an expense factor is presented by the seller, you should look beyond it at the actual expenses the property has experienced. It is important to note the expense factor in considering the likely reliability of the financial information you have received. It is also valuable in considering whether there is much likelihood of your reaching an agreement on the price and terms for the property. If the seller has told you that the expenses for the property are 20 percent, and you know they must be at least 40 percent, the seller is misrepresenting the expense factor in the hope that an ignorant purchaser will pay more for the property than it is worth. It is unlikely that you will get the kind of purchase you desire from this seller. Also, if the seller has misrepresented the financial information, you must ask yourself what other information has been misrepresented. It is difficult to deal with someone you know is lying to you.

When expenses are reported in detail by the seller, as they always should be before the buyer commits to the acquisition, the buyer should beware of the omissions. The best way to guard against omissions is to maintain a checklist of the expenses usually associated with property management and check the reported expenses against the list. I believe you will find the following list to be representative.

COMMON PROPERTY MANAGEMENT EXPENSES
Vacancy
    Promotional discounts
    Advertising
    Promotional literature
    Insurance—fire and casualty
    Insurance—liability
    Insurance—workers' compensation
    Insurance—employee theft
    Taxes—real property
    Taxes—personal property
    Taxes—federal income
    Taxes—state and local income
    Taxes—employment
    Taxes—sales and other
    Management—fees
    Management—salaries
    Management—fringe benefits
    Management—free apartment
    Supplies—office

Supplies—maintenance
Supplies—cleaning
Maintenance and repairs—salaries
Maintenance and repairs—materials
Painting and cleaning—labor
Painting and cleaning—materials
Utilities—electrical
Utilities—gas
Utilities—oil
Utilities—water
Utilities—sewer or septic service
Utilities—garbage removal
Auto and travel
Gardening and grounds—labor
Gardening and grounds—materials
Swimming pool—maintenance labor
Swimming pool—materials
Capitalized expenditures (improvement and replacement)
Legal and professional fees
Bank service charges
Bad checks
Over and short (handling of cash receipts)
Employee theft
Contract labor
Contract services
Petty cash (with or without expense detail)
Eviction filing fees and costs
Depreciation (noncash)
Amortization (noncash)
Debt service (interest or interest and principal)
Miscellaneous

Use the list above as a guideline. Yes, there is some overlap among expense categories. Yes, not every property will have expenses in every category. But remember that any grounds or recreational facilities such as a swimming pool won't maintain itself. Find out if the costs are buried in the maintenance category. If your preacquisition analysis omits expenses, those expenses will still have to be paid when you acquire ownership. If the property doesn't generate enough cash to pay all the cash expenses, you will have to pay the difference if you wish to maintain ownership. And, even if it isn't a question of losing ownership, if you omit expenses, you will be disappointed with the return you actually realize on your investment.

DEPRECIATION, AMORTIZATION, AND DEBT SERVICE

Depreciation, amortization, and debt service are frequently omitted from the operating expense consideration (and are not included in my guideline rate of least 35 percent) since the first two are noncash expenses and debt service is not an operating expense. But, also usually omitted by sellers, and frequently unquestioned by purchasers, are the capitalized improvements. It is a mistake to omit both depreciation and the cost of capital improvements. Remember, all expenses are to some extent recurring. You may not have to replace the roof each year, but, if the roof has to be replaced every ten years, that is roughly equivalent to replacing one-tenth of the roof each year. The same is true for the appliances, carpeting, parking lot, etc. Make sure that you adequately budget a repairs and replacements reserve.

When banks and other lenders look at financial statements, they are concerned with the debt coverage ratio. To calculate the debt coverage ratio, you calculate the revenue less cash operating expenses other than the debt service to arrive at a figure usually referred to as the property's *net operating income* (before debt service). You compare this figure to the debt service requirement to see how well covered the payment is—that is, how many times you could pay the debt with operating income from the property. If the net operating income from the property is $50,000, and the debt service payment is $40,000, the debt coverage ratio is 50,000 to 40,000 or 1.25 to 1. Banks are very pragmatic. They want to be sure that the debt is going to be paid. The greater the debt coverage ratio, the less the risk of default. Thus, in addition to its concern with the appraised value of the property, the bank will also insist on a certain level of debt coverage. Typically, the lender will require a debt coverage ratio of at least 1.2 to 1. You should be aware of the debt coverage ratio if you are going to refinance the property and are considering how much cash you can realize through refinancing.

MARKET RISK

In considering the expense factor and the importance of good management, it is important to consider the probability that those expense factors will continue to hold true. What we are considering on a broader scope is the whole question of market risk. If the rate of rent increases matches the rate of increase in the expenses for the property, the expense factor will remain the same. If rent increases exceed cost increases, the expense factor will decline, and if the rate of increase in the expenses exceeds the rate of rent increases, the expense factor will increase.

RENT CONTROL

Consider the political and economic environment in which you operate and its impact on the market risk. For example, what is the probability that the property will be affected by a rent control initiative? Often, when rent control is first introduced into the marketplace, it starts with a rent rollback to rent levels that existed at some point in time prior to the initiative. This is usually so because a rent control initiative, where successful, is a response to a market characterized by rapidly rising rent levels. The political response is to seek governmental or legal intervention. How would the property you are considering do with rent levels fixed at current levels, or worse, rent levels that have returned to the level of two years ago? Wouldn't you like to be able to roll back your operating expenses to the level of two years ago? Well, while rent levels may be rolled back, you know that expenses never will be.

Beyond the initial effect of rent control will be the continuing restraint that rent control puts on rent increases. Your operating costs will not be similarly restrained and are likely to be increasing at a greater rate than the rent. In a market that is controlled by rent control, you actually have the dual constraints of those imposed by the law and those imposed by ordinary market pressures. Thus, even if the rent control board would allow you to increase rent, the market might not support such an increase. If you attempt to increase rent in the face of a market that will not support the new rent level, the result will be high vacancy rate for your apartments. But you may have to increase rent in order to establish the base rent levels for future rent increases under the rent control restrictions. So, the cyclical market for rent levels may well be evened out under the pressure of rent control. And occasionally, the rent may actually be higher than it would be if rent control were not in effect.

Regardless of your political attitude with respect to governmental regulation, a fact of life in a controlled market is a limitation on the return to be realized from investments. It is unlikely that much new construction will be undertaken in such a market unless it is partially or totally exempt from the regulations. There is also very little motivation to maintain or improve the property. If the improvement costs can't be passed along to the tenants in the form of rent increases, those improvements will not be made. Similarly, the property will be maintained only at the level that the rent justifies. I will spare the reader my dissertation on the disadvantages of rent control. From an investment point of view, the prospect and chance of rent control should be considered an investment risk. It is a factor that should be considered in evaluating the potential return from the property.

Do not invest in a market where new rent control regulations are being considered. You might, however, consider investments in areas where rent controls have been in effect for a number of years. The initial effect of rent controls is devastating to property values. But after a period of time, values tend to adjust to this market condition. Many fortunes have been made in controlled rent environments like San Francisco and New York City, so I can't simply suggest that you avoid them. But you should consider the controls in your risk factor. It is interesting to note that rent controls impose an artificial constraint on normal free market functions, and vast amounts of money can be made by finding ways to circumvent the regulations. One example of which I am aware occurs in San Francisco, where rental properties of three units or less are not subject to rent control if the owner occupies one of the units. If a new purchaser buys a triplex that had controlled rent and moves into one of the units, the rents are controlled for one year and then the controls are dropped. There are a number of people who make a business of annually moving to a new building, living there for the minimum statutory period, increasing their rent (and property value) substantially, and then moving on to another similar property. They don't make the rules, but they know how to play the game very well.

CHANGING VACANCY RATES

Another risk factor to consider is fluctuations in the vacancy rate on the property. Since the end of World War II, there has been a tremendous increase in the market for owner-occupied and rental property. The market has been fueled by the population increase, but it has been growing more rapidly than the population increase due to the overall reduction in the size of households. The nuclear family is now the rule, not the exception. And increasingly, singles prefer to live alone and not share expenses with roommates. However, when economic times get tight, people make due with less than the most desirable conditions. Thus, in the early 1980s, much to everyone's surprise, the market for rental property, overall, died. There was actually a decline in the number of households for the first time since World War II. There were several reasons for the decline. In the hard times of the severe economic recession, there was a greater tendency for people to share housing. Children were somewhat less anxious to leave home, and, in general, less expensive housing fared better than the rest of the market. If the published literature of the time is any indication, this change in social practices was not anticipated by anyone active in the business. Suddenly, the overall vacancy rate for the United States was higher than at any time in recent memory. In certain markets that were adversely affected otherwise—by factory closings, falling prices for gasoline products, and other factors—the vacancy rate was nothing short of catastrophic. The falling rents affected the property values, and more than one owner either lost property or sold out at a substantial loss. How could this happen? Apartments have traditionally been regarded as a safe, if illiquid, investment. The feeling was that, even if unemployed, people "had to live somewhere." But the declining number of households revealed that even the most secure presumptions don't always hold true in the context of severe economic recessions.

Another factor affecting vacancy rates, in addition to the impact of the national and local economy, is competition from new construction. Strong current markets or the prospect for strong future markets will affect the level of occupancy by encouraging new construction. The additional supply of housing may or may not be absorbed by the market. Or the new supply may be absorbed at the expense of existing housing. But, under any circumstance, when the supply of housing exceeds the demand, the owners will suffer with higher vacancy and lower rent.

It is annoying when the new competition is provided by the government. When the government builds a housing development and you lose tenants to the project, it becomes difficult to vote for incumbents. These days there is a tendency for the government to subsidize a tenant's rent rather than build a new project. In constructing a low-income housing project, the well-intentioned government officials provide housing at the expense of human dignity. By accepting the housing, the poor people are required to endure the stigma of needing government support and having their address and accommodations show it. The children are brought up self-conscious of the place where they live and of their family's social and economic status. The government is also put to the burden of having to manage a housing project. Even if the government were good at managing property, which it isn't, a housing project imposes impossible management dilemmas. If you take a large number of low-income and welfare people and throw them together in a housing project, you are likely to create a new urban ghetto. The elderly people will find it difficult to feel secure, and the children will have trouble finding the "right kind" of friends.

If the government determines to provide for the housing of its less fortunate citizens through subsidy, it will find that it may house those people without the social stigma of life "in the projects." In addition, it will not alienate its local property owners by displacing tenants from existing privately owned properties. Therefore, I would strongly advocate subsidy over the construction of housing projects. Subsidy, however, is not guaranteed to bring the government and property owners together. It still can result in displacing tenants.

I have been both a beneficiary and a victim of government subsidy programs. Ironically, one government program benefited some property on which I have a partnership interest at the expense of another property that I own in another partnership. I was one of many downtown property owners in a city in the western United States. The primary housing for lower-income people in the city consisted of the older downtown apartment buildings. There was a city housing authority, but for many years it was funded inadequately to provide much assistance to anyone. Eventually, however, the city housing authority, on the strength of federal government matching funds, was convinced of the propriety of providing housing assistance. Then, with funding, the governmental agency sought worthy recipients of assistance and found them living in the downtown buildings. Determined to improve the lot of these poor unfortunates, the government subsidized their new apartments in the suburbs. They found many willing takers. If you had a choice between living in an older small apartment downtown and living in a spacious modern apartment in a garden court apartment complex in the suburbs, where would you choose to live? What if the downtown apartment rented for $125 per month, and your portion of the cost of the suburban apartment was $50 per month? The downtown buildings were marginally profitable when they were experiencing 95 percent occupancy. After a year of government subsidies, the average occupancy rate among the downtown residential apartments was below 80 percent. The occupancy of our suburban complexes was approaching 100 percent. The downtown buildings could no longer support themselves. Many property owners lost their investments, and the buildings fell into a state of disrepair. Now the bureaucrats are bemoaning the decline of the downtown business district, and the property owners are being sued by the city attorney's office to maintain their buildings better. Many property owners find it particularly curious that city officials fail to recognize that, even if they aren't responsible for creating the problem, they have certainly contributed to the situation.

In managing any property, you are concerned with managing a

business. Your goal should be to perform your business professionally and to manage your employees in a manner that will facilitate your ultimate business objective: to show a profit. The most important person to any business is the customer. Most successful businesses devote substantial time and attention to satisfying the needs of the customer. In the real estate business, the customer is your tenant. So why do landlords spend so much time, expense and effort fighting with their tenants? Unfortunately, it appears that there is a natural area of conflict in this business relationship, which we will explore in Chapter 8.

LANDLORDS VERSUS TENANTS | 8

As the title to this chapter implies, the landlord-tenant relationship is one that is quite often adversarial. This is unfortunate but quite understandable. There are many reasons that landlords and tenants are often at odds.

Landlords want to make money on their investments. They may also have some notion about providing superior housing or office space at competitive rates. But that is how they intend to go about making money; that is their product or service. It is not their objective, but rather the means to the end.

Landlords see themselves as reasonable businesspeople. They shop around for the best prices on supplies and services and charge as much for the rent as they can without incurring excessive vacancy. The image that landlords have of tenants depends largely on the landlords' experience. Generally, they do not dislike the tenants, but they are wary of becoming too close to them or too friendly with them. They suspect that, if they become too friendly with the tenants, the tenants will attempt to take advantage of the situation by failing to pay the rent on time or by asking for improvements to the property or the construction of additional amenities. So, landlords tend not to socialize with their tenants.

Tenants have a similarly positive self-image and a similarly neutral-to-negative image of their adversary. In the rental property context, the tenants are the consumers. As consumers, they are interested in obtaining the best value in their purchases. Prior to deciding on a purchase, they have probably shopped around among a number of rental properties, comparing amenities and rents. This is a major expenditure for tenants. The average person spends between 25 and 40 percent of take-home pay on housing. So, you would expect tenants to be careful or prudent in their acquisition. In addition, they know that, if they have made a mistake, it is unlikely to be discovered until after they have commenced occupancy and that it is not correctable for a potentially long period of time. All that tenants want is the benefit of their bargain—quiet enjoyment of the apartment, shelter from the elements, appliances and utilities that work, security, and attractively maintained private and public areas. They do not feel that it is at all unreasonable for them to demand that the landlord spend the money and perform or hire the labor necessary to maintain the building. But they view the landlord as a money-grubbing tightwad who is more interested in making money than in maintaining the property. They complain that they must request that repairs be made several times before anything is done and that, even then, the repairs are inadequate since the landlord is unwilling to spend enough money to do the job right.

If all of the foregoing sounds familiar, then the landlord-tenant relationships you have experienced have been typical. The relationship is not warm, but neither is it litigious. The parties have a healthy distrust for one another that will cause them to exercise caution in their dealings. Yet each side recognizes and appreciates the other. The tenant appreciates the landlord's efforts, and the landlord respects the tenant and his or her legitimate requests. Sometimes, however, the relationship is hardly one of mutual respect; the feeling that each side has for the other is nothing short of hatred. This unhealthy environment is likely to result in frequent and continuous litigation.

When the disputes between the landlord and the tenant indicate that the parties have strong feelings of dislike for one another, it is likely that the cause can be found well beneath the surface of the dispute. The dispute may well be a trivial matter that sparks the underlying animosity. These people do not like each other, and, if the reason is not personality conflicts, it is likely to be something approaching the traditional class struggle between the landlord class and the tenant class. Either side or both will perceive the reason for the animosity between them to be a function of the differences in their classes and stations in life, and if that is the perception, it can well become a self-fulfilling prophecy.

Such a perception, and the desire to resolve conflicts short of violence, is the motivation behind much of the landlord-tenant legislation that will be considered in more detail. As an experienced landlord, I can advise you on the issue of the class struggle as follows. You cannot avoid the issue by buying better-quality units. Although there are often fewer activists among the upper middle class, and they are less likely to organize the rest of the tenants, you may expect some conflict at any socio-economic level, even those with more wealth than you. Some people are simply convinced that you are villainous long before they meet you; regardless of your actions, you will not change this perception. Most of your tenants will be decent, hardworking people, regardless of their economic level. If you treat your tenants with respect, your tenant problems will be few. When conflict does arise, you will find more support from the tenants than will the rabble-rousers.

THE LOCAL LAW

As with many other issues in real estate, it is the local law and rules that will govern your relationships with the tenants. Real estate law is a state government matter supplemented by local regulations. Thus, an action that might be perfectly legal in one jurisdiction might be illegal in another. I was once examining an apartment building in a jurisdiction with which I was unfamiliar and came across a storage room filled with a considerable amount of valuable personal property. Among the items were stereos, typewriters, and television sets. I was advised that these items were seized personal property that would be sold in 90 days if the tenant didn't pay the delinquent rent. In another jurisdiction, I was advised that the policy of management when the tenant didn't pay the rent was to turn off the power and remove the front door. I was shocked by both of these policies, since the law with which I was familiar would not permit such actions. However, I confirmed their legality within the jurisdictions in which the respective properties were located.

In advising you on landlord-tenant matters, I must point out that you need to be cognizant of the local law. Any advice must be qualified and limited to the jurisdiction in question. Turning off the power and removing the front door will, in most jurisdictions, entitle the tenant to civil damages from you and in some jurisdictions may land you in jail. Therefore, the matter of evictions is one area in which you should utilize the services of a competent local attorney, until such time as you acquire enough experience to handle it on your own. Collecting rent and evicting tenants are, of course, but two examples of the many local laws that will affect your landlord-tenant relationship. Other examples of local laws are building codes, restrictions on lease provisions, restrictive covenants, health and safety ordinances, rent and deposit restrictions, and tenant rights legislation, just to name a few.

AREAS OF CONFLICT

PAYMENT OF RENT

For whatever reason, the tenant is not paying the rent that the landlord claims is due. The tenant may simply be unable to pay the rent because of unforeseen personal expenses or may be asserting that he or she doesn't owe the rent because of some failure on the part of the landlord or the property. It is important for you as landlord in this case to assert immediately and unequivocally the right to collect the rent and to proceed with whatever practical and legal methods are necessary to make the collection. You may sympathize with the tenant's situation and make provision for payment of the deficiency over a period of time. This is an understandable human reaction, and it often works out satisfactorily, but the chronically late tenant will in all likelihood eventually move out owing you money. And the amount owed will be greater than if you had enforced prompt rent collection.

SIGNING AND ENFORCING THE LEASE

I recommend that you always use a written rental agreement, whether the rental is for a month-to-month tenancy or a lease for a longer period of time. The agreement formalizes the relationship between the parties and will usually be signed by the tenant without question. Occasionally, the tenant may object to some of the provisions of the rental agreement, and you must decide if you can live with modifications of the standard agreement or if you want to avoid setting a precedent of modifying the standard agreement. You might also consider whether the requested modifications are an early indication of a problem tenancy. The conservative approach is to accept no modifications, but this may not take into account real-world practicalities.

Once you have a signed rental agreement, you have an enforceable legal document. Both you and the tenant have legal rights and obligations. The value of the document depends on its wording and the quality of the parties. If the tenant is not the kind of person who honors legal and moral obligations, you will find that it is impossible to enforce the lease and recover any deficiency once the tenant has vacated. On the other hand, the lease as a legal document can have an inhibiting effect on the tenant and will encourage the payment of the obligation since you can prove the legitimacy of your claim.

THE COSTS OF MOVING IN

How much are you going to charge the tenants to commence occupancy? Is it enough to charge the first month's rent? How about a damage deposit and a cleaning deposit or fee? How about a prepayment of the last month's rent? What do you charge in those circumstances in which the tenant requests substantial expensive improvements prior to occupancy? The answer to all these questions is that you will charge as much as the market will bear. In prosperous times of low vacancy, it is not uncommon to see charges of the first and last month's rent as well as substantial deposits and fees. However, when the market is soft, you will find property owners offering various incentives to promote occupancy, including promotional gifts and a reduction or elimination of some of the rental charges. In an extreme example of this, I was once offered six months' free rent and five dollars per square foot of complimentary tenant improvements (at the landlord's expense) in exchange for a three-year lease of a 2,000-square-foot office at an annual rate of $12 per square foot. The building was about 60 to 70 percent vacant in a very soft market of excess supply.

So, you collect as much as you can from the tenant, remembering that it is never enough if the tenant damages your property, but that it is always too much from the tenant's perspective.

INCREASING THE RENT

One area of recurring conflict between landlords and tenants concerns the level of rent, the method of increasing rent, and the frequency and amount of rent increases. The majority of the country does not have rent controls, and the level of rent is a matter of ownership choice constrained by market pressures. There may also be restrictions in the lease and rental agreement, and there will certainly be statutory notice requirements that the landlord must furnish the tenants informing them of an increase. As to how frequently the rent should be increased and by what magnitude; again, it must be noted that we are all constrained by the market and by traditional real estate practices. For example, it is very rare for rents to increase more frequently than semiannually. Therefore, if you attempt to increase rent monthly, even by one-sixth of your semiannual amount, you are likely to encounter resistance and vacancy problems. Your business practice is unusual and therefore suspect.

As to the amount that you should increase the rent, note that any amount is not going to be appreciated by the tenants, so you might as well make the increase large enough to justify the dissatisfaction. As Louie DePalma of TV's "Taxi" would say, "You want them to say, 'Ouch,' but you don't want them to move." As a practical matter, you must increase rents to experience appreciation in real estate values. You are constrained by market forces, and often you will have to forgo or postpone a scheduled rent increase until such time as the market justifies it. Other times, you will find that you are able to increase the level of rents at a significant rate without losing tenants. It all depends on the local market.

Frequently, landlords will apologize for rent increases or attempt to justify the increase in terms of increased operating costs or other factors. This apology or justification is included in the letter or notice informing the tenant of the increase, and I believe it is generally a mistake. You increase your rent because the market justifies the increase, and whatever excuse you present to the tenants will be perceived as just that, an excuse. Also, what will be your excuse the next time you wish to increase rent and haven't experienced the same kind of cost increases? Will you lie to the tenants about the costs? I think it is better to avoid the whole issue by not offering excuses for the rent increase; instead simply inform the tenants of the new rental charges.

ENFORCING TENANT OBLIGATIONS

Your tenants will have various obligations to you and the property in addition to simply paying the rent. For example, they will be obligated to maintain their individual units. This maintenance may be limited to keeping the property clean, or it might involve the obligation to make minor repairs. Also, the tenants will be obligated to refrain from interfering with the quiet enjoyment of the rest of the tenants. It is the landlord's responsibility to enforce the tenant's obligations, both for the maintenance of the appearance and value of the property and for the goodwill of the other tenants. One poor tenant can easily drive away several good ones, with loud music and obnoxious behavior. Undesirable tenants can also do serious damage to the property. Therefore, it is necessary to respond promptly to tenant complaints about other tenants. The offending tenant should be informed of the complaints but keep the complaining tenant's identity confidential whenever possible. And the offending tenant should be informed in no uncertain terms that you intend to maintain a quality property and that offensive behavior will not be tolerated. With the majority of tenants, one warning (every so often) is all that will be necessary. But for the more serious problem tenant, it might be necessary to commence eviction procedures.

While you must observe the tenants' right to privacy, it is also necessary to verify from time to time that they are not damaging the property. Therefore, I recommend periodic maintenance inspections. Provide the tenants with the legal written notice requirements, as specified by local laws, of your intention to inspect the property. Use the inspection for the dual purpose of identifying tenant damage and identifying items in need of repair. Make the inspection as positive as possible, complimenting those tenants who maintain their units and promptly following up on the repairs. This will reduce tenant resistance to the inspections. The remedial action will depend on the seriousness of the problem. If the tenant doesn't clean the carpets, perhaps it is because he or she doesn't own a vacuum cleaner and would be pleased to know that the manager has one available. Don't evict a tenant over trivial matters, but don't refrain from evicting a tenant who is engaging in harmful or illegal activities in the building.

HANDLING TENANT DEPOSITS

In a typical month-to-month tenancy or lease, the tenant will deposit funds with the landlord for various purposes. The most common deposit is a damage deposit, which is refundable to the tenant in the event that he or she meets rental obligations and leaves the property undamaged. Local law may require you to establish a trust account for these funds, or you may be permitted to deposit them in your operating account along with the rent.

When the funds are deposited in your account, it is difficult to remember that they aren't yours, and landlords in general have a notorious and much deserved reputation for failing to return the deposits to the tenants. Because of the abuse that has often been associated with the return of tenant deposits, most jurisdictions restrict the landlord's discretion. Consult a local attorney about the rules in your area.

Other common deposits include security deposits, cleaning deposits, and pet deposits. The purpose of the security deposit is to provide the landlord with some assurance that the tenant will honor the terms of the obligations. Frequently, this deposit is not refundable if the tenant moves during the initial term of the lease. The cleaning deposit is intended to cover the cost of cleaning and repairing the property for the subsequent tenant. It is intended to cover the cost of returning the property to its condition at the beginning of the lease, ordinary wear and tear excepted. Pet deposits are additional deposits levied against pet owners because of the additional damage that pets can cause.

All of the deposits may be partially or totally nonrefundable. To the extent that they are nonrefundable, they are more in the nature of fees than deposits, and some jurisdictions require labeling nonrefundable deposits as fees. The labeling is intended to protect consumers by providing them with notice that the fees in question are nonrefundable. I don't believe that the semantic change fulfills this purpose. However, it will occasionally catch unaware landlords with unintended provisions in their lease and deposit agreements. Another common regulation is restrictions on the uses of damage deposits. The most common complaint of tenants is that the property was returned in good condition and the deposit was not returned because the landlord has represented that it wasn't clean enough. No damage is alleged, and the tenant can neither prove nor disprove the cleanliness of the property. To prevent this abuse, many jurisdictions provide that damage deposits cannot be used for cleaning the apartment and that, if funds are to be used for cleaning, they must be charged in the form of a nonrefundable fee. This has the unfortunate consequence of punishing those tenants that return the property in good condition and encouraging the tenants to move out without making any attempt to clean. It is unfortunate that past abuses have resulted in this kind of regulation.

MAINTENANCE AND REPAIRS

The most common complaint of tenants, other than those related to rent and deposit requirements, is that the property is not maintained adequately. The complaint is related to repairs and maintenance of the common areas as well as repairs and maintenance of the rental unit. The usual complaints are that the repairs are slow and inadequate. The advice here, of course, is to make the repairs prompt and adequate, but the problem lies in evaluating the promptness and adequacy. If your tenant is hopping around on one leg because the toilet doesn't work, your promise to repair it tomorrow is not likely to be regarded as prompt enough. On the other hand, fixing one of the burners on a stove that has three others that work is not the kind of emergency repair that requires immediate action. Put yourself in the position of the tenant and consider the inconvenience caused by the defect.

Maintenance of the common areas and grounds should be an ongoing activity. Property that is not maintained begins to decline. You should budget for a certain amount of repairs every period, even if no need is evident. If you have no current use for the repair budget (an unlikely situation), set the funds aside so that they may be available when needed. A more likely scenario would involve a budgeted routine maintenance budget, with another list of major repairs for which funds and priority are being accumulated. The major items are the maintenance wish list, including such items as new refrigerators and air conditioners, new roof, and parking lot resurfacing. Eventually, all of these items will need to be purchased if the property is not to deteriorate.

Tenants will usually complain about the repairs, regardless of how rapidly and expertly the repairs are made. For that reason, it is difficult to evaluate the adequacy of the repairs and maintenance on your property. Sometimes you might reason that you are throwing enough money at the problem that it ought to be covered. But money is not a substitute for good management and control. One indication of your manager's concern with maintenance is the general appearance of the property. If the buildings and grounds are clean and attractive, you would suspect that the property systems are also well maintained. Listen to your tenants' complaints and consider their magnitude and nature. If a tenant complains that it took three weeks for your maintenance people to fix a broken toilet, the problem is much different from one in which a tenant is complaining that a broken fixture was patched rather than replaced. The first complaint is indicative of a serious problem with the property's maintenance labor, budget, or both. The second complaint, if trivial enough in nature, might actually be considered an endorsement of the maintenance staff's use of budgeted funds. We once had a tenant complain that a heated swimming pool was kept at 68 degrees. This was a complaint that we were pleased to receive since the manager was instructed to heat the pool to 68 degrees. The temperature might have been too low for this tenant, but heating the pool more would have been too hot for our budget. By filing the complaint, the tenant informed us that in this regard the manager was doing his job.

BUSINESSLIKE PRACTICES

If you are in the *business* of renting property, act like it. Conduct yourself in a businesslike manner and engage in businesslike practices.

THE WRITTEN LEASE

Among those practices that I have already suggested is the use of a written lease or rental agreement. The landlord will provide the rental agreement used on the property, and it will therefore be written in such a manner as to specify the rights of the landlord and the duties of the tenant. Always get the tenant to sign the written rental agreement before beginning occupancy or before taking possession of the property. After the tenant has possession of the property, if he or she refuses to sign the lease or objects to some of the provisions, you will find yourself in the awkward position of having to amend the agreement or evict what might otherwise be a good tenant.

When I was first considering the writing of this chapter, I thought that I would include a sample lease agreement that you might use on rental property. But I soon realized that the local laws vary so much that there is no such thing as a universal lease that might be used in various jurisdictions. Therefore, you must obtain a lease and other legal documents that comply with local law. If you have more money than you know what to do with, you might have a local attorney draw up your standard lease agreement and any other standard legal agreements. However, in most areas you will find that a superior and much less costly source of legal agreements is a stationery store that sells standard legal forms. The forms available at the store should be current and should comply with local laws. They will have been written for the forms supplier by an attorney familiar with the area. Also, since the forms supplier is not ignorant of the fact that his or her customers are landlords and not tenants, the forms will be written with the "appropriate" emphasis on the landlord's rights and tenant's duties.

RECORDKEEPING

Always keep meticulous books and records on the property and maintain a second set of records at a remote location. If you should have a fire or flood, your one set of records will be destroyed, but the remote records may be used to avoid the turmoil associated with lost or destroyed records. Use triplicate forms for cash receipts. One copy will be given to the tenant for his or her records, one will be kept at the property, and the third will be kept at a remote location, like a central office or your home.

Guard Against Embezzlement

Reconcile bank statements as soon as possible after their receipt. Frequently, banks make the error of posting deposits to the wrong account and do not discover this error unless informed of it by the customer. Also, it is important to verify that your managers are promptly depositing the money that they have collected. Look at the dates of the receipts and compare them to the dates of the deposits. A common fraud involves the lagging of deposits, which works like this:

Manager X collects and deposits the rent for the Goliath Apartment Complex. Manager X is broke because he hasn't had a winning horse in weeks. All the money he handles has proven too great a temptation, and Manager X has taken some of the money. He covers his fraud by taking subsequent receipts and depositing them as though they were the funds that he has stolen. Manager X recognizes that this is a temporary solution to his money problems, and he has the best intentions to restore the stolen funds, but he finds that his situation worsens, so he steals more and more, and the deposits lag more and more behind the receipts. Eventually, the fraud is discovered, and Manager X might end up in jail. The prospect that the landlord will recover the embezzled funds is poor, especially if the embezzler is sent to jail. So it is not uncommon for the landlord to refrain from criminal prosecution in exchange for restitution. Following the restitution, Manger X moves on to another management job in which he is again responsible for the handling of a large amount of cash.

How do you prevent this kind of fraud? There is no way, short of handling all the cash receipts yourself, that you can absolutely protect yourself from this kind of fraud. However, there are several things you can do that will diminish the likelihood of the fraud and minimize the damage when it does occur. The first is to do all that you can to eliminate the temptation. For example, you should keep the receipts of cash to a minimum. If possible, require the tenants to pay in checks payable only to the apartment complex. Provide the manager with a restrictive endorsement stamp so that the checks received can be deposited to the account of the apartment complex only. Be conscious of local banking rules and consider how difficult it would be for the manager to open an account in the name of the complex at a different bank, over which he or she has signature authority, so that checks received could be converted into cash. Establish and enforce a policy that all rent and other receipts are to be deposited on the same day received. Impress on the manager the importance of this policy and make sure that the management people know that you will be checking for compliance every month and will not tolerate noncompliance. Make it appear to the managers that there is no opportunity for fraud. Sometimes I find myself feeling sorry for managers that have embezzled funds when I know the landlords have very loose cash management procedures. There is no excuse for the embezzlement, but it probably would not have occurred if the landlord had not made the opportunity available.

Once you have discovered that a manager has embezzled any amount of funds, however trivial, remove the manager from the position that involves handling your receipts. This employee has shown you that he or she is not trustworthy. And while he or she may express a willingness to make restitution, the restitution should be made in such a way that does not require additional trust or expose you to additional loss.

CHECK REFERENCES AND CREDIT

Always get references, for both your tenants and your employees, from the last two places that the tenants have resided and the last two employers of the employee. Contact the references and don't rent to the tenant or hire the employee unless the references are unequivocally positive.

Use standardized forms for rental agreements, leases, deposit and fees receipts. If possible, you should also receive a credit report for the tenant or prospective employee to ascertain his or her credit worthiness and as an indication of character. While you may not be advancing credit to the tenant, do you really want to entrust your property to a person with a history of not honoring his or her obligations?

DO UNTO OTHERS...

Part of being professional and businesslike is performing your duties promptly and expecting the same from the tenants. It is not reasonable for you to expect prompt rent payment if you are delinquent in your maintenance obligations or in the return of tenant deposits. However, if you honor your obligations, it is not unreasonable to expect the tenants to do the same. So, if the rent is due on the first of the month, it is not unreasonable to assess late charges on rent received after the first. You may chose to grant a grace period of a few days, and you should be aware that any penalties must be part of the rental agreement, but penalties for late payment are generally an effective way of ensuring timely rent collection. And, if a prospective tenant objects to a reasonable penalty provision for late rent payment in the lease, you should take it as an indication that the tenant would probably pay late and that this is a tenant to be avoided.

While you must be businesslike and professional with your tenants, that does not mean that you must be unfriendly. The tenants are contributing to your lifestyle and wealth. You should rent to people that you like, and you should be friendly to them as well. Do not be aloof and inaccessible. If you are attentive and available to your tenants, you may expect them to treat you with similar courtesy.

ENCOURAGE COMMUNICATION

You will find that, as your investments grow and you acquire more and more property, you must form an organization to perform the work of managing and maintaining the property. In building the organization to perform your obligations, you should be wary of the possibility that you might be isolating yourself from the tenants. While you will want the tenants to contact the managers and maintenance people to perform the repairs and maintenance of the property, and while you will not want to be bothered with the miscellaneous details associated with management, you *will* want to be contacted in the event that the employees are not doing their jobs. Make sure the tenants know how to go over the manager's head and that, if they have grievances, they are encouraged to do so. Managers, both good and bad, will attempt to keep the problems on the property from you and settle matters on their own. This is fine if the managers are doing their jobs. But it is up to you to verify that you aren't receiving complaints because there aren't any complaints, not that the complaints aren't being received because of isolation and a lack of communication.

LEGISLATIVE TRENDS

In the area of landlord-tenant relations, the trend of the last few years is clearly a broadening of tenant rights and a regulation and restriction of landlord discretion. As previously noted, much of this protectionist legislation is a result of historic landlord abuse. It is to be expected that a state legislature, when confronted with documented evidence of abuse, will seek to protect the victims. This is especially true if it appears that the victims tend to be of an inferior economic class than the abusers. One would expect the legislature to provide fair legislation...that purports to provide both the tenants and the landlords with remedies for the abuses of the other, and most landlord tenant legislation is so structured. But the fallacy in this legislation is the underlying assumption that the landlords and tenants are equally suable. In reality, the landlord may generally be sued and has assets against which a judgment may be enforced, but tenants do not. So, the legislation that is designed to equate the rights of the landlord and the tenant often has the effect of shifting the favored treatment from the landlord to the tenant. Experienced abusive tenants know their rights and the restrictions placed on the landlord. They also know that, even if the landlord gets a judgment against them, his or her chances of collecting are minimal. So, the legislation designed for their protection tends to encourage their abuse.

On the other hand, much of the legislation is reasonable and appropriate. For example, many states have adopted just-cause eviction rules, which require the landlord to have just cause for evicting a tenant and prevent the landlord from arbitrarily evicting a tenant. A reasonable and intelligent landlord does not arbitrarily evict tenants. It is certainly not in the landlord's interest to evict tenants without cause. So, a reasonably administered just-cause eviction law should not cause a landlord any real consternation. But the problem comes in the administration of the law. If tenants are aware that landlords cannot evict them arbitrarily or in retaliation for their assertion of their rights as tenants, they will nearly always allege that an eviction is arbitrary, or retaliatory. And the landlord may be put to additional time and legal expense in accomplishing evictions. Similarly, health codes and safety legislation are seldom unreasonable on the surface, and you must investigate their application and administration to determine their reasonableness.

The trend in the law toward recognition and expansion of tenant rights should be noted by real estate investors since the trend is likely to continue and expand in the future. One trend that may or may not continue is that of rent control. The problems encountered in those jurisdictions with controlled rent are well documented and used by landlord associations to defeat most newly proposed rent control initiatives. However, it is too early to suggest that rent control is on its way out. Like most legislation and regulation, once it has passed and become effective, it tends to be self-perpetuating and unchallenged. It is reasonable to suggest that rent control as a socially acceptable regulation is in disfavor only when we observe it being voted out in the jurisdictions in which it has become entrenched. Until then, we could note that is has lost much of its momentum, but it is hardly being defeated. Rent control is a social experiment. As such, we cannot expect it to be defeated until such time as its failure is obvious to landlords and tenants alike.

The landlord-tenant relationship is one of inherent conflict, but it need not be one of depressing, expensive litigation. It may be conducted in a dynamic political environment that could effect substantial changes during the period of your ownership. It involves the real world of daily problems and problem solving. The relationship will commence with your acquisition of rental property and will endure until the point of sale. The problems of property ownership and tenant conflict may be a primary motivation for the sale of your property, or you may look back on the relationship as a satisfactory relationship with friendly, responsible people. Chapter 9 addresses the end of the landlord-tenant relationship, as the landlord prepares for and completes the sale of his rental property. It is the time when the landlord cashes in on all of the time, effort, investment, and aggravation that he has put into his property.

PREPARING FOR & COMPLETING THE SALE

9

Earlier, I advised you always to prepare for the sale in the purchase of investment property. If you followed that advice, you should already have a pretty good idea of when, where, how, and to whom you will sell the property. The price and the terms will be planned and the financing may be in place. You are ready to start the negotiations. But sometimes the best of plans encounter a snag or require modification, and a new sales strategy must be adopted. This chapter addresses the issues associated with the sale of the property.

WHEN TO SELL

There is no right time to purchase or to sell, but there are several events or occurrences that will make a property owner consider the sale of the property. If several of these elements occur in conjunction, you may face the overwhelming desire to sell the property, then you can truly say that it is time to sell. These circumstances are discussed below.

WHEN THERE IS A BUYER
The first obvious time to sell is when you are approached by an interested buyer who has the apparent capacity to purchase. Starting with the proposition that everything is for sale if the price is

right, it is a small sacrifice to alter your ownership plans if you are approached by an interested purchaser. Your plan might have been to hold the property for eight years, and the interested purchaser may approach you after only three. You (and the purchaser) might perceive a booming market in the near future, which dampens your motivation to sell. But all these elements can be factored into the price and terms that you are willing to consider. If someone is interested in buying your property, listen to what he or she has to offer.

WHEN THERE IS VALUE

Another time to sell is when it is worthwhile to do so. This happens when you have held the property for a period of time during which it has appreciated, and you have paid down on the debt, so that your equity in the property has increased. You know that, if you sell the property, you can pay the costs and the income and other taxes and realize a good profit. You may also find that you have "too much equity" in this particular property, which would be better invested in a larger property with greater leverage. The value of better-quality investments will tend to increase gradually over time, and there is no magic moment when you would decide that it is time to sell. However, as you begin to realize that the investments are worth substantially more than they cost, you will become more receptive to offers from prospective purchasers.

WHEN THE MARKET IS STRONG

While you want to buy when the market is depressed, you want to sell when the market is strong. You will want to sell when everyone tells you that you are crazy to do so. The popular sentiment will be that real estate is a good investment in which you can't lose. The prices for property will reflect this sentiment, and you will probably be able to sell your property with minimal difficulty. Everyone will say that you didn't get enough money and that you could have gotten more if you had held on to the property for a while longer. They predict that the boom is sure to continue and that you sold out too soon. However, if you see evidence that the boom is cresting and values moderating, you have waited too long. At that point, many property owners will recognize that it is time to sell, and your property will be one of many on the market. Also, the purchasers will want a better deal since they have a number of properties to choose from and the expectations for appreciation have moderated. Those who didn't want to sell when the market was going up may find that they are unable to sell when the market has peaked or is heading down.

WHEN YOUR RETURN ON INVESTMENT DECLINES
We have already considered the various elements of the return on real estate investment, including tax shelter, debt paydown, appreciation, and cash flow. We also considered how the return on investment tends to be cyclical on the one hand but compounding on the other. As you analyze your return on investment, either as a percentage of your original cost or as a percentage of your opportunity cost that you are giving up by maintaining this investment rather than buying other investments, you might find that your return is declining. Other potential investments appear more attractive than your property, and it appears to be time to sell. If you are selling because your return on investment is declining, the amount you realize on the sale will be a function of the cause of the declining rate of return. If the decline is a function of defects in or aging of the property, you may expect the price of the property to be affected. If the decline is a function of an overall softening in the local market, you may expect the value of this and every other property in the market to be affected. However, if the decline is a function of your unique circumstances, which do not affect the purchasers, you may find that you can sell and improve your return on investment without suffering a significant adjustment in value as a function of the decline.

WHEN YOUR TAX BENEFITS REVERSE
Real estate investments are purchased for their various attributes, including tax shelter. Frequently, the tax shelter benefits are the primary investment inducement. The problem is that the advantages of income tax shelter in real estate investments decrease over time. In those circumstances in which the investment is rapidly paying off its financing, the investment might actually produce taxable income in excess of the cash flow. At that point, the tax shelter has become a tax burden, and you should consider selling, trading, or refinancing the property to "freshen up" the tax shelter. Alternatively, you might recognize that there is more to real estate investment than tax shelter and might appreciate the rapid equity growth you are experiencing as a result of appreciation, cash flow, and debt paydown. The income tax you have to pay may be considered a small price to pay for such a return on investment. However, most investors that have purchased real estate investments as tax shelters will feel that it is time to sell when the tax benefits decline and past the time to sell when the benefits actually reverse.

WHEN THE SCHEDULED TIME ARRIVES
When you made the initial purchase, you had some idea of how

long you would hold the investment and under what circumstances it would sell. Perhaps you wanted to hold the property until it doubled in value. Maybe you wanted to shelter your income during your peak earning years. Perhaps you wanted to hold the property during a growth period in the local market. For whatever reason you originally made the purchase, that objective has been accomplished, and it is time to sell. Your original objectives may no longer be applicable and may have been modified over the years, but the investment has served its purposes and can now better serve the investment objectives of a new purchaser than your objectives.

WHEN YOU HAVE GIVEN UP HOPE

At the opposite extreme from the investment that has successfully served its investment objectives is the investment for which you have lost all hope of ever realizing a positive rate of return. The usual scenario involves a negative cash flow property that you have been feeding for a number of years. You have run out of money or patience or both, and you just want out. You probably recognize that you paid too much for the property and that whatever equity you might have in the property is not worth the continued cost of carrying the property and servicing the debt. It is time to sell at a loss as an alternative to losing out altogether and having the property foreclosed.

WHEN CIRCUMSTANCES HAVE CHANGED

Sometimes changed circumstances will make continued property ownership impractical or inappropriate. For example, if a husband and wife own a small rental property that they intended to use as a source of retirement income, and one dies, the surviving spouse may find that he or she no longer has the desire and interest necessary to maintain the investment. Or, worse, perhaps the deceased spouse was the one who performed the bulk of the maintenance and repairs on the property and the survivor finds it impossible to take over and prohibitively expensive to hire someone to do these tasks.

There are, of course, many less traumatic changes in circumstance that will also make real estate investments less appropriate. For example, the birth of a child and the formation of a young family may absorb the time that you would otherwise use for investment activities. But whatever the change, you must decide if it is so substantial as to compel the sale, regardless of the market conditions and other factors, or whether the continued ownership may be inconvenient but worthwhile, dictating a sale when market conditions improve.

WHEN LIQUIDATION OF ASSETS IS DESIRED

Real estate is an illiquid investment. It cannot quickly and easily be converted back into cash when the need arises. It is quite different from stocks and bonds, which can easily and rapidly be converted back into cash. Also, real estate is illiquid, whether it is a rental house, a vacant lot, or a limited partnership interest in property from a real estate syndicator. The fact is that there is only a slow and inefficient market for real estate, and it takes some time to liquidate property for its value. A quick sale will of necessity involve some discounting of value. Therefore, when you have the need or desire to liquidate your investments and obtain the cash, it may be time to sell. However, it may instead be time to refinance. If the value of the property is sufficiently in excess of the underlying debt, and the interest rates are acceptable, you may find that your liquidity needs are satisfied by refinancing, and you are able to liquidate your equity partially and still keep the property. Depending on the circumstances, refinancing proceeds may be available much sooner than sales proceeds. And if you refinance the property, you are able to get some cash while keeping the property. When refinancing is considered, don't lose sight of the overall objective of selling the property eventually; structure a loan that will be an attractive assumption for a subsequent purchaser. Don't solve your short-term liquidity problem at the cost of the longer-term objectives for the property.

PREPARING THE PROPERTY

When do you begin preparing the property for sale—when you list the property with a real estate agent, or a month before the listing date, or a year? I have previously suggested that you begin your preparation for the sale in the negotiations for the purchase. You should limit your purchases to those properties that you feel will be attractive to subsequent purchasers and attempt to structure your financing and other ownership attributes in such a way as to facilitate the sale and not restrain your options on the sale. Remember that the property is always for sale. It is unlikely that a sale shortly after your purchase will adequately cover your needs to justify the transactions, but it might. You should be in a position to sell at all times, and you should plan for a sale within a certain period that suits you individual investment objectives. For example, you may wish to sell within five to eight years after the acquisition, or eight to ten years, or whatever is appropriate. This plan should be loose and subject to modification if the circumstances require it. A soft market may require delaying the sale, a hot market may suggest an earlier sale, and a very soft market may dictate the immediate sale of the property at a loss because of your inability to continue to carry the property.

It is a mistake to have a fixed and inflexible plan. I know an investor who had the investment plan of holding a particular apartment for seven years, not five or six or eight. He felt that seven years was the appropriate holding period. He turned down a superior offer received five and a half years into his holding period because he reasoned that the time was not adequate. I supposed he reasoned that a better offer would be received when the time was right. At the time that his plan dictated the sale, the market was very soft, and he recognized that he should have taken the offer received a year and a half earlier or that he should hold the property until the market conditions improved. But, because he was so certain that he would sell after seven years, he scheduled balloon payments and other obligations that required him to sell the property regardless of the adverse market conditions. Naturally, his return was affected adversely.

The point is to have a flexible but reasonably specific plan for your investment in the property. And your actions in management and maintenance, repairs, and improvements should all reflect the plan or at least not be contrary to the plan. As you see your equity in the property grow, and your plans for it materialize, you should begin to formulate a plan for the sale. The plan should be developed at least a year before the actual intended sales date. This lead time is necessary so that you will be able to accomplish adequately the needed cosmetic improvements to the property that will facilitate the sale for your asking price.

MAKING COSMETIC IMPROVEMENTS

Most of the improvements that a property owner makes in preparing the well-kept property for sale are cosmetic in nature. They are inexpensive things—such as cleaning, gardening, and painting the trim—that make the property look better at a minimal cost. Even a property that is less than well kept will usually experience no more than cosmetic improvements in its preparation for sale. In the latter case, the improvements will not so much highlight the value of the property as conceal the defects. A good paint job can conceal significant structural problems and water damage, at least temporarily. The astute buyer will recognize this and look beyond the cosmetic improvements. But, however astute the buyer, he or she cannot help but be more favorably impressed with well-kept property or property that appears well kept over property that appears run-down and neglected. The effect of this will be seen in the negotiations: the property that has an attractive appearance will have a much greater chance of being sold for its value than the property for which cosmetic improvements have been neglected. If you start the cosmetic improvements several months before the intended sale date, you will probably provide yourself with adequate time to ensure their timely completion without giving the property the appearance of being rushed onto the market. The impression you wish to convey is that of a property that is well kept at all times, instead of a property that has merely been fixed up for the sale. But beware of commencing the cosmetic improvements too soon. Cleaning, gardening, and even new paint make a positive impression for only a limited period of time and may have to be redone if the sales process is delayed.

PREPARING THE FINANCIAL STATEMENTS
You should have recent financial statements for the property, including an income statement, balance sheet, statement of changes in financial position, rent roll, and other relevant financial data. You should also have available tax returns for the ownership entity for the past three years in case they are requested by the prospective purchaser. While I would refrain from volunteering these statements, I would suggest that you have them readily accessible so that you don't have to prepare them upon request. Negotiations are a delicate and fragile process, and they can easily be killed if the seller delays production of the financial statements. Also, the delay is likely to cause suspicion on the part of the prospective purchaser, who will wonder why they aren't readily available and what is being done to them. As a rule, delayed financial statements receive much more careful scrutiny than those that are produced quickly.

There are also certain cosmetic improvements that you will want to make to the financial statements. I am not suggesting that you should engage in any activities that are even remotely fraudulent. However, your objectives are changing, from wanting to report income conservatively and minimize income taxes to wanting to present a favorable picture of the profitability of the property. You may wish, for example, to capitalize certain expenditures rather than expense them, because capitalizing improves your operating income statement. If your property produces positive cash flow, but a loss for income tax purposes, you may wish to produce an operating cash flow statement that highlights this attribute more than the income statement. You may also wish to improve the apparent performance of the property by deferring discretionary expenditures for repairs and maintenance so that they aren't reflected on the income statements. However, you can defer certain repairs only for so long before they begin to affect adversely the condition of the property and the goodwill of the tenants. The purchaser should be wary of what appears to be an inadequate repairs and maintenance budget. It is not easy for the purchaser to determine the adequacy of the repairs and maintenance budget. Frequently, it is necessary to go back through financial statements for several years to determine if the current level of expenditure is adequate. Most often purchasers do not go to this much effort, instead relying on their experience to tell them how much the repairs and maintenance should cost. However, it is desirable to defer discretionary expenditures, both because they improve your financial statements and because you are unlikely to get the benefit of the expenditures. Improvements will benefit the purchaser and are unlikely to be reflected in the purchase price.

SUBSTANTIAL IMPROVEMENTS

Sometimes you will want to or have to make other than merely cosmetic improvements to the property that you wish to sell. In that case, you will wish to use the old rule of thumb that the improvements should increase the sales price by at least twice their cost (including the cost of labor) to be worthwhile. There is also the additional element of potentially adverse tax consequences that must be considered. For example, if you have a quality apartment with condominium conversion potential, and you sell the apartment as a single sale, the gain you realize will be primarily long-term capital gain. But if you choose to remodel the units and sell them as condominiums instead, you will find that the income you generate will be taxed at the higher ordinary income tax rates. Unfortunately, the higher rates will apply not only to the income that is a result of the conversion but also to the gain from holding the property, which isn't realized until the individual condominiums are sold. There are similar tax problems if you put improvements on your vacant land or take other action designed to improve the sales value of the property. Often the additional gain from the improvements and the change in the nature of the property is not worthwhile given the adverse income tax problems. Consult your tax advisor before making substantial improvements to your property and before accepting an offer to sell it.

HOW TO SELL

Selling real estate is no different from selling any other major purchase asset or major investment. The asset is sold through the negotiations procedure described in Chapter 5 and closed through the procedure described in Chapter 6. Here we will consider the sales options available to the seller and the seller's relationship with the purchaser and any agents that might be involved. We will also consider how the seller markets the product.

THROUGH THE REAL ESTATE AGENT

Most sellers feel unprepared to sell the property and prefer to utilize the services of a professional real estate agent. They will sign a contract with the agent in which the agent agrees to apply his or her best efforts to selling the property for the listed price in exchange for the agreed upon commission. It is important to note that officially the agent works for the seller and is paid by the seller out of the proceeds of the sale. However, the agent also has a fiduciary duty to the purchaser not to misrepresent the status of the property and to deal fairly with all the parties to the transaction. The use of real estate agents will be discussed in more detail in Chapter 12. Here I would just note that the agent performs essentially the same services that the prudent seller could easily perform on his or her own, for a commission that is not insubstantial. As a seller, you should not automatically use the agent. Instead, consider the following questions.

- How well do you know the property and the market?
- Do you have the time and expertise to market the property as well as the agent?
- Can you write an effective advertisement?
- Will the purchaser want you to discount the property anyway since you don't have to pay a real estate commission?
- How much attention will the agent devote to this property given the other property that he or she wants to sell?
- Which agent should you use?

Using real estate agents should facilitate the sales effort. The question should be whether the facilitated sales effort is worth the cost of the professional assistance.

DIRECT CONTACT OF PURCHASERS

If you are actively involved in the real estate investment business, you will know who the other purchasers are. They will be the individuals and groups that have purchased the other buildings in which you were interested. Many of them may still be in the market for additional acquisitions. If you are selling a property, why not contact those you know to be in the market to purchase? Also, why place an agent between yourself and the purchaser? You may be able to negotiate a sale better without the agent's intervention. Your knowledge of the other purchasers may well be more comprehensive than that of the agent. Review the types of property that the other parties have purchased and the deals they have negotiated. Some will be more interested in leverage, others in cash flow or tax shelter. If you can, structure your sale in such a way as to interest your target purchasers. This advice is especially relevant if you are considering structuring a like-kind exchange. You may well be able to accommodate the needs of both parties by exploring the possibility of a real estate exchange. One of the two parties will probably have to come up with cash to equalize the equities, but the transaction costs will be minimized if the principals deal directly with one another.

FOR SALE BY OWNER

You may simply choose to sell the property yourself. There is nothing that the agent can do for you that you can't do yourself, except perhaps involve other agents in the sale through personal contacts, other agents in the office, or the multiple-listing services. You will also find that you have a much more personal interest in the sale of this particular property than does the agent. You should follow the same procedures as the agent would have followed: place the advertisements, hold the open houses, contact and follow up on active purchasers or those who have expressed an interest in the property, and generally go to work selling the property.

Again, you are cautioned to be businesslike. One disadvantage of selling the property yourself is that you reveal a lot about what you are willing to settle for in your dealings with the purchaser. You don't have an agent to soften your reaction to the purchaser. And, assuming that you don't have the experience the agent has, you might find that you are giving away the store in order to make the sale. You may be overanxious and unwilling to let the first interested party get away.

To avoid the mistakes often made by the novice seller, I would suggest observation of the following rules:

1. Do not represent yourself until you have adequate experience as a result of participation in several negotiations as a purchaser and several as a seller.
2. Offer the property at a price and terms that are competitive and will interest purchasers but more than you expect to receive. I would suggest that the price be at least 10 percent higher than you expect.

3. Do not get upset when potential purchasers submit phony, nothing-down offers for substantially less than your asking price. Investors are being encouraged to submit such offers, and you may expect to receive some.
4. When you have a serious purchaser, carefully listen to what the purchaser is telling you he or she is willing to offer. Reread Chapter 5, on negotiations, so that the fundamentals are fresh in your mind.
5. Don't be afraid to ask for the sale. Don't be pushy but realize that there comes a time when the potential purchaser has asked all the questions, you have supplied all the answers, and it is time for the purchaser to submit an offer or for you to look elsewhere.
6. Don't react to offers, either positively or negatively, in the presence of the purchaser. Take the offer home with you and review it at your leisure. You may wish to have your accountant, financial advisor, or attorney review the offer as well.
7. Don't become impatient. If you must sell the property, use an agent. Property sold by the owner should not be property that must be sold, but rather property that the owner would like to sell but isn't compelled to sell.

TO WHOM TO SELL?

When you offer the property for sale, you will find that a variety of people will express an interest. You will, despite your attempts to remain objective, classify them on the basis of the likelihood of their purchase. You will never meet a greater assemblage of flaky people than when you offer property for sale. You will also find that there are a lot of lookers from whom you will not receive an offer. And you will experience a certain amount of frustration, wondering if and when you will ever get a serious purchaser with the capacity to complete the deal. So, considering the issue of to whom to sell might seem preposterous and actually no issue at all since you may not be presented with a choice of several good prospects. However, prospective purchasers *can* be categorized as follows.

THE FIRST PERSON WITH THE CASH
In fact, we could take this one step further and suggest that you might be interested in selling the property to the first person that

comes along that shows any interest in the property. This is usually a mistake since you will attempt to structure the deal to accommodate the purchaser at the expense of your needs and objectives. Take my word for it: there will be other purchasers. You have some idea what the property is worth and what you are willing to sell it for, and you needn't sell it to the first potential purchaser.

If the purchaser is offering cash or a substantial down payment, you should, of course, take him or her seriously. Counteroffer and negotiate in earnest. If he or she will cash out your interest in the property and assume your liability for the underlying debt, and the debt holder will release you, you don't have to know anything about the purchaser other than the color of his or her money. You will want to ascertain the purchaser's goals and objectives so as to negotiate better, but don't be concerned if he or she has some half-baked idea about using the property as a nudist colony. Whether the purchaser makes or loses money on the property is not your concern, provided that he or she has the capacity to purchase the property and complete the acquisition.

A FINANCIALLY STRONG PURCHASER

More often than not, however, financial strength of the purchaser as well as his or her management experience and expertise will be very relevant to the seller. If you provide some of the financing in the form of a second mortgage, deed of trust, or real estate contract, you will be very interested in the purchaser's capacity to perform. Also, the financial strength of the purchaser is relevant in considering the deal you are willing to structure. If the purchaser is very strong financially, you may not feel as insecure in structuring an acquisition involving a minimal down payment with considerable seller financing. However, if the financial strength of the prospective purchaser is unknown or weak, you will not wish to relinquish possession of your property until you have received enough money from the purchaser to cover your exposure to loss.

AN EXPERIENCED PURCHASER

Also relevant is the purchaser's experience in owning and/or managing property of the type in question. I would personally favor an experienced property manager as a purchaser over a financially strong purchaser. Of course, the ideal situation is one in which the purchaser has both financial strength and experience and you are confident that the purchaser will successfully own and operate the property. The experienced property manager/purchaser will run the property as well as the local economy allows, and the financially strong purchaser will provide the necessary support if that isn't good enough.

A DEFAULTING PURCHASER

You may find that you want to sell the property to a particular purchaser even though you know that the chances are very good that you will have to take the property back. Perhaps the purchaser has deeded back property in the past, or perhaps in your discussions with the purchaser it is obvious that he or she has no business experience and no idea what he or she is getting into. Why would you sell to such a purchaser? Because this individual or group is willing to pay your price and has enough cash that, even if you take the property back, you will not lose money. Just make sure that you have provided yourself with an adequate cushion. Foreclosed property is seldom well maintained, and you may find that an undesirable tenant population has driven away your good tenants. You will have costs involved in the foreclosure and additional costs on the property following the foreclosure. If your flaky purchaser is providing you with enough cash to cover these costs, go ahead and sell the property.

IMPACT ON SURROUNDING PROPERTIES

If you own adjoining properties, or it is important to you to maintain the goodwill of the surrounding property owners, the purchaser's intentions with respect to the property are relevant. While the use of the property will be restricted by zoning, the purchaser will have the capacity to affect the value and desirability of the surrounding property through this or her use of the property. It may be important, in this circumstance, to obtain some kind of assurance from the purchaser that the use of the property will not be inconsistent with the surrounding property and the surrounding property owners.

LOCATING REPLACEMENT PROPERTY

If you have experienced some degree of success with your real estate investments, you will intend to replace the property you have sold with other investment property unless you are retiring. So, you are always in the market for investment properties, looking for good deals, and reconfirming the value of your existing investments. If you intend to buy replacement property by structuring your sale as a deferred three-way like-kind exchange, you must (under the new rules for like-kind exchanges) identify the replacement property during a relatively short period of time (see Chapter 13). So, you will find that you are faced with the dilemma of wishing to negotiate seriously for replacement property but not having the capacity to make the purchase until your sale has closed. Indeed, this is often a problem regardless of whether or not a like-kind exchange is intended. There are timing difficulties in the sale of your old properties and acquisition of new properties.

It is a fact of the real estate business that there are always more properties and good deals than you will have the capacity to buy. If you are always in the market, you will be aware of these properties and will have the capacity to identify replacement properties rapidly. If, on the other hand you wait until you have sold your property before looking for replacement property, you are likely to discover two things. First, identifying a good acquisition and negotiating its purchase will be time-consuming and frustrating. Second, you may find that you didn't get the value you should have out of the property that you just sold. The market may suggest that a higher price would have been appropriate.

GROWING 10

Growing both physically and emotionally in the real estate business is a much easier task than getting started. There is a lot of inertia to overcome in getting started. But once you have gotten into the business, you will find that growth comes easily. In fact, it might be suggested that growth comes too easily. The opportunity for growth within the industry puts you in a position a lot like that of the man who is given enough rope to hang himself.

If you buy a rental house, duplex, or small apartment, you will probably encounter initial success. Despite your lack of experience, most of the decisions you have to make require nothing more than common sense. What is required for success, in addition to common sense, is time and attention to the investments. If you have only a small number of rentals, you will probably watch them very carefully, and you will probably be successful. Those mistakes that you make will be made on a small scale. They will not "bring you down." They will contribute to your base of knowledge.

If your property produces a positive cash flow, the economics of your prior investments will not restrain your growth. If you have long-term financing on your investments, you will not have to retain the capacity to self-finance an approaching balloon obligation. The constraints that you do experience will be those of

171

your own making. For example, you may wish to spend part of the cash flow and set aside only a portion each month for future acquisitions. If this is your only source of investment capital, and if you are unwilling to take the risks associated with minimum down payment purchases, you may expect your rate of growth to be slow but controlled.

Actually, though, your rate of growth need not be so constrained. There are several ways in which you may accelerate your rate of growth. This chapter explores the desirability and risk associated with growth and the methods by which the rate of growth may be accelerated.

TAKE IT EASY—DON'T GET OVEREXTENDED

Growth is intoxicating. It is a fun fantasy to consider yourself an empire builder. There is also the personal satisfaction that comes from being able to claim to be a self-made millionaire. But growth is not mandatory. You may decide for a variety of reasons that you want to limit the size of your investment business to, say, 20 or 50 units. You may feel more comfortable with the business when its size is limited. If you wish to make all the repairs personally, you'll obviously have to limit your expansion. You may wish to meet all the new tenants and execute the lease agreements personally. So as to better keep an eye on them, some investors limit their investments to a certain geographic area, and this may impose practical constraints on the number of rental units that may be acquired.

As you grow, you will continue to make mistakes. Hopefully, the mistakes will be made less frequently than when you were just getting started, and hopefully they will be somewhat different mistakes, reflecting that you have learned from your errors. However, a bigger business means your mistakes are likely to be bigger too, and your safety net might be smaller. For example, when you buy your first rental house, you could probably make the payment on that house, as well as on your own, out of your salary. If the house sat vacant for six months, it would not wipe you out. But it is unlikely that you would have the capacity from other sources to carry a loan on a large apartment complex.

Also, your learning experience may not be as adequate or as accurate as you think it is. If your experience comes from buying and operating rental houses, you might be unprepared for the operation of apartment buildings. In your rental houses, the tenants will generally pay all the utility bills. They will maintain the property and the grounds. They may even make small repairs. If the housing is desirable, the tenants will tend to turn over infrequently. And when the vacancy rate in rental property is climbing, rental housing as opposed to apartments will be the last to feel the strain. But apartments are quite different. First, the landlord will pay some or all of the utility bills. The tenants will also expect the landlord to make nearly all of the repairs and to maintain the property and the grounds. And since rental apartments are, on the whole, considered to be less desirable than rental houses, they tend to have a higher vacancy rate. As discussed in Chapter 7, you may be quite surprised by just how much it costs to run an apartment building and how little cash flow is left over for payment of the debt service or distribution to the owners. Your experience in rental houses has given you the mistaken impression that apartments will experience the same kind of expense history and profitability. Hopefully, you will not have invested too much in apartments on the strength of this erroneous assumption.

REFINANCING

Refinancing property is a traditional method of obtaining investment capital from your existing investments for the purpose of expanding into other investments. Refinancing has the advantage of being able to generate investment capital short of the sale of the property. You therefore keep your existing property and acquire the capacity to obtain additional property.

The cash you obtain through refinancing your property will not be taxable. You haven't sold the property to generate a taxable gain; instead, you have merely borrowed additional funds secured by the property. The refinancing may produce a situation in which you have debt in excess of your basis. So, if you should sell the property later, you will be facing a taxable gain in excess of your proceeds. But that is a problem for the future and not a concern at the time of refinancing.

Refinancing has not been as applicable during the last few years as a result of high interest rates. If you have a low interest rate on the property, it is hard to justify paying off that low-interest-rate loan in order to borrow more money at a higher rate on the whole debt. High interest rates have made refinancing expensive and all but infeasible in most cases. Consider the following example.

A building is encumbered with a $100,000 loan at 10 percent interest. The building has been approved for a new first mortgage of $160,000 at 15 percent interest and about $10,000 in loan costs. The owner could net $50,000 from the refinancing, but the cost of these dollars would be substantial. One way to look at it is to consider the effective rate of interest on the $50,000. The $50,000 pays interest at 15 percent, and there is an additional 5 percent interest (15 percent less 10 percent) on the original balance of $100,000, which is effectively an additional 10 percent on the new $50,000, and the fees are an additional debt that generates an interest expense of 15 percent on $10,000 or effectively an additional 3 percent on the new $50,000. So, the owner is already up to 28 percent interest, and we haven't yet considered the fact that the owner will receive $10,000 less upon sale or refinancing in the future as a result of the loan fees. The magnitude of this latter expense depends on when it is incurred. The further into the future, the less significant the expense. In any event, it appears that the cost of the new money is in excess of 30 percent.

From this example, it should be obvious why there is very little refinancing taking place in a high-interest-rate market. Fortunately, there are alternatives.

Given the substantial cost of refinancing the property, that second mortgage that was offered to you at 22 percent no longer looks so outrageous. Also, the fees and costs are likely to be lower since you are looking at fees as only a percentage of the second mortgage, not the whole property indebtedness. Also, banks are becoming more sophisticated about wrapping loans. If you don't have to pay off the low-interest underlying indebtedness, why do so? If the bank wraps the underlying contract, it may be able to give you a better rate since the bank will be able to take advantage of the low interest on the underlying loan. Banks refer to this as "blending" the rate. Referring to the above example, if the bank were to wrap the underlying debt and charge you 15 percent on the total debt, the bank's yield would be over 30 percent, which would be excessive and unnecessary. Therefore, the bank might be willing to loan you money at, say, 12 percent. In that case, your interest expense and the bank's yield on the $50,000 of new money would be calculated as follows:

12%	stated rate on the new loan
+ 4	effective rate on $50,000 of $100,000 original loan balance 2% higher
+ 2.4%	interest on fees of $10,000 at 12% effective rate on $50,000
18.4%	total before consideration of the effective cost of the fees

Once again, the magnitude of the loan fees will depend on when their cost is realized. The further into the future that the property is either sold or again refinanced, the less significant are those fees. At least two observations are appropriate from the blended fee example. First, you should note that the rate being charged will be more than the bank would have been willing to charge you on the new first mortgage. In this example, the rate being charged is something over 20 percent of the loan fees, while the bank was willing to charge you only 15 percent on the new mortgage. But the bank is entitled to a higher rate of interest since it is in a secondary position to the underlying loan and therefore has more risk exposure. Second, although the example is merely illustrative, the rate you may be expected to be charged is almost certainly less than the rate you could expect to pay on a second mortgage.

We will look forward to some time in the future when refinancing will again be possible, without so significant an economic cost. However, there can be no assurance that the financial markets will ever again be as accommodating to real estate financing as they once were.

THE IMPORTANCE OF A TRACK RECORD

Your experience in investments and the degree of success or failure that you experience is referred to in the profession as your *track record*. Your capacity to grow will depend to a great degree on the quality of your track record. Banks will be inclined to trust your creditworthiness if you have a history of performing well on previous debts. Investors will trust you with their money if you have performed well for them or for their friends or acquaintances in the past. It is a simple matter of going with a winner, investing in success.

Stock brokerage firms analyze the track record of promoters before recommending investments. It is part of their "due diligence" requirements. A favorable relationship with a brokerage firm and a positive recommendation for your firm can open the door to unlimited growth potential.

You should be aware, however, that establishing a positive track record, adequate to impress the brokerage firms with your firm's merit, is a long-term proposition. Many stock brokerage firms will not recommend an investment firm unless it has been syndicating for at least five years. And measuring success in real estate investment is, by its nature, a long-term proposition. It takes some time in the typical real estate investment to determine if success is forthcoming. In fact, you will generally be unable to determine if the investment has truly been successful until it is sold because the sale gives you the capacity to measure the overall success or failure of the investment. Up to that point, you can only speculate as to the level of success the investment will yield.

While it takes a long time to measure the success of your investments, it takes much less time to measure the failures. The highest level of risk associated with your investments will be experienced in the first year of ownership. It is during the first year that cash flow is at a minimum or may even be negative. Also, this period is one in which you will have the least knowledge about the property and its operating peculiarities. If there is an opportunity to lose money, and perhaps lose the property, it will come early in the holding period. After a period of ownership, the cash flow should be better, and it is only the cyclical fluctuations or balloon payments that are likely to cause you to lose the property. So, the successes will tend to be only speculative for a long period, during which your failures are blatantly and painfully obvious.

There are ways to doctor a track record, to make to appear that the performance is better than it has been. One method is to hold on to those properties that are not doing well and sell only those that will show a substantial gain. It will appear that all of your investments are doing as well as those that have been sold. Continuing to hold marginal or losing properties, so that their performance is not reflected in your track record, is a policy that reflects questionable judgment, but there is nothing fraudulent about the practice. A much more disreputable practice is that of doctoring track records through the creation of transactions that are not at arm's length, that is, transactions that are engineered by the promoter and a related or accommodating party, designed to appear better than the real performance. The transactions could simply be fraudulent. More likely they are real transactions that are structured by very sophisticated buyers and sellers to accommodate the need to create the appearance of superior performance. It may be an accommodating situation in which two promoters buy each other's property and overpay by offsetting amounts. Another common practice is to engineer a high selling price through unrealistically attractive terms. We will consider, in a different context in Chapter 13, how manipulation of the interest rate on the seller financing can substantially affect the performance appearance of the property. In addition to the interest rate, there are other terms that can be manipulated to inflate the selling price, including the term of the loan and the down payment arrangements. You could sell with a nonrecourse loan, which is particularly attractive to limited partnerships. You might even have a loan with negative amortization or a contractual cap on the negative cash flow.

You might also manipulate the nonfinancial characteristics of the transaction, perhaps structuring it to maximize the tax benefits for the purchaser or augmenting the benefits of the transaction through such measures as a contractual rent guarantee. The latter is a contract between the seller and the purchaser in which the seller guarantees to the purchaser that the rents for a stated period will be at a certain minimum level or the purchase price will be adjusted to reflect the rent loss. There are many variations on the provisions of such contracts. The point is that, instead of just the property, the purchaser is getting other benefits from the transaction that may not be apparent to a casual observer and may even be hidden from the experienced professional.

One way to get exactly what you want from a transaction is to be on both sides of it. This is called *resyndication*. When property is resyndicated, it is sold by one partnership formed by the promoter to another partnership formed by the same promoter. Surprisingly, this may be a perfectly legitimate transaction. Perhaps the original partnership has accomplished its objectives in the ownership of property. It has taken advantage of the tax shelter, received several years of operating cash flow, held the property during a period of appreciation, and even made modest reductions in the underlying debt. It is time for the first partnership to sell. Now, the promoter knows that the property is a good investment; he has owned and operated it for the other partnership for a number of years. The property would be perfect for a new partnership that he is putting together. As long as the promoter is honest about his relationship to both partnerships and has revealed the potential conflict of interest to all the parties, I don't see that the partners have any basis for complaint. However, the promoter does find him- or herself in the delicate position of having a fiduciary responsibility to two conflicting parties. The creative promoter will accommodate the interests of both parties by creating partnerships with differing objectives. For example, the promoter might have a partnership that was formed for long-term investment purposes sell to a partnership that is structured to make shorter-term investments and maximize the tax shelter. There are many examples of ways in which partnerships with differing objectives can be utilized by accommodating parties to improve the overall performance of all parties concerned.

Even when the track record has not been manipulated and accurately reflects the performance of the promoter, what does it really tell you? It indicates the degree to which the promoter's prior investments have been successful. There is some value in this in that, if the promoter has been successful in the past, he or she will probably be competent and capable of repeating that performance in the future. But there are many things that the track record does not reveal. It does not give an indication of the personal reputation or the quality of the promoter. It doesn't indicate the degree to which the superior performance was due to skill and what was simply good luck. It provides very little indication of the performance of the property that is still owned by the promoter's prior partnerships. It also gives no indication as to whether the promoter has learned from his or her mistakes or if they are likely to be repeated. A track record, like any other financial information, is meaningful only if augmented by other information necessary to give a clear picture of who the promoter is and what his or her performance is likely to be.

USING OPM

The key to growth in the real estate or any other investment business is not only investing your own money successfully, but also taking advantage of the opportunities available through the use of OPM. Have you figured it out yet? *OPM* stands for "other people's money." And you will find a ready supply of it if you have encountered success in investing your own money, as reflected by your track record.

You may obtain other people's money through either debt or equity financing. In the former case, you borrow the money from the other people; in the latter case, you join the other people in a partnership. The categories of debt and equity are becoming somewhat blurred. The traditional differences between the two are no longer so obvious.

Debt used to be characterized by an interest-bearing note secured by a security interest in the property. The note would amortize at a fixed rate and either pay off or become due well in the future. The note and security instrument remain, but the nature of the indebtedness has changed substantially. Now it is unlikely that the interest rate will be fixed or the commitment long-term. Also, the debt is likely to have equity characteristics, like profit participation, in which the lender is entitled to a share of the profits on the sale of the property.

Equity financing has also experienced some changes. Traditionally, the equity investor put up money in exchange for an interest in the property or the partnership purchasing the property. The equity investor had unlimited opportunity for gain, but no guarantee that he or she wouldn't lose his money. And the equity investment was in an inferior position to the debt investors in the event of the insolvency of the partnership. Now the equity investor is looking for something more. Like the debt investor, he or she is holding out for better terms on the money invested. One way to give the equity investor something more than he or she had was to provide a preferential return for the limited partners or the monied general partners before the split with the active general partner promoter. This is nothing new. Contracts have often provided that the investors putting up the money were to receive their money back before the working partners were entitled to split the profits. There are many variations on this contractual provision. But now the preferential rate of return has become pervasive in the industry to the extent that it has even been codified in the guidelines published by the National Association of Securities Dealers, Inc.

When you have reached a level of experience that enables you to take advantage of the use of OPM, you will find that it enables your rate of growth to increase significantly. While you will be sharing the investment with your investment partners, you will be able to buy significantly greater amounts of property. And it is better to have a part of something than 100 percent of nothing. Also, the investment activities are not mutually exclusive. In other words, you can invest on behalf of the partnerships and for your own account without violating any kind of duty to the partners. There is only the practical constraint that you might perceive as a result of the pressure from the limited partners to let them in on "all the good deals." Accurate or not, if you are investing for partnerships and for your own account, the investors are going to perceive that you are saving the best deals for yourself. This perception may cause ill will among your partners and may inhibit your ability to raise money for the partnership acquisitions. But whether you choose to invest solely for the investment groups or for the investment groups and for your own account is a personal matter for you to decide.

When you are investing other people's money, you are not free to do whatever you want with the money. You have a legal fiduciary duty to the investors to invest the money as you have represented. You may not use the money for your own purposes or convert it to your own uses. Instead, you must invest it in the partnership property or in the expenses incurred in furtherance of the partnership business.

YOUR FIRST JOINT VENTURE

Your first experience in using other people's money for your investment activities will probably be the informal formation of a joint venture or partnership among your friends for the purpose of purchasing a building of interest to the group. You may have only one partner, or several, but you will probably not go through an elaborate sales presentation to sell the investment idea. Instead, you will form the group from interested parties and formalize the already friendly relationship with a partnership agreement. The agreement may not even be that formal. The partners may have an oral gentleman's agreement that the money will be contributed and the profits split. As the promoter, you may take the property in your own name, with or without reference to the fact that you are purchasing on behalf of an investment group. Sometimes, the property is purchased in the name of the general partner promoter with the simple designation "nominee" for an undisclosed principal. The designation alerts subsequent purchasers that the property is being purchased by the promoter but is being acquired for someone or something else. The nominee is an agent for the investment group and generally has the authority to bind the partnership and, if he or she chooses, to sell the property. It is in everyone's best interest to formalize the relationship between the parties with a formal partnership agreement. That way there will be fewer problems later in determining who represented what to whom and to what the parties agreed. Don't assume that your understanding of the agreement between you and your partners is the same as their understanding. Put the agreement in writing and then see who objects to it.

You might think that these first investment groups, involving friends and relatives, represent a good and comfortable way to experiment with the investment group format for making investments. But you may find that the disadvantages of investing the money of your friends far outweighs the advantages. Initially, the relationship will be friendly. The investors all know one another, and they are entering an investment together with high expectations for the performance of the property. They trust you; they feel that you are competent and will do the best you can to achieve success in the investment. They know that you won't steal their money and leave the country. But, rather than be comfortable, you will feel a strong personal responsibility to these investors to achieve their expectations. You might not feel too bad if the investment doesn't work out and you lose your own money, but losing the money of your friends is a different matter. These are not some casual investors who are taking a chance with surplus cash. These are people with whom you are close, who are trusting you with money that you have to assume is very important to their wellbeing. You must ask yourself if you are ready to assume this level of responsibility.

I previously recommended against business relationships with family members. To the list of undesirable partners I would now also add friends. The friendship may or may not endure an unsuccessful business relationship, but why take the chance? Consider the importance of your friendship and whether it is worth risking its loss for the investment opportunity that you might otherwise have to forgo. Also, consider whether the investment opportunity is worth the psychological pressure that you will experience as a result of investing your friends' money. You will always feel the need to perform for your partners and for yourself in your investments. That is an inescapable part of investing but, the kind of pressure you feel to perform for family and friends is on a completely different level. In fact, the pressure is so substantial that it might lead to the mistakes that you are trying to avoid. If you are preoccupied with the possibility of failure, you may find yourself unable to take prudent risks. Therefore, the investment may not yield what it could, and it may in fact fail.

If you have experienced success in your business activities, there will be people who will want to invest with you for business reasons, without being unduly influenced by the fact that they might be your friends. You should inform your friends that you have a policy against allowing your friends to invest with you. This may make some of your friends angry. They might suggest that you are treating them as if their money isn't good enough. This is a delicate situation. You should tell them that their friendship means far more to you than any investment opportunity can possibly be worth, that there is a degree of risk involved in any investment, and that you could not perform as the active general partner if you had the prospect of losing their money hanging over your head. They are nearly certain to respond that they know the risk and are willing to take the chance. They will probably add that they have faith and confidence in you. That is where the problem comes in: the subtle pressure that comes from the expectations of your friends. You should be polite but firm. It is a particularly troublesome fact that either way you jeopardize your friendship. Either your friends will be put off by the fact that you won't let them in on a good deal or you will allow them to invest with you and face the risk that the future of the friendship will depend on the performance of the investment.

Perhaps the best policy is not to tell your friends that you are in the real estate investment business. If you have the capacity to keep your investment activities confidential, you will not experience the pressure from them to become involved. If they ask you what you do for a living, tell them that you are either a rodeo clown or a septic tank cleaner. In either case, you won't get caught in a lie. They won't know enough about being a rodeo clown to talk about it, and they won't want to talk about your septic tank cleaning business.

Now, I know that my advice against investing your friends' money will go largely ignored. It is a very common practice for friends to get together in investments. In fact, more partnerships are composed of friends than are composed of merely business acquaintances. And this is true despite the fact that the promoters recognize that the situation is undesirable. Why are there so many partnerships composed of friends? There are basically two reasons. The first reason is that friends may be necessary or convenient. Perhaps the promoter has an inadequate track record to attract nonfriendly money and will be unable to make the investment without taking the money of friends. The promoter is confident that the investment will be successful, and is flattered by the faith and trust of friends. The second reason is that, although the promoter has plenty of experience to obtain investment capital from other people he or she either wants to or consents to let them in on the deal. He may feel that the investment has low risk and represents a tremendous opportunity. In that case, why should the promoter deprive friends of the opportunity that he or she makes readily available to business associates? Or he or she may simply lack the backbone to turn them down when they ask to be included in the investment group.

For whatever reasons, there are many partnerships composed of friends, and this will likely be your first exposure to the use of other people's money. If there is a good side to the partnership composed of friends, it is that the pressure cooker environment of the friendly partnership will likely prepare you for the different kind of pressure that is imposed by investors that were not first your friends. Such investors have no interest in you personally and care only about your performance with their money.

FORMING PARTNERSHIPS

Partnerships are marriages of convenience. Generally, they are formed at the instigation of the promoter because the promoter wants to invest in something that cannot be acquired without financial assistance. The promoter may or may not put his or her money into the investment. Typically, in early investments, the promoter will buy a portion of the investment and will bring in partners to make up the difference. There is a large variety in the quality of the deals being offered by the inexperienced investor/promoter. Frequently, the promoter will give far more than would a more experienced promoter. The promoter feels the need to make the deal particularly attractive to compensate for lack of experience. Representative of the early partnerships formed by the novice promoter is the following example.

A small apartment complex requires $100,000 of equity to make the purchase. The promoter has $20,000 to invest and has four friends that each have $20,000, for a total of the $100,000 needed. Each partner will own one-fifth of the partnership and through that interest a one-fifth interest in the building and land. The partnership is no-load, which means that the promoter is not charging the partnership anything for his or her own contribution in finding the property, negotiating the purchase, forming the partnership, and raising the money. The promoter will manage the property, also without fee, for the benefit of the partnership and will report the results of operation of the property to the partners on a monthly or quarterly basis. The promoter will also assume the responsibility for complying with local laws and for filing the partnership income tax returns.

In this example, the promoter is doing an awful lot for the partnership without receiving compensation. Why would anyone do that? What is in it for the promoter? The promoter has identified what he or she considers to be a very superior acquisition. The promoter feels that there is nothing comparable that can be acquired without forming the partnership. That is, there is nothing that can be bought for $20,000 down that is comparable in terms of the yield expected from the investment. The promoter also perceives the need to provide substantial services in order to interest the other partners in the deal. While the promoter is not receiving fees for his or her services to the partnership, neither is the promoter being charged for the valuable training and experience gained. Like establishing credit, the promoter is building a track record, acquiring a major investment on behalf of all the partners, and setting the stage for greater acquisitions in the future.

As you acquire experience as a promoter; you increase your value to the partnership and are in a position to charge more for your contribution and services. You might start by charging the partnership an organization fee, or you might receive your unit of ownership without paying the capital contribution required of the other investors. Eventually, you will charge a management fee comparable to those charged by independent management companies in the area. Also, you may find that you are able to increase the percentage of ownership that you require in the investment and the degree of authority and autonomy that you are able to exercise. But it's important not to get too greedy too quickly. You still have to sell the partnership interests to your investors, and the more you take for yourself, the harder the sale will be. But there is a certain psychological advantage in charging the fees that your services are worth. In charging those fees, you are communicating to the investor your feeling that you are worth the fees charged. You are competent, experienced, and far from cheap. They will be paying for your services, but they will be getting superior services of substantial value. If your self-perception is very favorable, and this perception is communicated, it will tend to be shared by the investors. For some investors, your aggressive fee structure might actually break down sales resistance rather than contribute to it.

The biggest problem with selling interests in general partnerships is that the partners have to have infinite faith and trust in you since that is the measure of their liability to the partnership creditors. The level of risk may not be very great. It is unlikely that an investor will suffer major exposure from an apartment investment, which can't be insured against. But, while the chance of loss may not be great, the magnitude of the loss is unlimited.

Another potential disadvantage is that the contribution of the promoter versus those of the partners is obvious, and the partners might find the favorable treatment given the promoter to be objectionable. I am not suggesting that you mislead the investors, but neither am I suggesting that it is necessary continually to highlight items that the investor might find objectionable.

Limited Partnerships

If there was ever an investment vehicle perfectly suited to real estate investment, it is the limited partnership. In the following chapters, we will consider the tax advantages and liability advantages of limited partnership investments. It should go without saying that these substantial attributes greatly enhance the salability of limited partnership units. That does not require further elaboration. Here we will consider the flexibility of the limited partnership structure and the additional legal requirements of it. We will also consider the applicability of limited partnership formation to the relatively inexperienced promoter.

One reason that the limited partnership is so ideally suited to real estate investment is that the form is so flexible. The basic structure is a partnership composed of at least one general partner and one or more limited partners. The general partner, like the partners in a general partnership, has unlimited liability. But, when structured properly, the limited partners' liability is limited to the amount of their investment. The limited partners may assume greater liability for the debts of the partnership, but the structure is designed to give the investors the benefits of the partnership form of business without the liability exposure of the general partnership. The general partner or partners may be individuals, corporations, and/or other partnerships. The limited partners may also be individuals, corporations, partnerships, and also estates and trusts. There may be a single general partner or thousands, or anything in between. Similarly, there are no legal restrictions on the number of limited partners, though there are different legal regulations, affecting limited partnerships, depending on the number of limited partners and whether those partners are from more than one state.

The general partners will usually perform the business of the partnership. They are the active parties in the business scheme. The limited partners are not actively involved in the business. They are making a casual investment in real estate for investment and tax shelter purposes. Anyone who wants to be actively involved in the business shouldn't be a limited partner. Limited partners who become actively involved in the business jeopardize their limited liability status. What is the point in becoming a limited partner if you are going to forgo the limited liability?

The responsibilities of the various general partners and the profit and loss sharing arrangements between the general and limited partners and among the general and limited partners will be determined by the limited partnership agreement. The National Association of Securities Dealers, Inc., publishes guidelines for what it considers reasonable fee levels and sharing arrangements for limited partnerships. The intent is to regulate promoters and general partners, to prevent the abuse of limited partners. The IRS also has guidelines for what it considers reasonable sharing arrangements. The purpose of the IRS rules is to prevent abuse of the income tax law. In general, the IRS is concerned only that the sharing arrangement have substantial economic effect and not be solely for the purpose of avoiding income taxation. But, within these general guidelines and rules, the partners are free to structure whatever agreement they choose. The regulations pose very little constraint on the parties.

Limited partnerships are regulated by state laws. Each state regulates the limited partnerships registered within that state. Unlike general partnerships, limited partnerships are required to be registered with the state. The limited partners want to obtain the limited liability unique to limited partners and shareholders of corporations. To obtain this limited liability, corporations and limited partnerships are subject to similar filing requirements. Usually, the limited partnership is registered in the state in which the investors live and the property is located. But this is also flexible, and it is not unusual for the limited partnership to be registered in one state, the investors to reside in another part of the country, and the property located in still a different region. Why register the limited partnership in a remote location? States compete for the business of registering limited partnerships to a lesser extent but in the same manner as they compete for the registration of corporate business. The competition takes the form of laws favorable to the partnership and, in particular, favorable to the promoter. Also, the fees may be lower in some areas and the filing requirements less burdensome. But by and large, all the states have similar rules, regulations, and laws. The fees are not substantial. It is therefore not worth shopping for a more favorable jurisdiction except in unusual circumstances.

Should the relatively inexperienced promoter consider limited partnership formation? The answer is an unequivocal yes. The interest shown in recent years by investors in real estate limited partnerships has greatly exceeded the amount of quality offerings available. It is an open market, with great potential for promoters. However, the promoter must be a good organizer. If you plan to promote a limited partnership, you must make arrangements to supplement your skills with those of your partners, employees, and outside professionals. There is no substitute for professional planning, organization, and performance.

Forming your first investment limited partnership is very similar to acquiring your first investment. The first one is always the hardest. It is important not to speculate on your capacity to sell units of your first proposals. Instead, before risking earnest money and reputation on successful projects, you should presell the idea to your investors. Don't bite off more than you can chew. Find a suitable investment that requires a small number of limited partners and doesn't require them to put up a lot of money. For example, a small apartment that requires from $50,000 to $100,000 down is ideal. You will have fewer than ten investors, each of whom will be required to invest $10,000 or less. If all the investors are from one state, the partnership offering will probably be exempt from state or federal registration. It must still comply with the laws regulating such partnerships, but you may not need to register the partnership prior to seeking investors. This is what is generally referred to as the *private offering* or *small offering exemption* from registration. When the number of investors you are approaching increases beyond about ten, the states will require more substantial registration and impose greater regulation. If the number of investors exceeds 35, you will certainly have to obtain the approval of the appropriate state securities office, which in most states is a division of the secretary of state's office. Also, if you use the mails to solicit investors, or if your investors come from more than one state, you will be subject to Securities and Exchange Commission regulations. The reason I suggest starting with a smaller offering is twofold; first, you will have a greater probability of having the capacity to complete such an offering, and second, you will avoid much of the hassle associated with the larger public offerings and their regulatory requirements.

SYNDICATING
Marketing interests in limited partnerships is called *syndication*. Syndication can be conducted on any level, from that of small private offerings marketed by the general partner to large public offerings marketed by the national securities firms.

Syndication is the ultimate use of OPM. Not only are you financing 100 percent of your acquisitions with the use of other people's money, but you are also charging them for their participation in your investments. You're sharing the investments and their profits with the investors, but they are putting up all the money. Of course, the general partner may put up some of his or her own money. But syndication provides the structure for raising 100 percent of the down payment and costs from the investors. In addition, the structure has the capacity for protection against negative cash flow through an assessment clause. The assessment clause is a provision of the limited partnership agreement that allows the general partner to assess the limited partners for the funds necessary to meet the obligations of the limited partnership. The clause may be limited to negative cash flow from operations or broad enough to provide refinancing proceeds. It may be limited or unlimited in amount. The existence of a broad assessment clause may impair the salability of the limited partnership units, but the absence of an assessment clause greatly increases the risk of the investment. It's a matter of balancing the desirability of an assessment clause against the reluctance of the limited partners to obligate themselves beyond the amount of their initial investment.

Consider whether and to what extent an assessment clause is necessary. Write the assessment clause that is necessary, but don't ask for more than you need. I have advised investors against investing in limited partnerships that have broadly worded discretionary assessment clauses. If there is an assessment provision, you must assume that it will be exercised. You may be advised that the syndicator hardly ever makes assessments, but you must assume that, if the clause exists, it will be used. Assessment provisions should be limited and nondiscretionary. The limitations should apply to both the amount of the assessment and its authorized uses. Investors shouldn't object to limited assessment provisions designed to limit their loss exposure; however, they have good reason to object to general assessment provisions left to the discretion of the general partner.

When you syndicate interests in limited partnerships, you are selling interests in the limited partnership, not in the property that the partnership is to acquire. Given that fact, you might question whether or not the property has to be identified when the partnership is formed. In other words, if you have investors who want to invest with you and trust your judgment, can't you receive their investment now and determine what property to invest in later? Yes, this is permissible. A limited partnership formed before the property is identified is called a *blind pool*. In a blind pool, the syndicating general partner will describe the kind of property he or she intends to buy, and he or she may detail the price and terms anticipated. But there can be no assurance that such deals will be available. You are relying exclusively on the reputation of the general partner and his or her ability to perform as indicated. For obvious reasons, it is very difficult to sell interests in a blind pool. Sometimes, the partnership property will be partially identified and partially blind. Rather than form two or more smaller partnerships, the syndicating general partner has determined that he or she can receive better economies in the syndicating sales effort by identifying the first property or properties that he or she intends to buy and indicating that other similar acquisitions will follow. The more the property is identified, the easier it will be to sell the investors in the limited partnership. You will be reducing the uncertainty and giving the investors a better description of what is being sold.

Note, however, that whenever it is possible to form a blind pool successfully, you should do so. There are tremendous advantages for the general partner if the money is in before he or she has to commit for property purchases. The general partner will know that the commitments can be honored without speculation as to whether he or she can syndicate the partnership units. The general partner is in a position to close quickly, which should aid the negotiations. Aside from the need to acquire property soon so that the tax write-offs will be substantial, the general partner is under less pressure to acquire property quickly. When the general partner is under pressure to acquire property quickly, there is a tendency to compromise and get less than was desired. There is also a tendency to make mistakes.

One word of caution in real estate syndication: recognize its importance and contribution to the investment effort. It is easy to think that the reputation of the firm or the reputation of the promoter sells the limited partnership units. To some extent this is true. But the limited partnership units do not sell themselves. They must be sold by one or more of the general partners, by employees of the firm, or by the independent securities firm or firms. There is a tendency not to recognize the contribution of the securities salespeople. Frequently, their compensation is substantial, and their contribution to the partnership ends before the work of the majority of the firm begins. Also, good salespeople make it look easy. Their business is done over lunches, at golf courses, and in private clubs. If you are working 70 hours a week on the partnership business, it it hard not to be jealous of your syndication partner, who drifts in at around ten o'clock, takes a two-hour lunch, and leaves for the club at three-thirty. Yet, this is the nature of his or her work. And, this partner may be doing a lot more of it than is apparent. He or she is working evenings and weekends and, provided that the partner's performance is adequate to meet the firm's needs, you should try to avoid second-guessing his or her contribution or methods. Don't close your eyes to underachievement and don't hold any partner or employee above criticism, but try to avoid criticism that is fostered by ignorance or jealousy.

Initially, you will find it necessary to syndicate your own projects. Securities firms are looking for a substantial period of positive track record in both property ownership and management and in prior syndication efforts. Depending on the volume of acquisitions you wish to make, and the volume of limited partners you must attract, it might be advisable to add a partner whose sole function is the real estate syndication. It is better to err on the side of overproviding for the syndication function than it is to come up short and be unable to complete the acquisitions.

Eventually, you must decide between expanding the syndication capabilities of your firm internally and contracting with independent syndication firms. There are advantages in either course of action. The syndication portion of your firm should be organized as a "profit center" and should contribute to the income of the firm. You must decide if you are in a position to forgo the profit from the syndication sales commission in order to obtain the greater growth potential from independent syndication. Also, you must decide if you wish to give up the internal control you have over the syndication effort. You must consider the faith and confidence you have in the syndication firm and whether you have faith in its ability to perform. Finally, you must consider if even a profitable syndication division is worth the time and effort it requires. Giving up the commission profit may prove to be a bargain when the overhead and hassle of the effort is eliminated.

In any investment effort, you should focus your time and attention on the objectives of the business. In our case, this is real estate investment. Syndication is a means to an end. You may or may not profit from your syndication effort, but you should not lose sight of your objective of acquiring profitable real estate investments.

REAL ESTATE AS PART OF A BUSINESS ACQUISITION

Frequently, real estate will be purchased as part of a larger acquisition involving other assets; for example, when it is part of a business acquisition. If you buy an automobile dealership, you will buy the franchise from the auto manufacturer, the business reputation and goodwill that has been generated by the seller, and perhaps also the parking lot and the buildings. In this example and many others, real estate constitutes a large portion of the total purchase price. This is a somewhat peculiar anomaly, since the purchaser intended to enter the chosen business, not to invest in real estate. Yet the need to buy a substantial amount of expensive real estate might well prevent the purchaser from entering the business. It is therefore desirable to explore the role of real estate in an active business, the desirability of its purchase, and the alternatives to purchase.

IS THIS REALLY NECESSARY?
There is nothing that you can buy that you can't lease. The reason that real estate is usually included as part of a business acquisition is that the business seller owns the real estate. The reason is seldom better or worse than that. Sometimes, the business and the real estate are synonymous. For example, a warehouse business or a railroad could hardly operate without the real estate. A person who is selling a warehouse business is really selling the building, which just happens to have the warehouse business as its current use. The sale price that you negotiate will be a function of the value of the building and the business. If the business is truly the best use for the building, the value of the business will determine the sale price. However, if the building has a better use, the selling price might be far more than the business is worth. Then you might expect to see the building converted to the higher use, perhaps the construction of more overpriced condominiums for the upwardly mobile young professionals.

In those cases where the building or real estate *is* the business, as with apartments, motels, warehouses, and the like, the need to purchase the real estate as part of the business acquisition is not questioned. But there are many instances where, although the real estate is a necessary part of the business in that it needs shelter, it isn't a part of the business in the sense that particular space or construction is needed. For example, most service firms that are primarily office functions should be relatively indifferent as to which first-class office space they occupy. Where specific real estate is not important, there is less of a tendency to own the property.

Other considerations are the unique requirements of the business. If the business requires a special-purpose structure, it may well be that the business finds it necessary to acquire or construct the structure. This again is an integral part of the business. Other times the property will have only minimal used sales value or minimal salvage value. It is very difficult to lease property that has only a limited secondary market and minimal salvage value. The leasing company has too much exposure in the event that the lessee defaults. To cover its exposure, the leasing company will require security deposits that might be more than would be required as a down payment if you purchased the property.

For some reason, certain businesses tend to own their buildings while others tend to lease. For example, a law firm will almost always lease its offices, and a retailer will often lease its stores, but a restaurant owner will frequently own its buildings. In this case, the reason that some businesses tend to own their buildings, while others tend to lease, is tradition. But neither the seller's ownership nor tradition is a good reason for the purchaser of the business to purchase the real estate as well. The seller will insist that he or she "has no interest" in continuing to own the real estate after selling the business. So, although the seller may carry the contract, he or she will probably insist on a sale rather than a lease. Perhaps the seller will allow for a short-term lease with a purchase option. In that case, the seller will expect you to complete the purchase in a rather short period of time. But the seller will probably insist that the building and real estate are part of the business sale and insist that the "whole" business be purchased. Therefore, it will probably be necessary for the purchaser to acquire the business and the real estate at least temporarily, until an alternative method of financing the real estate can be put together.

REASONS NOT TO BUY THE REAL ESTATE
The principal reason not to buy the real estate is that you may have other more important uses for the money that would otherwise be tied up in the down payment and equity in the real estate.

Cash flow is often tight in new (and established) businesses. Also, the down payment required for the real estate might put a significant dent in the operating capital of the business. In addition, this money is tied up for a long period of time in an illiquid asset. If the money were spent on other assets, like materials or inventory, at least you could expect the inventory to "turn" and become cash again in a relatively short period of time. The real estate, on the other hand, may not convert back into cash, or operating capital, until the business is sold or liquidated.

Another reason not to buy real estate is that businesses tend to be dynamic rather than static. Businesses either grow or decline; they seldom remain the same size for very long. So, if you buy the space in which the business operates, you will likely find that the business either outgrows the space or has excess capacity within a short period of time. Thus, success and growth could become a burden when you have a substantial amount of cash tied up in facilities that cramp your growth and operations. You may find it inconvenient or impossible to move to a new facility until the old facility is sold, and there may be no market for your old space. This is the primary reason why I advise against buying condominium office space. In addition to being overpriced, it might service your current business needs but not the future needs.

If you buy the property, you will have to maintain it. You won't fully realize all the services that the landlord performs until you have to perform them yourself. From items as small as janitorial service or gardening to something as substantial as facilities maintenance, you will find that all functions will become the responsibility of the owner-occupant.

Start-up businesses are seldom in a position to utilize the tax advantages of real estate ownership fully. They usually show plenty of start-up period loss without the need for depreciation on the real property. If they cannot utilize the tax advantages, and they buy the buildings in a competitive market populated by investors who could utilize the tax benefits, they will probably pay too much for the value they receive.

REASONS TO BUY THE REAL ESTATE

There are also many reasons that you might wish to buy the real estate. To begin with, it might be an excellent investment. You might be tired of sending a lease check to the landlord each month with no equity to show for it. You may be concerned with the stability of your occupancy. The landlord may be threatening to raise your rent or displace your business in favor of a more appealing tenant. On the other hand, you may have a tremendous bargaining advantage over the landlord in negotiating the purchase of your building. This is especially true if you are flexible and in a position to move if necessary. Consider what the building would be worth if you were not the tenant. Commercial and office space may sit vacant for long periods before a replacement tenant is located. You might, therefore, be able to negotiate a bargain purchase with the implied threat that, if you are not allowed to purchase the property, you will move. In this case, the building is worth more to you than it is to the landlord. If you purchase the building, you know it will be occupied by a tenant of the quality of your business. However, if the landlord doesn't sell the property to you, he or she may be stuck with an empty building. The next time your lease comes up for renewal, consider this among your options.

Real estate is also a hedge against inflation. Each year you will probably pay more rent than the year before. If, instead, you buy the property, especially on a fixed-rate mortgage, you will come closer to fixing the costs of your occupancy. Naturally, the costs of maintaining the property and overhead costs like utilities will continue to be inflated along with the rest of the economy. But rent or debt service, which is a major cost of occupancy, will be nearly fixed. Over the years, this cost of occupancy should become a relative bargain.

Another reason to buy the real estate would be to tie up the valuable space. If you have a profitable business for which location is an important attribute, you will want to operate forever in the same location. This is especially true if the neighborhood is stable or improving. If someone else owns the property, the owner will undoubtedly recognize the importance of this location to the tenant and seek to benefit in the form of increased rent. The advantageous location will command a premium sales price or rent, which may offset the benefit of the location.

If you have been renting your business location for any length of time, consider how nice it would be to have no landlord, which would be the case if you purchased the property. For better or worse, you are on your own. The landlord's personality and whims will cease to have an adverse effect on your business.

Depending on the nature of your business, owning your building may not impose a constraint on your growth. It may be unnecessary to have all of your business functions at one location or under one roof. You may choose to purchase the building that houses your corporate offices and, if the business grows, move some of the functions like computer programming to a remote location. Also, there are many businesses that grow on the basis of a defined business unit. If you operate a highly successful shoe store

in a mall location, you may well find it advantageous to expand
the business by opening a new store in a different mall rather than
expanding the store in the first mall. You should have more traffic
and make more sales with two small stores than with one large
store. In this case, it would not be disadvantageous to purchase
each of the locations if we limit the analysis to the question of the
adequacy of the space.

If you have a profitable business, the business may find it advantageous to purchase its building. It may utilize the tax shelter
that the building generates. In addition, it may be a use for the
profits of the business approved by the government to avoid im-
position of the accumulated earnings tax. These obscure tax considerations are beyond the scope of this book. However, it might
be noted that there are many considerations beyond the scope of
simple common sense that might make the purchase of the building desirable. Accountants and tax lawyers will be more than
happy to advise you in these matters, on a noncomplimentary basis, of course.

SALE AND LEASEBACK

One method used by businesses to rid themselves of the burden
of tying up their operating capital in their buildings is through the
mechanism of the sale and leaseback. In this case, the business
would sell its building to an investor or group of investors and
lease the building back at terms that are satisfactory to the business. The business will be writing its own lease, so there is the
temptation to write one highly favorable to the business in its capacity as a tenant. The problem with this strategy is that, if you
place too favorable a lease on the building, you will not be able to
realize much on its sale. In doing that, you will defeat the purpose
of the sale and leaseback. It is intended that the sale generate cash
and the leaseback preserve occupancy.

Sometimes the sale and leaseback is arranged with a friendly
party who is better able to take advantage of the ownership of the
building than you are. The friendly party might be an individual
owner of the business or perhaps a major shareholder. By owning
the property, the individual is able to utilize the tax loss without diluting the benefit with the offsetting income from the business.
Also, the business may be able to utilize the lower corporate tax
rates. The overall intent is to realize the maximum after-tax advantage by minimizing the total tax liability of the owner and his
or her business.

It would be ideal if the sale and leaseback could be arranged as
part of the acquisition of the business. In that case, you wouldn't

have to finance the purchase of the building that you don't really want (or can't really afford), even temporarily. Unfortunately, the ideal is hard to realize. There are problems with trying to convince the seller of a business to split the package between a purchaser of the buildings and another purchaser of the business. Also, you need to sell the building purchaser on the value of your business as a tenant for the property. New businesses have a tendency not to succeed, so they are not the best of credit risks. Therefore, it is often much easier to structure a sale and leaseback after your business has some operating history, some track record on which the purchaser of the building can rely. However, if you can utilize the friendly party as noted above, you may have the capacity to engineer such an acquisition.

LONG-TERM LEASE
A long-term lease may accomplish the advantages of ownership without the investment requirement. You will sacrifice the investment opportunity, but you may be able to enter the desired business with a much lower cash outlay. The provisions in the lease are up to the parties. You may be able to structure a lease with a fixed rent level for 20 years if the landlord is willing to lease at those terms. If you find any such landlords, give them my name and phone number. I think we might be able to do some business. But in this marketplace you are more likely to encounter landlords who are unwilling to fix the rent for that long a period. You can also expect that the lease provisions are not going to be as favorable as those that you could arrange through a purchase. Just consider that to be part of the cost you pay by choosing not to purchase the property.

A long-term lease is not a riskless commitment. You may have the right to assign your lease benefits and obligations, and the lessor is under a legal obligation to attempt to mitigate your damages in the event that you default on the lease; however, if you sign a 20-year lease, you are legally obligating yourself for a 20-year period. This is an obligation that should not be taken lightly. You might wish to take other precautions to limit your exposure, like forming a corporation to buy the business and enter into the lease. If this is a concern of yours, you should refuse to personally guarantee the obligation of the corporation and the lease.

YEARS AND YEARS OF LEASE OPTIONS
Perhaps the best of available options for the new business is to attempt to secure its necessary occupancy with a short-term lease and a series of options covering the period of anticipated need for

the property. The business's legal exposure on the lease will be only for the original or optioned term, not for the period not yet optioned. The business may be able to obtain the benefits of secure long-term occupancy, without the cost of acquisition or the legal exposure of the long-term lease. You might expect that the cost of your occupancy will be more than if you were willing to obligate yourself to a long-term lease, which, as already mentioned, would be more than the costs of the debt service associated with ownership. The availability of such an acquisition that includes lease options for the property rather than the seller's requiring you either to lease the property for a long-term or to purchase the property will depend on your considerable negotiation skills. When selling a business, usually the last thing the seller wants to do is to take it back. Your attempt to structure the transaction to limit your exposure in the event of default communicates to the seller your concern over the possibility that you might fail and default. The seller might interpret your caution as good cautious business judgment or may determine that those who plan to fail usually do.

Everything that a business acquires is for the use of the business in generating profitable operations. The businessperson must be pragmatic and attempt to acquire the most value for his or her money. You must not buy property for the business without giving thought to the alternatives for acquiring the use of the property. As far as an investment goes, the property may well make a good investment, but that is a separate consideration from your business's needs. Don't buy the building simply because your business lives there.

FINANCE 11

In real estate investment books written 20 years ago, there was hardly a mention of financial considerations. Real estate finance was not a very sexy subject. In fact, it was something of a given. Mortgage interest rates were relatively stable and low and had been for a long period of time. Inflation also was relatively stable and low. Keynesian economics and deficit spending were still more theory than practice, and the national debt didn't concern economists and scare the rest of us.

Real estate finance reflected the stability of the rest of the economy. The period for the financing was routinely long-term, with 30-year financing being common. By today's standards, the rates were low and, contrary to current trends, fixed. In case you don't remember, fixed rates are those that remain stable throughout the term of the loan. The old loans were also quite "accommodating." The loans were generally assumable by a new purchaser, without fees, restrictive approval provisions, or interest rate adjustments. Also, the loans generally had no prepayment restrictions or penalties. You had the option of paying off the loan if you thought for any reason it was in your best interest to do so. It was a simpler age in many respects.

Twenty years ago, it was easier to make money from the operations of real estate. There are those who would quickly disagree with this statement. They are wrong. First of all, the statement is narrow. I didn't say that you could make more money, in general,

197

in real estate 20 years ago than today. I limited the statement to a consideration of the profit potential from property operations; that is, the monthly cash flow that the property produced. There were several reasons why the cash flow was better, but at least one reason why it may have been worse. The cash flow was better because the property was purchased for the economic considerations. Cash flow was important. Since the rate of inflation had not been very high, property didn't sell for inflated values in anticipation of inflated income and property values. Also, the tax advantages of real property ownership were not so great as they are today. The tax considerations didn't so dominate other considerations as to crowd out economic considerations. It didn't make sense to buy property that produced negative cash flow that made economic sense after tax. If the investment didn't make sense before tax, it wouldn't make sense after tax. And, with a low rate of inflation, if the property produced negative cash flow when you bought it, chances were very good that the property would continue to be negative for a long period to come. So, property was bought for its positive cash flow.

One factor that would partially offset the others and tend to reduce the yield was lower standards and expectations. In an environment that shows a 3 percent rate of inflation, a 5 percent cash flow has a higher value than the same cash flow in an environment of a 10 percent rate of inflation. Inflation has affected our expectation as to what constitutes a reasonable rate of return. And it will be some time before expectations are readjusted to the levels of 20 years ago.

The advantages of the long-term, fixed-rate mortgage were substantial. For one thing, by fixing the payment, you were assured that the cash flow from the property would improve over the period during which you owned it. If interest rates dropped, you could refinance the property and realize the savings; but if interest rates increased, you could continue to take advantage of your low-rate mortgage. Banks especially liked that arrangement. Another advantage in the long-term, fixed-rate mortgage was the general availability of mortgage financing. It was not necessary for the seller to provide financing and improve on what the market could provide. As a result, sellers were generally able to do what every smart seller wants to do, and that is to cash out.

SELLER FINANCING

Seller financing grew out of necessity. The banking system and financial markets failed to provide adequate financing for real estate transactions. Those sellers who wanted to sell real estate in such a market found it necessary to provide financing themselves, defer the sale, or discount the price.

What happened specifically was that, beginning in the latter half of the 1960s and continuing through the 1970s, interest rates increased. The increase wasn't regular, but it was pervasive. And real estate wasn't the only industry affected. The whole economy was adjusting to new expectations as to the cost of money and what constituted a reasonable return on invested money. What investors and banks wanted was a real rate of return on invested dollars in an inflationary economy. The problem with real estate in this economy is that it is a heavily financed investment. It is not uncommon for the amount of debt in a real estate transaction to exceed 90 percent of the purchase price. This contrasts with manufacturing and other industries, where it is uncommon for the debt-to-equity ratio to exceed two to one. Thus, a manufacturer is usually considered to have excess debt if the debt exceeds 67 percent of the manufacturer's capitalization.

As with any other expense of ownership, if costs increase, the yield on the investment decreases and the property value should fall. However, interest rates were high in an environment of high inflation throughout the economy, including rents. The cost increase associated with high interest was offset with increased revenue from the higher rents. And there are many other factors affecting property values. Therefore, I doubt that the inverse relationship between real estate values and interest rates has ever been documented scientifically. But the relationship is intuitively obvious and is evidenced by such things as the increased role of seller financing.

When the seller provides the financing for the sale of property at a rate that is lower than the rate available in the financial markets, the seller is actually discounting the price of the property by the difference in the rate provided and what would be available in the financial markets. Most sellers fail to consider seller financing in the context of a discount on the price. If they stopped to consider the amount of the discount that the financing provides, they might find that less of a discount is necessary for a cash-out sale.

Another way to look at the cost of seller financing from the seller's point of view is to look at what the seller is giving up by providing the financing. This is called *opportunity cost*. If the seller is investing in leveraged investments in real estate, it is likely that the seller's investments are yielding in excess of 30 percent after taxes. If the seller carries the contract at 12 percent before taxes and is in the 50 percent marginal income tax bracket, the financing that the seller is carrying is yielding only 6 percent after tax. What seller can afford this kind of opportunity cost? Yet many sellers routinely pay that cost on every sale by carrying the paper on the deal. I am sure that many sellers have never stopped to consider the cost of carrying the financing. Many others are vaguely aware that it is undesirable to carry the financing, but they know no viable alternative. And there may well be no viable alternative, but the important thing to consider is the cost you are incurring.

To make an intelligent decision on financing alternatives and their impact on your return on investment, you must know the cost you are paying. One reason that sellers frequently make the mistake of carrying undesirable financing is that they think of their property in terms of its value. They think of the value as absolute, not as a function of the many attributes of the property, including the financing on the property. In order to get that price, the seller offers to provide financing that is highly desirable to the purchaser. The financing offered will be at below-market interest rates, may be for a long term, and may be assumable by a subsequent purchaser. With these attributes, the seller may expect to carry the financing on the property for the full term of his or her contract with the purchaser. Pragmatically, the purchaser can't do better than the financing offered by the seller, so the purchaser will have no desire to pay it off or refinance.

PROS AND CONS FOR THE PURCHASER

As a purchaser, you may find seller financing highly desirable. It may have most of the attributes of the traditional long-term, fixed-rate mortgage. And, if it is assumable by your subsequent purchaser, you will be following my rule of always planning for the subsequent sale when you make the purchase. One problem is that the seller will have a continuing interest in the property. The typical seller will have a tendency to second-guess your management decisions for the property and may question the propriety of rent increases, find fault with your management personnel, and criticize your maintenance of the property. In summary, the seller will probably show far more interest in the property than would the institutional lender. And, as long as the seller provides the financing, you will have to deal with his or her personality. Sometimes that personality is accommodating and friendly, other times it is disruptive and annoying. And since all sellers are trying to sell their property and will try to appear cooperative and accommodating, you will generally be unable to determine who will be a problem until it is too late.

You might consider the seller's intrusion into your ownership as being just one of the costs of ownership and as part of the cost of the desirable financing. However, if you find such seller intrusion to be intolerable, you may attempt to avoid it by seeking more information about the seller from others who have had dealings with him or her. If others tell you that the seller was accommodating after the sale, you may wish to continue negotiations for the property, but if they tell you that the seller tends to be an intrusive and uncooperative creditor, you may wish to withdraw from the transaction or consider the transaction's cost without the seller financing.

Sometimes I think that some sellers are particularly hard to deal with because they realized after the fact that they are obligated to provide below-market financing for a long period of time, and they hope that by being difficult they can encourage the purchaser to cash them out. Unfortunately, this tactic is often successful.

THE SELLER'S VIEWPOINT

As the seller, you want to dispose of the property. You want to realize as much as you can for the property through negotiations that are as swift and comfortable as possible. You may find that you have "too much equity" in the property to cash out. And since other sellers are willing to carry a contract in order to sell their property, you too may find it necessary to carry a contract in order to sell the property. If you find yourself in this situation, you will want to minimize the cost of carrying the financing.

Wraparound Loans

One method of reducing the cost of seller financing is to wrap around existing financing. For example, say that you want to sell a small apartment building for $100,000, and the purchaser has agreed to the price but can manage a down payment of only $10,000. On contacting banks, the best loan you could obtain would be for $75,000 at 15.5 percent interest only (none of the payment applies to a reduction of the principal) but due in five years. Assume further that the property has an assumable mortgage of $40,000 at 8 percent interest and payments of $520 per month. The underlying mortgage has about nine years to pay off. Consider the following three alternatives.

Alternative A: New financing of $75,000 is obtained, and the seller carries back a second mortgage of $15,000 at 12 percent interest only, due in five years.

Alternative B: The new purchaser assumes the underlying mortgage of $40,000, and the seller carries back a second mortgage of $50,000 at 12 percent interest only, due in five years.

Alternative C: The seller carries a second mortgage of $90,000 at 12 percent interest only, due in five years, wrapping the underly-

ing mortgage of $40,000. In other words, the seller charges inter-
est to the purchaser on the total debt, and the seller continues to
make payments on the underlying first mortgage.

Description	Alternative A	Alternative B	Alternative C
Monthly rent	$ 1,200	$ 1,200	$ 1,200
Operating expenses (40%)	− 480	− 480	− 480
Net before debt service	$ 720	$ 720	$ 720
Debt service	1,118.75	1,020	$ 900
Monthly cash flow	$ (398.75)	$ (300)	$ (180)
Cash to seller on closing*	$45,000	$10,000	$10,000
Net cash to seller monthly	150	500	380
First month debt paydown on underlying	n/a	n/a	253
Seller's net monthly benefit	$150	$500	$633

*disregarding closing costs

In this example, we see a highly leveraged purchase in which the
purchaser is acquiring property with a value of $100,000 for only
$10,000 down. Under each of the three alternatives considered,
the purchaser will have negative cash flow from the property, at
least initially. The negative cash flow is worse in the context of the
new 15.5 percent financing. And, while the seller might prefer to
obtain such financing since he or she will be able to obtain considerably more cash in the closing, the purchaser is likely to object to
the high interest rate and conditions of the financing and might
withdraw from the deal. The negative cash flow is lowest in Alternative C, in which the seller is wrapping the underlying loan. Even
though the purchaser is paying a higher rate of interest by having
the seller wrap the low-interest underlying contract (12 percent)
rather than the purchaser's assuming the underlying contract
(which would have a weighted average interest rate of 10.22 percent), the cash flow of the purchaser is improved since the underlying loan is amortizing so rapidly. The purchaser may be unable

to take advantage of the low-interest underlying financing because he or she is simply unable to pay off the debt so quickly. The seller, on the other hand, by reducing the cash flow received per month from $500 to $380 or by only $120, is receiving the benefit of paying off the underlying loan by $253 in the first month and an increasing amount each month thereafter. In addition, the seller is really loaning the purchaser $50,000, the difference between the underlying loan and the amount of financing required. But the purchaser is paying the seller interest on $90,000 at 12 percent. The $40,000 difference costs the seller interest of 8 percent. So, the seller is effectively loaning the purchaser $50,000 at 15.2 percent interest.

The seller would still probably prefer to cash out his or her interest in the property rather than carry the financing. But, by wrapping a low-interest underlying loan, the seller can substantially ease the burden of carrying the financing by generating a significant yield on the money lent.

THE DURATION OF THE SELLER FINANCING

Another consideration in seller financing is the period of the loan. The purpose of the seller's providing financing for the purchaser is to facilitate the transaction and enable the purchaser to buy property from the seller that the purchaser wouldn't be able or willing to buy otherwise. In this context, the seller should question whether or not it is necessary to provide long-term financing for the property. It is not uncommon for sellers to provide long-term, low-interest financing on the property they sell without balloon payments, due-on-sale provisions, or other mechanisms to obtain cash prior to the amortization schedule of the property. With most purchasers, this is probably unneccesary. If the seller provides financing for a period of five to ten years, most purchasers will consider that adequate and not attempt to adjust the price to reflect the cost of the new financing that will be necessary to replace the seller financing.

As a purchaser, however, you should attempt to get the seller to provide longer-term financing. For example, if the seller agrees to provide financing with a balloon payment due in seven years, that may seem like a long period when you purchase the property and more than adequate. But, if you hold the property for five years before you attempt to resell, the remaining period on the first seller's financing will be only two years. Regardless of how attractive the financing is, a new purchaser who buys property from you will not be able to realize much benefit. Therefore, this financing will have only minimal benefit to you when it comes time for you to sell. You will then pay the cost of violating the rule of always setting up the subsequent sale when you make the purchase.

ASSUMABLE FINANCING

The seller should also consider whether or not he or she wishes to make the financing assumable by a subsequent purchaser. Pragmatically, assumable financing is not very desirable for the seller. If the financing is assumable, it is less likely to be paid off in a subsequent sale, and the first seller will likely carry the loan through several subsequent purchasers. The subsequent purchasers may not be as creditworthy or responsible as the first purchaser to whom the seller sold. The subsequent purchasers may not be people with whom the seller would want to have a business relationship, especially the relationship of creditor-debtor. Frequently, the purchaser insists that the financing be assumable. Otherwise, the benefit of the seller financing is limited to the first purchaser. A reasonable compromise is to provide that the seller would have the right to approve the subsequent purchaser, which approval and consent to assumption shall not be unreasonably refused. The courts in the various states have interpreted the reasonable consent clause differently, but generally the clause imposes little constraint on the choice of a subsequent purchaser, provided that his or her creditworthiness and net worth are comparable or superior to that of the first purchaser. The first seller is able to avoid the subsequent sale of the property to significant credit risks, but he or she continues to have significant exposure on the assumption of a subsequent purchaser.

SPLIT DOWN PAYMENT

A variation of the seller financing with a balloon payment is the sale with a split down payment. The split down payment has become very popular in many markets. In a sale with a split down payment, the seller agrees to defer receipt of a portion of the down payment until subsequent years. For example, the seller may agree to receive a 25 percent down payment for the property, with 10 percent paid on closing and 5 percent paid for each of the next three years. This arrangement will enable the purchaser with the 10 percent down payment on closing to acquire the property and the seller to receive a significant amount of his or her equity (25 percent of the purchase price) within three years. The deferred portion of the down payment actually constitutes a series of deferred but short-term balloon payments.

Why would a purchaser agree to purchase property with a series of short-term balloon payments? The mechanism of splitting the down payment may enable the purchaser to purchase more property than would otherwise be possible. The purchaser may feel that the property is of superior quality or has other attributes worthy of purchase. But a primary motivation of the split down payment purchaser is to maximize purchasing power after tax. By buying the property with significant leverage and depreciating the building and personal property, the purchaser could develop a significant tax shelter. This would enable him or her to make the deferred portion of the down payment in dollars that would otherwise be paid in taxes. It is particularly appealing to the high-bracket taxpayer to see funds that would normally have been paid to the government in income taxes used instead to buy equity in investments. When this is structured properly, the high-bracket purchaser could be "out of pocket" only the initial down payment and any negative cash flow, with subsequent payments on the deferred down payment made entirely out of tax savings.

Seller financing is here to stay. Until such time as financial institutions are once more competitive with the rates, terms, and conditions that are willingly offered by the sellers of property, you may expect to see seller-financed acquisitions dominate the marketplace.

BANK AND OTHER INSTITUTIONAL FINANCING

Traditionally, when you were negotiating the purchase of investment property, a bank, insurance company, or other financial institution was contacted during the negotiations to obtain a commitment for financing the debt portion of the acquisition. Sometimes the original bank was contacted for the assumption of the existing loan, but more often a new bank was involved, since additional debt was required for the new purchaser and to cash out the seller. The bank would appraise the property to determine the amount it would loan. It had a major impact on the terms of the acquisition, since the purchaser would have to provide whatever funds the bank would not provide. The amount of funds that the bank would provide was primarily a function of the appraised value that the bank determined. A further constraint was the purchase price and terms negotiated between the buyer and seller. The bank wanted to see "some commitment" on the part of the purchaser and would often restrict the amount of secondary financing it would allow. The percentage of the purchase price that the bank would finance depended on the stability of the market, the availability of financing proceeds and the creditworthiness of the borrower. An additional consideration was the debt coverage ratio that the property provided. But, in the traditional environment of positive cash flow properties, debt coverage was a condition of the financing that seldom posed a significant constraint. That situation changed as interest rates increased.

As interest rates climbed, it became increasingly difficult for investment property to service its debt. An interest rate of 16 percent has twice as much interest expense as an interest rate of 8 percent. Debt coverage became a significant constraint in financing and reduced the amount of financing available for the property. Typically, banks are looking for a scheduled debt coverage ratio of 1.2 or 1.25 to 1. So, if the property requires a monthly payment of $400, the bank will want to be convinced that the property will generate a net income before debt service of about $480 to $500. At this rate, the bank officers will feel relatively comfortable that the loan will be serviced promptly. At 8 percent interest only, a $400 monthly payment will service a debt of $60,000. At 16 percent interest only, the same $400 monthly payment will service a debt of only $30,000. With the rent from the property able to service less debt, the amount of bank financing available as a percentage of the price of property began a steady decline. One might suggest that the property was becoming progressively less valuable also, but as previously noted, there are many factors other than debt service that affect the value of property. If the perception was that interest rates would remain high for an indefinite period of time, and if the sellers were unwilling to provide acceptable financing, it is likely that the value of property would have fallen as interest rates rose. But, among other factors affecting the value, inflation in both rents and the cost of new construction had the effect of maintaining property values.

Gradually, the market adjusted. Fewer and fewer new loans were being written by institutions, and more and more were written by sellers and other private parties. Much planned new construction that couldn't tolerate high interest rates was simply not built. And, where new loans were obtained from institutional sources, borrowers became accustomed to loans of lower percentage of the price or value.

CREATIVE FINANCING, NEGATIVE AMORTIZATION LOANS

Where there is a problem, creative minds will attempt to find a solution. In the context of institutional financing, the problem was and is high interest rates and a resulting lack in the availability of debt financing. Specifically, it cost too much each month to make the debt payments. The property didn't generate enough money to service the debt necessary to purchase the buildings. So, how could you reduce the monthly payments in a manner acceptable to the banks? One possibility was to shift to a longer and longer amortization period for the loan. But, after you have stretched out the amortization period beyond 30 years, payments cannot be reduced much more by further extending the period. The next logical step is to interest-only financing and, beyond that, to negative amortizations. In other words, with a negative amortization loan, you owe more debt after you have owned the property for a period of time than you did when you purchased the property. If the property has appreciated in value, you may still have a significant equity position in the property, even with the negative amortization. From the bank's point of view, a negative amortization loan is new and exotic, so they are going to be reluctant to participate in it. However, if there is adequate equity so that it is unlikely that the bank would lose money on the loan, it may be convinced to initiate such a loan. If you are going to attempt to convince a bank to write a negative amortization loan, you should come prepared to show the bank how the loan will subsequently be converted to an amortizing status and/or how you intend to retire the loan. Banks are going to be reluctant to write negative amortization loans for a very long period. At best, a negative amortization loan should be viewed as a gap loan; that is, a loan that is taken out to fill the gap until better financing can be obtained.

EQUITY PARTICIPATION LOANS
    Another method of reducing the payments to the bank each month is to give the bank something other than interest as an incentive to write the loan. The incentive that many banks want and many borrowers are willing to give is an equity participation in the property. What that means is that the bank will get a percentage of the profits generated on the sale of the building. In exchange for this equity participation, the bank will charge a reduced rate of interest on the loan. The bank will calculate the amount that it is willing to reduce the interest rate by calculating what it expects its share of the profit to be. The bank will require a higher rate of return on this deferred and somewhat more speculative loan than it would on a more conventional loan. For example, if the bank was willing to write a loan for 15 percent on a standard amortizing loan, it would want to yield in excess of 20 percent (per annum compounded, including participation in the sales proceeds) on an equity participation loan. However, even with the increased cost, the equity participation loan may be attractive to the borrower be-

cause it is more serviceable. The equity participation loan may yield a break-even cash flow, while a conventional loan might result in a significant negative cash flow that the purchaser would find impossible to service. More likely would be the scenario in which the equity participation loan would yield enough proceeds to acquire the property, while a conventional loan would not yield enough to buy the property.

If it comes down to a question of being able to acquire the property with an equity participation loan and being unable to acquire the property otherwise, what choice does the purchaser have? One choice is to acquire the best equity participation loan you can find. The variety of loans is limited only by the creativity of the financial institutions. Banks, of course, are proud of their lack of creativity, but strained market conditions have made some creative financing desirable.

One problem with equity participation loans is that your banker becomes your partner. The bank and your banker might turn out to be a good partner, imposing very little on your management decisions and objectives, or it may turn out to be a problem partner, severely restricting your decisions and second-guessing your management decisions. Any partner will have some restrictive effect on your options. The bank evaluates risk on the basis of how long the financing is carried. Therefore, the bank will in all likelihood encourage you to sell the property before it is in your best interest to do so. Since the bank will probably be unable to utilize the tax advantages of the property as well as an individual investor can, the bank's objectives for the property are likely to differ substantially from the purchaser's. Also, because the bank perceives itself as bending over backward to satisfy your needs, it will want a substantial "slice of the pie" for such an accommodation.

One provision you may be able to obtain in an equity participation loan is a ceiling on the participation that the bank is to be paid. When you first suggest this provision, make sure that your banker is seated and not holding coffee or anything else likely to spill. Part of the motivation the bank has for writing an equity participation loan is that its possible yield on the loan is infinite. On the negative side, the bank will impose a floor on the interest rate by providing that a certain amount of interest is to be paid monthly and perhaps a certain amount of the initial proceeds are to be applied to interest before being split among the owners (including the bank). Since the bank shows no reluctance in insisting on a floor, I believe the borrower should show a similar lack of reluctance in suggesting a ceiling. This, of course, depends largely on your bargaining position with the bank and the availability of alternative financing in the marketplace. You might suggest, for example, that if the bank's conventional loans are being written at 15 percent a ceiling be imposed on the effective rate of interest on your loan as a function of the equity participation and the interest payments at, say, 20 percent. The bank may accept the ceiling, reject it, or perhaps suggest a higher ceiling of, say, 25 percent. Analyze the financial market, the strength of your negotiating position, and the return you expect from the property. Consider the value of a ceiling on the bank's yield to you, the borrower. And remember that, in your proposal of a yield ceiling on the financing, you are in a negotiating posture in the same way as when you are negotiating the purchase from the seller. To succeed in the negotiations, you will have to satisfy the bank's objectives as well as your own.

Don't go into you bank expecting to negotiate a fixed-rate, long-term loan. You will be disappointed. Banks were severely hurt during the 1970s when the costs of their borrowed funds exceeded the yield on their fixed-rate, long-term loans. To recover from this situation, banking policies have changed substantially. The first change was a reduction in the term or period of the loans. The amortization might be calculated on a 30-year schedule, but the loan would be due in a much shorter period of, say, five to ten years. If you wanted a fixed-rate loan, you could expect that fixed rate to be very high. Banks weren't about to duplicate the problems of the '70s. As a practical matter, bank financing became variable. The rate would vary with some index, like the prime rate or perhaps the bank's cost of funds.

ADJUSTABLE-RATE MORTGAGES

A more acceptable form of financing for banks is the adjustable-rate mortgage (or ARM). In an adjustable-rate mortgage, the interest rate on the mortgage starts out low and increases over the life of the loan. Unlike in a floating-rate loan, the interest rates to be charged on the adjustable-rate mortgage are fixed at the beginning of the loan. The interest rate and payment obligation at the beginning of the loan are below the market rates for fixed- and floating-rate loans. This advantage is offset by the higher interest rates later in the loan, which may be above the market rate. Generally, the loan will have prepayment penalties to prevent the borrower from using the early loan rates without paying the cost of the higher, later rates.

Adjustable-rate mortgages are particularly popular in highly leveraged investments during periods of high inflation. They enable the purchaser to service more debt than would otherwise be possible. The hope is that, as the interest rate and payment obligations increase, so will the rental receipts as a result of inflation.

The overall interest rate on adjustable-rate mortgages tends to be higher than that on either fixed-rate mortgages or floating-rate mortgages. This is justified by the institution as compensation for the accommodation of the early loan rates and the added risk associated with increasing payment obligations. This extra cost, coupled with lower rates of inflation, is among the reasons that adjustable-rate mortgages are less favored today. Many investors who used adjustable-rate mortgages and budgeted continued compounded inflation at a rate of 10 percent per year were not able to meet the increasing payment obligations and thus lost the property.

A type of adjustable-rate mortgage that is becoming more prevalent with institutional lenders and sellers and individual lenders is the step-rate loan. A step-rate loan is one in which the interest rate increases at a prescribed rate over the life of the loan. A step-rate loan may or may not involve negative amortization during the lower-interest-payment, earlier years of the loan. An example of a step-rate loan would be one in which the interest rate is 10 percent in the first year, 12 percent in the second year, 14 percent in the third year, 16 percent in the fourth year, and 18 percent in years five through ten, with the principal due after ten years. The higher interest rates in the later years of the loan may be intended to encourage you to refinance or simply to recover for the lower interest in the first few years. In the latter case, it is likely that, if the loan is retired prior to its maturity, a prepayment penalty will be imposed. Step-rate financing has some appeal since, if the property value and rent levels increase, you may expect it to be easier to make the higher-interest-rate payments in the future than it is to make a higher-interest-rate payment in the year of acquisition.

ASSUMPTION FEES AND OTHER CLAUSES

Other features common in new bank and financial institution financing are clauses calling for assumption fees, prepayment penalties, due-on-sale provisions, and call features. All of these provisions reflect the recent status of the financial market in which borrowing was at a substantial disadvantage and banks pressed the advantage to structure loan provisions more to their liking. Unfortunately, banks seem to have developed something of a take-it-or-leave-it attitude with respect to such provisions, attempting to exclude such clauses from negotiation. A common explanation is that the assumption fee is a matter of bank policy. This is no explanation at all. When you were four years old, and you asked your mother why something was the way it was, how satisfied were you when she said, "because I say so"? Eventually, banks may find the capacity to treat borrowers with more respect.

RECOURSE VERSUS NONRECOURSE DEBT

If the debt on the property is nonrecourse debt, the lender is limited to the property for security on the debt. In the event of default, the lender may foreclose on the property. But, if the property is inadequate to pay off the debt, the lender has no recourse beyond the property. If there is a deficit, the lender will lose money. Recourse debt is debt that is secured by the property and by either other property or the personal guarantee of one or more of the owners or both. The lender is said to have recourse to the other property or to the assets of the guarantor. The extent of the liability of the guarantor is determined by state law and varies among the states. For the purposes of this book, assume that no individuals are responsible for nonrecourse debt and that the guaranteeing partners are liable without limitations for recourse debt. If the property is secured by nonrecourse debt, and the property is losing money, the owners are free to abandon the property without exposing their other assets. On the other hand, if the property is secured by recourse debt, one bad investment could result in the loss of many. Obviously, you would be well advised to purchase only property that is secured by nonrecourse debt. The problem is that banks and other lenders, for equally obvious reasons, want to write only recourse debts.

Another reason that nonrecourse debt is favored by investors, especially limited partnerships, is a peculiar provision of the tax law that favors nonrecourse debt. If the property is secured by recourse debt, the only investors that can use the debt to establish basis for write-off purposes are those investors that are liable for the debt, usually the general partners. But, if the debt is nonrecourse, and none of the owners of the property are liable for the debt, the basis that the debt represents is apportioned to the owners according to their loss sharing ratio. Thus, nonrecourse debt will create basis for the limited partners, while recourse debt will not. In the usual circumstance, the general partners in a limited partnership are the promoters who organize and promote the business. The limited partners are the high-bracket investors who are investing more or less casually and have the most to benefit from the tax write-off. Therefore, it is important to structure the acquisition to give maximum advantage to the class of investors that can use it best. This will help the general partner sell the transaction to the limited partners. So, nonrecourse debt is important not only to the limited partners, but also to the general partners and the partnership as a whole.

Without nonrecourse debt, the promoter might not be able to put together the limited partnership to acquire the property.

FINANCING THE EQUITY

Investment "income" property will carry and service a certain amount of debt, and it will also carry and service a certain amount of equity. The debt is serviced by the interest payments and amortization of the loan. The equity is serviced by the utilization of the tax benefits, the cash flow after debt service, and the appreciation. As with any other investment, people invest in real estate to generate a profit. That profit may be generated from tax dollars saved, from the sale of the property at a gain, or from the profitable operation of the property. Whatever the source, the objective is the same: to end up with more money than you started with (hopefully much more).

Over the years, there has been an evolution in the nature of real estate investment. Twenty years ago, a beginning investor would purchase a rental house and become a landlord. The rent on the property less the operating expenses would service the debt and yield a small cash flow. The property would also provide some tax shelter and would be expected to appreciate. If the ordeal of managing the property and dealing with tenants was not too much for the investor, his or her holdings could be expected to increase from reinvestment of cash flow from the property, or from the reinvestment of the tax benefits, or from additional contributions of capital from the investor. Eventually, the investor would graduate into apartments and other investment property.

This scenario still occurs today; in fact, I recommend it as a method for obtaining experience and expertise in real estate investment. But the beginning investor is seldom in a very high tax bracket. At least the type of investor who goes out and buys a fixer-upper rental house is seldom in the higher tax brackets. If the investor had such a substantial income, he or she would probably find a more convenient, if lower-yield, investment vehicle. The result is that the traditional small investor is not in a position to utilize the tax advantages generated by his or her investments as fully as a higher-bracket taxpayer would. And, as previously noted, the tax benefits have become so considerable as to crowd out the other benefits of real estate investment. To the small investor, the other benefits that real estate investments used to generate, like cash flow, are very important. Many small investors would supplement their incomes from cash flow from their rental property. Now that is very difficult to do since the cash flow generated from the property is not significant and may in fact be negative. These days, it is not uncommon for small investors to talk about the yield on their investments after tax that cost them only a certain percentage (in negative cash flow) to carry. So, it is increasingly difficult to be a small investor in real estate.

On the other hand, there has never been more opportunity to make money at all levels of real estate investment than there is now. Investors are aware of the many benefits to be obtained from real estate ownership and are eager to form partnerships with entrepreneurs to undertake such investments. The usual vehicle for such an investment is the partnership, whether a limited or general partnership. The promoter may or may not have any of his or her own money in the project. Perhaps the investors are financing 100 percent of the equity necessary to purchase the property. If this is the case, the promoter must be a very good salesperson. The promoter must convince the investor that his or her experience is worth his or her share of the investment proceeds and ownership interest. So, again we find a stumbling block for the novice investor. It is more difficult than before to get satisfactory starting investments, and until such time as you have marketable experience, it is difficult to get other people to invest with you. Chapter 2 is devoted to the subject of getting started and explores in detail the opportunities and limitations facing the novice investor. At this point, it should be noted that, since investors are investing more money than ever before in real estate partnerships, the opportunity for the promoter to get rich through real estate investments has never been better.

BALLOON PAYMENTS

Balloon payments are substantial equity payments made at specific times according to the terms of the purchase or financing. The purpose of the balloon payment is to retire the debt on the building more rapidly than the amortization schedule calls for. For example, the loan may have a 30-year amortization schedule with a five-year balloon. It is the intention of the lender to advance the loan proceeds for a five-year period only. It should be anticipated by all the parties that it will be necessary for the owner to refinance the property at the time the balloon payment is due in order to make the balloon payment. The reason that balloon payments are used rather than simply shortening the amortization period on the loan is that, if the amortization period were shortened, the property couldn't service the debt. Generally, loans are structured so that the operating property can service the monthly debt service with an acceptable coverage ratio, and it is anticipated that the balloon payment will require either additional investment on the part of the owners or refinancing.

Balloon payment loans are often referred to as *bullet loans*. The bullet analogy is used because it is necessary for the owner to dodge the bullet in order to maintain ownership. If the balloon is due in five years after the closing date, the owner has five years in which to obtain replacement financing. If the seller is providing the first financing, it is likely that the financing is at below-market rates. The purchaser will not wish to refinance until it becomes necessary, because the new financing will be obtained at an increased cost. Remember, the closer you get to a bullet, the more difficult it is to avoid. If you fail to refinance the property and make the balloon payment, you may lose the property. You might find that you lose a property in which you have a substantial equity interest. Your capacity to refinance may depend on the short-term conditions of the financial markets at the time of refinancing. If market conditions are such that property will support new debt equal to only 50 percent of the market value, the available financing may well be inadequate to pay your balloon payment obligation.

The simple advice would be to avoid investing in property where the financing requires a balloon payment. Unfortunately, this is a naive approach. The market for financing as it exists today is predominated by financing that requires balloon payments. If you avoid all property that requires balloon payments in the financing, you will find that you have very little left to purchase. More sophisticated advice would be to cover yourself in whatever way you can. For example, a small balloon is better than a large balloon. Plan for the balloon and set aside a sinking fund, if possible. Have a contingency plan to provide for the financing if the market will not provide for adequate financing. For example, make sure that the limited partners are aware of the balloon obligation and are prepared to be assessed to make the payment to the extent that it cannot be financed. Consider whether other property owned by the individual or partnership could be pledged as additional collateral for the loan and, as a result of the additional collateral, more proceeds could be realized. Finally, don't wait until it is too late. Processing the loan will take some time. Don't wait until 30 days before the loan is due to plan the refinancing. I would suggest that preliminary inquiries be submitted at least a year before the loan is due. If the financial institution wants to advance the funds before it is necessary to retire the first loan, perhaps the additional cost in terms of higher interest is worthwhile to avoid the insecurity of waiting until the last minute. If you have five years from the closing date to obtain financing, you will experience a variety of financial market conditions during that period. If you reach a period during which it is advisable to refinance, do it. Don't wait simply because the loan is not yet due. And don't wait too long because you are hoping for lower rates.

Each time you refinance a property there will be fees and costs involved. You should not refinance on a whim. Instead, refinance only to improve your position or to maintain your position with a minimum of loss. If you have one year remaining of financing at a 10 percent interest rate, and the best replacement financing you can obtain carries a 15 percent rate, consider asking the lender for a forward commitment. A forward commitment is a commitment to loan a fixed amount of money according to contract conditions (either at a fixed rate or variable, tied to a specific index) at a specific time in the future. A forward commitment will require additional fees of between .5 percent and 5 percent of the loan proceeds. The amount of the fee will depend on the amount of time before the loan is to be funded, the volatility of the market, and how much the bank thinks it can get away with charging. If the market improves substantially, and you no longer wish to obtain the committed financing, you will generally not be obligated, but the contract will require certain withdrawal fees and you will sacrifice the forward commitment fee. But, even with these financial penalties, you are better off with the commitment and the capacity to pay the balloon obligation. You will be able to utilize the 10 percent loan to maximum advantage, receive a commitment for refinancing proceeds to retire the balloon payment, and still retain the capacity to obtain better financing if the market improves substantially.

LOAN AND MORTGAGE BROKERS

Before you have been in the real estate business for long you will find it necessary to shop for a new mortgage on either a property you own or one you are considering buying. If you do much mortgage shopping, you are nearly certain to encounter a mortgage broker. A mortgage broker is an individual who, for a fee, will endeavor to obtain a mortgage for you. Ostensibly, the mortgage broker will draw on his or her expertise and valuable contacts to obtain the best possible loan for your project. In reality, the only thing you need to become a mortgage broker is a telephone and perhaps a garage in which to open an office. But the garage isn't really necessary.

The mortgage broker will begin the relationship with you by requesting information on your project and also by requesting a check. He or she will represent that the check is to cover the broker's costs in reviewing and marketing the loan. In addition, the broker will be entitled to fees as a percentage of the loan proceeds on his or her obtaining of a loan commitment. The amount of up-front fees that the broker will charge varies substantially among the brokers, but any amount is too much. Why should the brokers be paid regardless of whether or not they perform? Many attempt to charge so much in fees that it is actually unnecessary for them to obtain a loan. The amount you are charged will depend on the amount that the broker determines you are willing to pay.

The pig theory applies especially to your relationship with your mortgage broker. The mortgage broker will indicate that he or she can obtain a loan for you that sounds too good to be true. However, the broker probably will not commit to specific loan terms, but rather will represent that he or she will obtain the best financing available. If you agree to the financing proposed, the broker is entitled to the balance of his or her fees, regardless of whether or not you actually fund the loan. In order to collect fees in advance from you, the broker will relate his or her vast experience and discuss loans that he or she has arranged in the past. The terms of these loans will in all likelihood bring out the pig in you. But, remember, once again, that it is the pig that gets slaughtered.

In general, mortgage brokers should be avoided. They have no professional status or qualifying institution. You cannot rely on them to perform in accordance with your expectations. You will have to sue them for fraud in order to recover the fees you paid to them on the basis of their representations. And, even if you are successful in winning the suit, recovering on the judgment will prove to be quite a challenge.

Even those loan brokers that are not outright frauds are unlikely to provide you with much service that you could not have obtained on your own. Financial institutions are in the business of writing loans. They will endeavor to advise you on what is necessary to make a financial presentation to them, without fees, unless the loan is committed. Also, you will generally find bank loan officers to be very helpful in placing your loan with another bank or in giving you a contact person if they are unable to write your loan but the proposal has merit and is "bankable." If the loan is not "bankable," you may find that a higher-risk lender like a finance company is willing to make the loan. You may expect to pay a higher interest rate on the loan if it is written by a higher-risk institution. Most banks are also in the loan brokerage business. They will offer to place the loan with a preferred bank customer in order to provide service to the customer and collect fees from both of you.

INVESTING IN INFLATION

An important part of real estate investment and real estate finance is consideration given to the importance of inflation. Politicians will tell you that inflation is evil. In the real estate context, we have chosen to differentiate between the good and evil of inflation by differentiating terminology. The good is called *appreciation;* the evil *inflation.* It is perfectly acceptable to invest for appreciation and still maintain that inflation is evil. But substantial appreciation is dependent upon inflation. To obtain appreciation, you can start by making a bargain purchase. You can improve the property and improve its operating efficiency, resulting in increased value. A better-managed, better-kept building will command a higher rent level. However, substantial rent increases will not occur unless there is inflation.

Inflated dollars will not buy as much as noninflated dollars. However, through the use of leverage, you may be able to generate a lot more inflated dollars than you had noninflated dollars. And the combination of inflation/appreciation and a leveraged investment can result in a substantial rate of return. How much return can you expect as a result of inflation? Well, that depends on how much inflation you experience and how leveraged your investment is. The higher the leverage and the higher the inflation (appreciation) rate, the higher the potential rate of return and the higher the risk. The reverse is also true.

The following tables illustrate the before-income tax yield of investments at 4 percent, 6 percent, 8 percent, and 10 percent appreciation respectively. It is assumed that the investor starts out with $10,000 and that his or her proceeds on sale of the property are reduced by 5 percent transaction costs. The tables illustrate the value of the investment equity, net of transaction costs, assuming down payments of 10 percent, 15 percent, 20 percent, and 25 percent. To convert the dollar amounts in the tables to the total percentage return, subtract $10,000 from the dollar amount and divide by 100. This will yield the total percentage return, not the annual rate of return.

The tables illustrate several aspects of investments that are impacted positively by compounded appreciation. For one thing, each table illustrates that, at any rate of inflation, the more leveraged the investment, the greater the rate of return. You should be cautioned that this benefit is offset by a greater risk of

4% ANNUAL APPRECIATION				
DESCRIPTION	10% DOWN	15% DOWN	20% DOWN	25% DOWN
Investment	$10,000	$10,000	$10,000	$10,000
Property purchased	$100,000	$66,667	$50,000	$40,000
Value after:				
1 year	8,800	9,200	9,400	9,520
2 years	12,752	11,835	11,376	11,101
3 years	16,862	14,575	13,431	12,745
4 years	21,137	17,424	15,568	14,455
5 years	25,582	20,388	17,791	16,233
6 years	30,205	23,470	20,103	18,082
7 years	35,014	26,676	22,507	20,005
8 years	40,014	30,009	25,007	22,006
9 years	45,215	33,477	27,607	24,086
10 years	50,623	37,082	30,312	26,249
11 years	56,248	40,832	33,124	28,499
12 years	62,098	44,732	36,049	30,839
13 years	68,182	48,788	39,091	33,273
14 years	74,509	53,006	42,255	35,804
15 years	81,090	57,393	45,545	38,436
16 years	87,933	61,956	48,967	41,173
17 years	95,050	66,701	52,525	44,020
18 years	102,452	71,635	56,226	46,981
19 years	110,151	76,767	60,075	50,060
20 years	118,157	82,105	64,078	53,263

6% ANNUAL APPRECIATION				
DESCRIPTION	10% DOWN	15% DOWN	20% DOWN	25% DOWN
Investment	$10,000	$10,000	$10,000	$10,000
Property purchased	$100,000	$66,667	$50,000	$40,000
Value after:				
1 year	10,700	10,467	10,350	10,280
2 years	16,742	14,495	13,371	12,697
3 years	23,147	18,764	16,573	15,259
4 years	29,935	23,290	19,968	17,974
5 years	37,131	28,088	23,566	20,853
6 years	44,759	33,173	27,380	23,904
7 years	52,845	38,563	31,422	27,138
8 years	61,416	44,277	35,708	30,566
9 years	70,500	50,334	40,250	34,200
10 years	80,130	56,754	45,065	38,052
11 years	90,338	63,559	50,169	42,135
12 years	101,159	70,773	55,579	46,463
13 years	112,628	78,419	61,314	51,051
14 years	124,786	86,524	67,393	55,914
15 years	137,673	95,116	73,836	61,069
16 years	151,333	104,223	80,667	66,533
17 years	165,813	113,876	87,907	72,325
18 years	181,162	124,109	95,581	78,465
19 years	197,432	134,955	103,716	84,973
20 years	214,678	146,452	112,339	91,871

8% ANNUAL APPRECIATION				
DESCRIPTION	10% DOWN	15% DOWN	20% DOWN	25% DOWN
Investment	$10,000	$10,000	$10,000	$10,000
Property purchased	$100,000	$66,667	$50,000	$40,000
Value after:				
1 year	12,600	11,733	11,300	11,040
2 years	20,808	17,205	15,404	14,323
3 years	29,673	23,115	19,836	17,869
4 years	39,246	29,498	24,623	21,699
5 years	49,586	36,391	29,793	25,834
6 years	60,753	43,836	35,377	30,301
7 years	72,813	51,876	41,407	35,125
8 years	85,838	60,559	47,919	40,335
9 years	99,905	69,937	54,953	45,962
10 years	115,098	80,066	62,549	52,039
11 years	131,506	91,004	70,753	58,602
12 years	149,226	102,818	79,613	65,690
13 years	168,364	115,577	89,182	73,346
14 years	189,033	129,356	99,517	81,613
15 years	211,356	144,238	110,678	90,542
16 years	235,464	160,310	122,732	100,186
17 years	261,502	177,669	135,751	110,601
18 years	289,622	196,415	149,811	121,849
19 years	319,991	216,662	164,996	133,997
20 years	352,791	238,528	181,395	147,116

| 10% ANNUAL APPRECIATION | | | |
DESCRIPTION	10% DOWN	15% DOWN	20% DOWN	25% DOWN
Investment	$10,000	$10,000	$10,000	$10,000
Property purchased	$100,000	$66,667	$50,000	$40,000
Value after:				
1 year	14,500	13,000	12,250	11,800
2 years	24,950	19,967	17,475	15,980
3 years	36,445	27,630	23,223	20,578
4 years	49,090	36,060	29,545	25,636
5 years	62,998	45,332	36,499	31,199
6 years	78,298	55,532	44,149	37,319
7 years	95,128	66,752	52,564	44,051
8 years	113,641	79,094	61,820	51,456
9 years	134,005	92,670	72,003	59,602
10 years	156,406	107,604	83,203	68,562
11 years	181,046	124,031	95,523	78,418
12 years	208,151	142,101	109,075	89,260
13 years	237,966	161,978	123,983	101,186
14 years	270,762	183,842	140,381	114,305
15 years	306,839	207,893	158,419	128,735
16 years	346,522	234,349	178,261	144,609
17 years	390,175	263,451	200,087	162,070
18 years	438,192	295,463	224,096	181,277
19 years	491,011	330,676	250,506	202,404
20 years	549,112	369,410	279,556	225,645

default in the more highly leveraged investment. Comparing the tables, it is revealed that the greater rate of inflation (or appreciation), the greater the appreciation in value. And the rate of appreciation is far in excess of the difference in the inflation rates. This magnified difference is also a result of the leverage. You are experiencing appreciation on not only the property that you purchase with your cash down payment, but also the property that is purchased with borrowed funds. If the property is able to service the debt, your return on equity from appreciation may be substantial.

The tables also show the substantial benefit to be derived from long-term investments. In the first few years, the return is reduced by the relatively high transaction costs. However, with a longer holding period, even if the transaction costs are higher in nominal terms, since they are a percentage of the sales price, they will have less of an impact on the rate of return.

Reviewing the appreciation tables is an interesting exercise in considering the benefits of a constant rate of appreciation. In reality, the rate of appreciation is not constant but is subject to the same cyclical market pressures as the rents and expenses on the property. Market values may remain flat for a number of years or may experience rapid appreciation. If property values remain flat in an inflationary environment, the owner will actually experience a loss in purchasing power as a result of holding the investment. This is especially true if the analysis is limited to appreciation.

It should finally be noted that a 10 percent compounded rate of appreciation for a 20-year period is very unlikely. It is questionable if a 4 percent rate is realistic, pessimistic, or optimistic. The rate of appreciation is likely to follow a volatile pattern of, say, 4 percent one year, 10 percent the next year, 6 percent the third year, etc. There is always the possibility, especially over a short period, that property values will actually decline. In a deflationary environment, the benefits of leverage are reversed. Instead of compounding the benefits, you compound the costs. If you experience a 10 percent decline in the value of property that you purchased for 10 percent down, after the decline you will have no equity in the property. If you are able to hold on and maintain your ownership, inflation will probably bail you out in the long run.

USING PROFESSIONALS 12

As in any other field, you will find that the business of real estate investment has its professional advisors, who are more than willing (and may even be able) to provide you with professional help, for a fee. There are many steps in real estate investment, from the initial analysis to the acquisition, management and development, and the final sale, and you may seek professional help with certain aspects of each.

You should obtain professional help to supplement your skills and make up for your deficiencies. Until such time as you acquire the experience and expertise in the various disciplines involved, you will be well advised to make use of the skills of others. Some of the help may be contributed by employees. Other help might require a partner. And still other help is best acquired from an independent contractor or professional for a fee. In considering the cost of professional help, it is easy to make the mistake of being too cheap and trying to avoid the costs. This is likely to end up costing you more in the long run. For example, you might be tempted to make your experienced acquaintance a partner on the theory that you will save costs up front and only have to compensate him or her with a share of the profits. You might feel it is better to compensate this person later, with part of the investment, than up front, with money that you don't have. However, a partner's share of the profits would likely be far greater than if you paid for the services and maintained your ownership. Worse, you might be tempted to avoid professional help all together, relying on your own good judgment and instincts. You may be very skilled and capable, but avoiding needed professional help is likely to cause you substantial grief. That's the bad news. The other bad news it that, even if you purchase professional help, you may not always avoid substantial grief. Unfortunately, the quality of professional help in many areas leaves a great deal to be desired. This chapter offers you specific advice on the various professions and professional help available so that you may be an informed purchaser of the services.

REAL ESTATE AGENTS

The first professionals that you are likely to encounter in your real estate investment business are real estate agents. The vast majority of the investment property and commercial property classified advertisements are placed by real estate agents. In responding to such an ad, you will come in contact with an agent. The reason that you responded to the advertisement must have been that the property described appeared to meet your investment criteria. The property interested you. The agent will have advertised the attributes of the property that are important to investors in the agent's opinion. The agent is a salesperson and will try to highlight the positive attributes and gloss over the deficiencies. For example, if the property is particularly attractive, but the seller wants too much money, the agent will point out the advantages of the "pride of ownership" property and may acknowledge that the seller has a "high opinion" of the property.

Frequently, agents find themselves in a situation analogous to that of a salesperson in a shoe store that has only brown shoes for sale. When a potential customer comes in looking for black shoes, the salesperson has a problem. The salesperson could advise the customer that nothing is available that meets the customer's requirements, but that isn't going to lead to many sales. More likely, the salesperson will try to interest the customer in the darkest shade of brown shoes, perhaps acknowledging that the proposed merchandise is "not exactly" what the customer had in mind but that it is the best that is available. Alternatively, the salesperson may scoff at the customer's insistence on black shoes and detail the many virtues of the brown variety. Pulling off this ploy could result in the sale of that "hard to move" pair of tan shoes on the back shelf.

It all depends on the skill of the salesperson. Those who have the personal skills to sell what they have available are the envy of salespeople everywhere. However, as a purchaser, you should not appreciate them. If you want black shoes, that is what you should get. Don't close your mind to alternatives, but don't get talked into buying something in which you are not interested.

Unfortunately, most real estate agents are not skilled in selling investment property. Most are unable to differentiate a good deal from a bad one. Because of its complexity, they do not understand the product that they are trying to sell. This would be analogous to a shoe salesperson who is color blind. The handicap may or may not affect the ability to sell the product. Such individuals will waste a tremendous amount of your time by presenting for your consideration investments that are not even close to your area of interest. You might be advised to be rudely frank with such agents to avoid the time drain. Simply inform them that they have presented nothing of interest to you. Further, you have seen nothing in their progress to indicate that they ever will present anything of interest. So, they should avoid wasting both their time and yours and not make future presentations. It is frustrating to be presented with the same poor deals by a multitude of agents who are more interested in making the sale than in satisfying your investment objectives. The problem is that such an agent might just stumble across an excellent investment right after you summarily dismiss him or her.

The real estate agent is paid by commission. The commission rate is determined in the contract between the seller and the agent. So, it is usually represented that the commission is the seller's obligation and is of no concern to the buyer. Don't believe it. In considering the offer that you have made on the property, the seller will evaluate his or her net receipt of cash (price and terms) after closing costs, including the real estate commission. In reality, the purchaser pays all the costs of the transaction, whether they appear on the seller's closing statement or purchaser's. In most cases, the purchaser funds the transaction, and the seller yields (or obtains) whatever cash is left over after paying all the costs. Those costs are in the middle and represent a barrier between the buyer and seller. And, while it may be an overstatement to suggest that the buyer pays for everything, it is also inaccurate to suggest that the buyer should have no interest in the commission agreement.

SELLER'S AGENT AND BUYER'S AGENT

In larger real estate transactions, it is not uncommon to have more than one agent involved. This occurs in the common circumstance where the listing agent has no customer that is interested in purchasing the property. The listing agent will then contact other agents, either personally or via the mechanism of the multiple-listing service, to inform the marketplace of the availability of the property. The listing agent will indicate the proposed commission-sharing arrangement between the agents on the multiple-listing agreement or through a formal or informal agreement between the agents. It has become a common practice for listing agents to seek out buyers represented by other agents rather than seek the buyers directly. Listing agents have found that offering to share the commission is often necessary to make the sale.

The market has evolved to the point where the more productive commercial agents tend to specialize as either buyer's or seller's agents. The seller's agent will seek out property owners and inquire as to their interest in selling the property. A buyer's agent will seek out investors who are actively purchasing property and seek to establish a relationship with them in which the agent represents them in negotiations for a piece of property. This arrangement is in the best interest of all the parties. The listing agent is not alone in being in a position between the buyer and seller. He or she shares that responsibility with the buyer's agent. In the event that the negotiations break down, the blame is more diffused. Also, the agents are in a position to "soften" the reaction of the principals. If the seller throws the buyer's offer into the trash can, the seller's agent may simply inform the buyer's agent that the seller has declined to make a counteroffer and would like to see a stronger first offer. If the parties were allowed to react toward one another in person, it is more likely that the reactions would kill the negotiations.

However, by placing more people between the principals, you are also placing more opinions between the parties, and the quality of information received by the principals is impacted adversely. For example, I know that I have told agents that there is no way that I would pay more than, say, $500,000 for an apartment building, only to have the agent say that I "indicated a reluctance to pay more than $500,000 for the property" but that he thought that I would pay $520,000. Given this information, the seller is likely to counter at $550,000 in the hope that I would up my offer to $520,000. The seller may have been willing to accept $500,000, and had my statement been accurately communicated, we would have had a deal. But, the seller's counteroffer indicated an unwillingness to sell for my highest and final offer, so negotiations would break off. Like everyone else, real estate agents have opinions. They are frequently asked to express those opinions, and they show no reluctance to do so. I think that they would be more successful if they would refrain from offering their opinions so frequently.

Another advantage in differentiating seller's and buyer's agents is that the agents, while still having a fiduciary responsibility to the parties, are freer to advocate the position of their client. A good agent will study the client and determine the client's interests and motivations. By doing this, the agent can perform a screening process and save the client a lot of time. If the client is a potential purchaser, the agent can review the many listings available and present only those that will be of interest to the buyer. If the agent represents the seller, the agent can inform buyer's agents that they would be wasting their time if they presented offers that did not fall within certain parameters.

The screening process that the buyer's agent performs enables that agent to adopt a rifle rather than a shotgun approach. Most agents will use a shotgun approach in their dealings with you. They will throw at you all of their listings that even remotely meet your requirements. They are hopeful that, by throwing the mass of information at you, they will be offering something in the pile that will be of interest to you. In adopting this approach, they are deferring the rejection decision to you. They actually are providing you with a service of some value since they are exposing you to a wide variety and large number of offerings. If you are unfamiliar with the local market, this may be a good initial approach. However, the agent who screens the property for you provides a better service in that he or she limits the presentations to those properties that have the potential for a deal. The screening agent takes a rifle and attempts to shoot down only the good deals. The nonscreening agent takes a shotgun and attempts to hit anything that *might* be of interest to you. You will see the agent with the shotgun far more frequently than the agent with the rifle, but the time spent with the latter will be more worthwhile.

In the same way that the salesperson who can sell tan shoes is respected by the other shoe salespeople, the real estate agent who can "control" his or her principal is respected by other real estate agents. This is exactly the opposite of the way that an agency relationship is legally supposed to work. The principal is supposed to make the decisions and instruct the agent to carry them out. In fact, the principal/agent relationship has been likened to that of master/servant. I suppose the servants of the world would be impressed with a servant who could control his or her master. But this element of control is not expected. in the context of real estate agents, an element of control is expected and to some extent necessary. If the agent cannot rely on the principal to perform as represented, the agent will waste a lot of time pursuing deals that have no chance of coming together. On the other hand, it is wrong to expect the agent to be able to push the parties into a deal that is not satisfactory. If the agent is in any way pressuring you into a deal that is not what you want, tell the agent that he or she is doing so and that it's not appreciated. If the agent wishes to continue the relationship with you, he or she will have to refrain from such tactics in the future. It is not necessary to tolerate abusive agents. There are plenty of competent reputable agents with whom you can deal.

As a commissioned salesperson, the agent is highly motivated to close transactions. Generally, agents are not paid if, for any reason, the deal fails to close. The occupation is one of feast or famine. The commission the agent receives on a large commercial transaction may be enough to feed a family for several years; however, there may be long dry spells during which the agent earns nothing. In addition, out of the commission, the agent must pay all of the costs of doing business. These overhead costs will continue, regardless of whether or not the sales are being made. That is why real estate agents are reluctant to negotiate or to cut their commission structure. However, they *will* do so. The larger the deal, the lower the percentage you may expect to pay in commission. It is better to get 1 percent of a $10,000,000 deal than it is to get 7 percent of the sales price on a $100,000 house. It is important for you to know the amount that the seller has agreed to pay the agent, but you will find this information difficult to obtain. The contract between the seller and the agent is a private one to which you have no legal access. But, if the seller and the agent have agreed to a 10 percent commission on a $1,000,000 deal, which the market would indicate is worth a 4 percent commission, the seller is "wasting" the 6 percent or $60,000. Since you will have to satisfy the seller with your offer, after transaction costs, the seller is effectively wasting your money and making the deal that much more difficult to consummate.

Some, especially agents, would argue that the higher commission is not wasted since it motivates a higher level of performance from the agent and increases the likelihood of selling the property. I suppose that anytime that you excessively compensate someone, you might expect a higher than average level of motivation, but that hardly justifies the excessive compensation.

The fact that the purchaser really pays the costs of the transaction has furthered the practice of purchasers hiring their own agents. These purchaser's agents are paid directly by the pur-

Using Professionals **229**

chasers and will earn a commission when the deal is closed. Occasionally, the purchaser's agent is compensated through salary rather than commission, but this is unusual. Generally, an active purchaser may contract with an agent to locate and negotiate the acquisition of property at a relatively modest commission. The purchaser's agent is free to contact property-owning principals about the sale of their property without having to ask them for a listing or a commission. If the agent is good at the job, the relationship may be very satisfactory. But, if the agent is of questionable repute, he or she can cause you considerable difficulty. As your agent, he or she may have the capacity to obligate you beyond your intention. Therefore, you must restrict the agent's authority and make all of his or her negotiations subject to your inspection and written approval. Act promptly and responsibly so that the agent maintains credibility, and you may more efficiently consider a larger amount of property.

If you are considering hiring a purchaser's agent, limit your consideration to those agents that have a proven track record of understanding and satisfying your needs. The designation of the status of purchaser's agent should indicate that the agent has a preferred position with you because he or she understands your investment objectives. The designation should accomplish two objectives. First, it should reward an agent for superior performance. Second, it should improve the agent's status and might reduce the commission rate he or she receives. I am not saying that we are rewarding the agent with a reduced commission. Rather, although the rate of commission will in all likelihood be reduced, the number of commissions will increase. Thus, the agent may expect to make more money as a buyer's agent than the agent made before.

Aside from the circumstance in which the purchaser's agent deals directly with the seller on unlisted property, it is unlikely that the purchaser's agency agreement will actually save you any money on the commission expense. More often than not, the opposite is true. Despite your efforts, the buyer's agent's commission is often just added to the listing agent's commission in the transaction. You must consider whether the superior service is worth the additional cost involved. An alternative would be to limit the buyer's agency agreement to unlisted properties.

Finally, the buyer's agency agreement should not be exclusive. It is presumptuous of the agent to request an exclusive-agency agreement, yet many will do so. If you are foolish enough to sign an exclusive-buyer's-agency agreement with a real estate agent, you may entitle the agent to the receipt of a commission from you for the purchase of any property you acquire during the period of his or her agency, regardless of whether the agent had anything to do with the acquisition. No agent, regardless of how skillful, is worth that cost.

THE PROS AND CONS OF USING AGENTS

The seller and the purchaser have different reasons to consider the possibility of attempting to avoid real estate agents and dealing directly with each other. The seller will be motivated by the possibility of avoiding the commission expense. The purchaser will be motivated by the opportunity to avoid a substantial amount of closing costs to get a more leveraged purchase. Additionally, each party is likely to feel that he or she has superior skill and knowledge and will be able to take advantage of the less sophisticated adversary in the negotiations.

In considering the costs and advantages of the agency arrangement, purchasers must consider the fact that the vast majority of property is listed by agents. Buyers who choose to consider only unlisted property will substantially limit their options. Additionally, they will be without the benefit of the agent's professional opinion as to the value of the property and its potential problems. Purchasers who are knowledgeable and experienced in real estate transactions may well find some circumstances in which it is to their advantage to buy property without the benefit of an agent's professional help.

Seller's will wish to avoid the commission, pure and simple. If they could obtain the services of the agent without paying the commission, they would certainly choose to use the agent. They recognize the agent's contribution and the value of the agent's services in expanding the visibility of the property and its exposure in the marketplace. They just don't want to pay the cost. Seller's may find the opportunity to avoid real estate agents if they are approached by a potential purchaser for their property before considering selling. Also, sellers may be able to sell their property if they are in contact with active purchasers or are in no hurry to sell because, in all likelihood, it will take sellers considerably longer to sell their property without an agent.

Commercial real estate agents comprise a wide variety of individuals. It is therefore difficult to make general statements about them. It is also difficult to define a standard of performance on which you can rely. A good agent is more than worth the commission; however, a bad one may be a substantial impediment to negotiations and may perform a disservice to the seller and purchaser. The problem is that it is difficult to determine the quality of the agent until you have had dealings with the individual. At that point it is too late, at least for the deal at hand. The best that you can do is to rely on commonsense rules. In general, an intelligent, ambitious, successful agent is preferable to a stupid, lazy failure. But intelligence is hard to evaluate, and success is a highly personal matter. You should not be too quick to judge.

The most successful, intelligent agent with whom I have dealt was a quiet, unassuming man from a small rural town. His background was in selling land, not in acquiring apartments. But the economic recession of the early 1980s drove him to the cities (temporarily, and against his will) to make a living with real estate syndicators until the rural economy improved. He was a quick study and a good listener, and his hard work resulted in many commission checks. He was the best negotiator and the most diplomatic person I have ever met. Yet he was so unassuming as to be easily dismissed by those who didn't know him well. When I first met him, I didn't expect him to be very productive. I was wrong. Fortunately, I did not express my pessimism and discourage him before he got started.

ACCOUNTANTS

It is not surprising that the movie *Revenge of the Nerds* was a big hit. Accountants are stereotyped by the Wally Cox personality type. But if the stereotype is accurate, so is the revenge. The accounting profession, especially in the elite "Big Eight" certified public accounting firms, has become the glamourous profession of the latter half of the 20th century. The reason that accountants are doing so well is that the service they perform is so valuable. What is more important to a business than financial advice, auditing, and tax service?

Unfortunately, as the accounting profession has grown in contribution and importance and sheds its bookkeeper image, it has also shed its inhibition about fee structure. Accountants, particularly CPAs are among the best compensated of the professionals. And the high compensation level is encouraging more highly competent people to enter the profession. Nothing succeeds like success, and the success is self-perpetuating.

Certified public accountants are great people from whom to get financial and tax advice. They are trained in business and finance. Most of them actively review proposals and investments. They are well educated, and most are intelligent. For all these reasons, they are valuable sources of financial advice, but the most important reason may at first escape you. Certified public accountants are particularly valuable sources of financial information because they have nothing to sell besides their services. Their objectivity is not hampered by a desire to sell some investment product. They are in a superior position to real estate agents, stockbrokers, certified financial planners, and just about anyone else who is in the business of offering you financial advice. The advantage of objectivity may be offset partially by the general nature of the accountants' background. They may simply have less specific real estate background than other professionals.

Hiring an accountant is a difficult undertaking. The value and accuracy of the advice you receive from the accountant may not be evident to you until the IRS audits you. At that point, if the advice was in error, it is you who will suffer. Bad tax advice is particularly troublesome because it isn't discovered until after the fact and after you have the opportunity to do anything about it. If you knew that a particular investment would not produce enough tax shelter, you could buy additional tax shelter. However, if the inadequacy isn't discovered until audit time (after the end of the year) you will no longer be in a position to do anything to correct the problem. So, if you need accounting and tax advice, it is important that you get a good CPA and get reliable advice.

The top college graduates are hired by the elite accounting firms. This perpetuates the dominance of the "Big Eight" and the large national firms. A safe, if somewhat expensive, approach is to hire one of these firms. A problem is that many of the topflight graduates use the large firms as a practical graduate school. With all the opportunities available to top graduates with "Big Eight" experience, you will find that the turnover among these firms is tremendous. It's very frustrating to have the personnel at your accounting firm change every year. The accounting firms contribute to the problem by adhering to an "up or out" philosophy in which, if an employee isn't advancing and being promoted within the firm, he or she is expected to move on, either voluntarily or involuntarily. The result is that these young accountants are getting their experience and cutting their teeth on your account. You will, however, generally receive good and competent advice. The advice offered by the less experienced people on the staff will be reviewed by their superiors prior to dissemination. The result is good advice, competent efficient work, and horrendous fees. Do not be shy about talking over fees with the firm. If you are fee-conscious, you will be billed less for the same services than if you are more complacent. Also, if you receive bills that you consider excessive, confront the firm about the value of the services received.

An alternative to hiring one of the international or national firms is to hire a respected local firm or an individual practitioner recommended by a business associate or friend. Limit your consideration to certified public accountants. The CPA designation indicates that the professional has at least a bachelor's degree in business, accounting, or economics and has passed one of the toughest of the professional examinations. To illustrate how difficult the CPA exam is, it might be compared to the bar exam. The average state bar exam is passed on the first sitting by about two-thirds of the applicants, while the CPA exam is passed on the first sitting by only about 5 percent of the applicants. So, when you hire a CPA, you know that you are hiring an educated professional who, if nothing else, is good at taking tests. Of course, you will probably want more assurance of quality service than that, and there are a few things to watch out for.

Beware of CPA's who have moved around too much. Anyone who has one year's experience with four different firms is probably washing out. Because of the courtesy shown by the firms, that person may never have been fired, but instead was "encouraged" to move on. Movement is an indication that some problem may exist.

Another problem, both practical and personal, is the difficulty in performing the service in a small one- or two-person firm. When dealing with a CPA who is a sole practitioner, you must recognize that the CPA's advice is reviewed by no one. This is a precarious situation, regardless of how competent the professional. It is valuable for professionals offering advice in an uncertain field to have other professionals to bounce their ideas off. Sole practitioners may have personality problems in their relationship with other professionals, or they may simply prefer to practice alone. Whatever the case, they are at a disadvantage. Another problem with the small office is that the highly skilled professional must perform all of the services. In a larger office, a paraprofessional or starting person might perform the routine tasks like filing tax returns. The more experienced professionals will limit their input into routine matters to providing a review of the work. Using this method results in better service at lower billing rates. It's difficult to justify hiring a sole practitioner when you are likely to get lower-quality service and perhaps pay as much as if you had hired a "Big Eight" firm.

In considering the cost of good advice, don't overlook the considerable cost of bad advice. I would advise the hiring of a good firm, whether international, national, or local. Then, I would advise working with the people assigned to your account until you understand them and their advice and until you develop a rapport.

Following that, I would advise loyalty to the individuals with whom you have worked more than to the firm. What is a service firm other than a collection of working people? If the CPA with whom you have worked leaves the firm to move to another firm, I would suggest that you move your account as well. You will find the CPA very appreciative and he or she will endeavor to provide you with superior service at competitive rates. However, if the CPA moves twice within a three-year period, consider the possibility of seeking other professional service. One movement might be a career advancement move to obtain a better position for the professional, but, multiple moves should cause you to suspect the personality and/or competence of the professional. Either flaw could cause you problems.

LAWYERS

Law is probably the most overrated profession in America today. To become an attorney, the common procedure is to attend an undergraduate school and then a law school, which is a graduate school. Thus, prospective lawyers can expect to spend at least seven years in college before graduating and sitting for the bar examination. Then they must pass the bar examination before practicing law. After all of this, the amount of practical knowledge that the new attorneys bring to the profession is minimal. Legal education is like a liberal arts education. You study the law within the confines of the law school, and you study legal theory more than practical application. It is quite possible to graduate from law school without ever seeing the inside of a courtroom, to pass contract law without ever seeing a legal contract, and to pass real property law without ever seeing a deed. The law schools do not purport to give the student a practical education. Such practical education is to be learned in practice (presumably at the expense of the first few clients).

So, what is the value of recent law school graduates? Well, for what do you want to use them? If you are interested in discussing the social implications of a complex legal theory, you may have found the right people. However, if you wish to draft a real estate contract, you would be well advised to consider other help. Recent law school graduates are worse than worthless. Their training has not contributed to any worth at that point, and their advanced education makes them conceited. Do not waste your time and money with such people. Hire attorneys who are experienced in real estate law. If you become involved in securities transactions as a result of partnership formation or other business transactions, make sure that your attorney is experienced and skilled in these areas as well or is associated with other attorneys who are so experienced.

Unlike the accounting profession, the legal profession is not dominated by a small number of very large national and international firms. There are some firms that provide services overlapping adjoining state boundaries or have offices in Washington, DC, as well as in the state. But generally, lawyers are involved in a very local practice. They will become familiar with local ordinances and the state law, as well as the national law as it affects their particular jurisdiction.

By and large, the legal profession has resisted specialization. The bar examination remains a general exam, and in most cases, it is illegal for a lawyer to advertise or even indicate a specialization. As a result, it is very difficult to determine if the attorney you are considering hiring is skilled in those areas in which you need help.

The biggest problem with the legal profession today is that there are simply too many attorneys. The law schools continue to turn out more attorneys than are needed for the legal work in the United States and I fear they are diluting the quality of the services performed. If for no other reason than their sheer numbers, they are decreasing the average experience level of the profession. If you are practicing in a crowded profession, and a potential client walks through the door, you will be inclined to attempt to provide that potential client with service, even if it is outside your area of expertise. There are simply too few clients to let some get away.

Also, there is a tendency to attempt to expand the profession into areas that are not historically those of the legal profession. For example, lawyers are increasingly becoming involved as agents for professional athletes, negotiating contracts and otherwise advising the athletes. This might be considered a positive development, as the athletes are able to benefit from the legal training of their agents. But there are many negatives associated with the crowding of the profession. There are too few quality positions in the better firms for the number of capable trained professionals. The result is significant frustration for many young attorneys. Worse, there is a tendency to find legal answers to nonlegal questions. We are becoming a litigious society, and the number of underutilized attorneys is fueling this undesired trend. The result is a profusion of frivolous lawsuits and a waste of resources in both bringing and defending such lawsuits. There is also a vast number of new laws and governmental regulations designed to regulate our lives and provide employment for our many attorneys.

Another problem with the crowded profession is that the quality of the experience is declining. Twenty years ago attorneys

Chapter 12

might have expected an interesting caseload in working for a major firm, but now they can expect a long internship characterized by boring and monotonous routines. Also, they can expect much earlier and much stronger pressure to specialize. As specialists they will increase their value to the large firms and may decrease their potential as sole practitioners. This is true because many specialties can be performed only when supplemented by other professionals in the large firms. When you are considering a lawyer or law firm, you don't have to limit yourself to the large, highly specialized firms. However, you should consider such firms since largeness often equates with prestige, and the prestigious firms tend to draw and hold the best graduates.

Common sense should play a big role in your choice and use of an attorney. Find an attorney with verifiable experience in real estate, contracts, syndication, and any other area of your business and seek his or her advice in these matters. Legal fees may be a significant expense for you, especially when you are just starting out, so you may be tempted to do without the advice. If you are not experienced in real estate, and even if you are, this is probably a mistake. A common complaint among attorneys is that the clients don't obtain advice until after they are in trouble. At that point, the attorney can't do nearly as much as he or she could have done to head off the problem in the first place. Preventive law is a lot like preventive medicine. It is better to detect and solve problems early than it is to let them get out of hand. So, have an attorney review your real estate contract or lease. Hopefully, the small amount of dollars spent up front in preventive legal fees will be money well spent. If it is well spent, you may not realize it, but if the money is not well spent, it will be quite obvious.

As a real estate investor, you may expect to experience more problems than benefits in dealing with the legal profession. Lawyers will represent your adversaries in both legitimate and frivolous lawsuits. They will represent tenants in landlord-tenant disputes, enforcing laws that incorrectly assume that landlords and tenants are equally suable. Lawyers will work for governmental organizations that must justify their existence by passing and enforcing new regulations, which restrict your options and cost you money in compliance requirements.

The legal profession best contributes to society when used sparingly. Using a lawyer and suing to recover damages should be considered only as a last resort after nonlitigious negotiations prove unproductive. When a dispute deteriorates to the point of litigation, both parties will lose and the only winners will be the attorneys.

APPRAISERS

Many real estate appraisers are the prostitutes of the real estate investment business. They produce an appraisal to suit a purpose. The purpose, rather than the actual value, will determine the value figure produced. Also, like any good prostitute, the appraiser usually pays close attention to who is paying for the service and what the client wants. Within limits, you can direct the appraiser to produce the value that you desire. There are many reasons why you might want to acquire an appraisal, but accurately determining the value of the property is not one of them.

Frequently, an appraisal is required in conjunction with obtaining the financing on property. The bank will require an appraised value of some dollar amount in order to approve a loan of some lesser amount. Usually, the bank will require you to pay for the appraisal and allow you to choose an appraiser from among a list approved by the bank. The bank's list will include appraisers that the bank knows to be reliable and conservative. But that doesn't mean that the appraiser can't be influenced substantially. The appraiser will solicit your input into the appraisal process, including providing income and expense information and indicating the appraised value that you desire. Unless you are seeking a totally unrealistic value, you will generally find that you can purchase an appraisal for the value you desire. All that you have to do is make your desires known and "help" the appraiser in whatever way necessary to arrive at the appraised value you need for the loan.

Appraisals are also frequently used in negotiations for the purchase or sale of property. Here again, you will be less interested in the accuracy of the appraisal than in its usefulness in indicating that your asking price is reasonable or a bargain for the purchaser. Purchasers might also use appraisals to indicate that the asking price is excessive. Appraisals are used in this manner for advocacy, not accuracy, and both parties should recognize this element in their preparation. Frequently, the purchaser of the appraisal makes the mistake of believing the information purchased. When that happens, the appraisal may inhibit the sale rather than assist in the sale. The property is not worth its appraised value. The appraisal was made to fool the other party and influence his or her assessment of value of the property. If you are fooled by your own engineered, bought, and paid for misrepresentation, what does that make you? For additional discussion and analysis of appraisals, review Chapter 4.

As to hiring and using appraisers, my advice is simple if unsatisfactory. You might find it distasteful to use appraisers and endure

Chapter 12

the misrepresentations that are a common part of the industry, but that is the way the game is played. You aren't going to change it. I find it distasteful myself, and I have avoided using appraisals whenever possible. I do not use them in negotiations, because I find them to be counterproductive. I will, however, provide them in the context of bank financing and will do whatever is necessary to assist the appraiser in value determination. Banks should recognize that appraisals are inaccurate, but if they don't, I can't, or won't, change their perception at the expense of my loan request.

BANKERS

It is difficult to underestimate the capabilities of your banker. Banking as an industry has a problem in drawing quality people because the pay scale is so low compared to other options for business graduates. To compensate for the lack of monetary reward, the banks have attempted to make positions appear more prestigious by making nearly anyone who isn't a teller some kind of bank officer. Banks have managers, assistant managers, and vice presidents to suit any purpose. The result is a competency level that is frankly scary. This is especially true given the amount of money that they handle and the position of trust that they enjoy.

Bankers are in the business of selling the use of money. As with all money lenders, they are concerned with preserving the money and generating a profit. Despite appearances to the contrary, bankers really do want to write the loans requested. They are paying depositors for the money in the bank, and it is important for them to loan that money out, to keep it "working" and to generate a profit. What the bankers want is satisfactory proposals on which they can justify making loans.

Often overlooked is the fact that bankers are salepeople. Their product is just as important to the manufacturing process as the raw materials, just as important to the construction business as the carpentry. Some bankers recognize the sales element of their profession more than others, and it is reflected in their attitude toward borrowers and other potential clients.

Appearance and attitude are particular problems for bankers. It is important for them to appear professional. They fear that, if they don't appear to know what they are doing, borrowers might become tempted to default on the obligations. This, of course, happens only in extreme cases. The appearance of professionalism is important to the banker in a positive way as well, since, if the client is successful and growing, he or she is likely to become a more important customer for the bank. The banker will want to give the impression of being competent to handle the client's increasing business needs.

Attitude is a problem for many bankers, since they have difficulty in avoiding the temptation of assuming the role of the creditor. It is easy for bankers to adopt a superior attitude when they are associated with the lender and are dealing with borrowers. After all, if you have to borrow money, you must not be as important as those who are lending. Not only is this attitude insulting; it is also ignorant. It disregards the fact that the vast majority of the private fortunes in this country were made through, among other things, the judicious use of borrowed money. Borrowers pay the bills and generate the profits of the bank; therefore, they deserve better treatment.

Banks do not place high value on creativity in their employees. A good banker, in their view, is one who generates a high volume of conservative loans with a good payment record. Creative financing and refinancing schemes are regarded with suspicion. Strong personalities are also not considered particularly praiseworthy. The kind of personality that is approved by the bank is that of the conservative businessperson/banker image, the nononsense professional. No one is born a no-nonsense professional banker; it is an acquired act. Frequently, the bankers have difficulty in determining when they should wear their banker's face and when they should be ordinary people.

While the vast majority of bankers are marginally competent, there are some few who are very competent, intelligent businesspeople. In the context of your dealings with bankers, you are bound to run across these few professionals. If possible, you should establish a rapport and working relationship with them. Take them to lunch at a place they can't otherwise afford. This is anyplace better than McDonald's—remember, these are not highly compensated people. You should talk with your banker about your financing needs, your investment goals and objectives, and where you see financial institutions fitting into the plan. If the banker is good, he or she will tell you what is wrong with your plan from a financing and banking viewpoint. For the cost of lunch for two, you will acquire some insight into the workings and loan criteria of the bank, and you will receive financial advice that would have cost you several hundred dollars if you had used a consultant.

One problem you will encounter is that bankers' turnover is about as high as that of any profession. The compensation and opportunity available within the bank is unlikely to hold the quality performer, and the incompetent is given plenty of opportunity to wash out. The "personal banker" assigned to my account at one bank once changed four times in a six-month period. This makes it difficult to cultivate a banking relationship.

Despite the obstacles, it is necessary to develop a banking relationship. You should have a working arrangement with several banks. Ideally, you will want to get the banks competing for your business. If you work on establishing relationships with at least three bankers at three major banks, you are prepared in the event that one of your bankers quits. A goal of the real estate investor should be the establishment of substantial credit with at least those three banks, which can be drawn upon quickly when necessary to make a bargain purchase or otherwise service short-term needs. Judiciously obtained and carefully nurtured, the banking relationship is as valuable as any other asset that you will acquire.

INSURANCE AGENTS

In acquiring property, you will find it necessary to secure fire and casualty insurance on the buildings and general liability insurance on your whole business. The more property you acquire, the more insurance expenses you will incur and the more important the liability protection. Shopping for insurance is very difficult since you will have trouble comparing the various coverages, limitations, and clauses. Insurance contracts are written by insurance attorneys, and determining the quality of your protection borders on the impossible. Also, it is difficult to determine if the $1,000,000 policy for $2,000 per year is really a better deal than the $1,000,000 policy for $2,400 per year. The test of the value of your insurance coverage comes when you have a claim. At that point, you will find out whether the bargain rate policy is truly a bargain. The important consideration is prompt payoff when you have a legitimate claim. If you have problems, your first accident might have been a fire; the second will be the insurance settlement.

Because insurance is a complex area, and since there are many firms marketing coverage, the field of independent insurance agents has evolved. Ostensibly, these people are in the business of shopping the various companies who provide insurance coverage to determine where the customer gets the best value for the insurance cost. Also, there are many agents that work solely for one of the larger insurance companies. While most insurance agents work on a straight commission basis, some in the employ of the larger companies work for a salary plus bonus. At any rate, most have come to your office to sell you insurance. They will pitch their product and do their best to convince you that what they have to sell is what you want to buy.

You hope never to collect on an insurance claim. The insurance company especially hopes that you never collect on an insurance claim. Unfortunately, some will attempt to make sure that you don't collect, even if you have a legitimate claim. If you have never attempted to collect on an insurance claim, you may be shocked at the contortions that the insurance company puts you through in order to collect. You might also be surprised to find that your policy is worth far less than the face value of the insurance policy that you thought you were purchasing.

An extreme example of this occurred in the insurance of an older building that we purchased, which suffered a total loss. We originally purchased the building for $80,000. We put an additional $40,000 into improvements. It was our desire to buy replacement value insurance on the property, so that in the event of a loss the building would be rebuilt. We were informed that replacement value insurance could not be purchased on an older building like this, since it would cost over $1,000,000 to build the building today, and it was simply not worth that much. Instead, we were sold a net cash value policy in the face amount of $200,000. The $200,000 value was our estimate of the market value of the building after improvements. We were advised by the agent that *net cash value* was defined as replacement cost less physical depreciation. The agent estimated that the building would cost $1,000,000 to replace and was built to stand for 100 years. Since it was 50 years old, we might expect the value of our coverage to be $500,000.

The explanation of our coverage was confusing, so we asked, "Why don't we insure it for $500,000?"

"Because you paid only $80,000 for it, and the insurance company would be suspicious of a value of $500,000," he answered.

"So, how much coverage do we have—$80,000, $200,000, $500,000, or what? Our concern is that we have $200,000 of insurance coverage in the event of a total loss and that we have enough coverage to rebuild in the event of a partial loss."

"Well," he explained, "as I pointed out to you before, since you are insuring so much property with one company, you are in a position to get special treatment. In this case, the company is waiving the coinsurance clause, so any loss you suffer, whether partial or total, is covered 100 percent, and the amount of the coverage is the net cash value of the property, that is, replacement cost less physical depreciation. Perhaps that will amount to $500,000, but you may expect it to be at least $200,000. Your losses would have to exceed your policy limits, in this case $12,000,000, before you would have any exposure to loss."

The cost of insuring this building was about $800 per year. We had insured the building during our ownership for over three years before the building was destroyed by fire. At that point, we submitted an insurance claim for the total loss of the building. We were informed by the insurance company that the insurance agent had used the incorrect definition of *net cash value* of the building. The term, as he used it, was the historical definition used within the state. However, recent legal precedents said that *net cash value* was actually the *net market value* of the property, as determined from the best available data. The insurance company proceeded to buy an appraisal that concluded that the property was not economically viable and so was worth only its salvage value. The estimated salvage value was $35,000 (before the fire), but the cost to raze the building was $34,900, so the estimated values of the building before the fire was $100. The insurance company offered us a settlement of $100. *This is not a hypothetical illustration; this is an exact description of what happened.*

We told the insurance company that its settlement offer was ridiculous. The company made it clear that we would have to litigate to receive anything beyond the $100 offer. In the process of settling the dispute, we tore down the building and were paid over $8,000 "net" from a salvage company for what was left of the building that had been 90 percent destroyed by the fire. This was for a building that was worth only $100? We filed suit and a complaint with the state insurance commissioner's office. Eventually, the insurance company settled with us for $80,000, and at this writing we are still negotiating with the insurance brokerage firm for its portion of the settlement. We also obtained appraisals that indicated a market value for the building in excess of $160,000 and a replacement cost less physical depreciation net cash value of about $450,000 to $500,000.

I won't speculate as to what we might settle for with the insurance brokerage firm or what a court might eventually award. However, I know that whatever we might make in profit over our costs in the building from the insurance coverage has more than been absorbed by legal fees. Settling with the insurance company took more than one year. Settling with the brokerage firm may well take more than two years.

So, I would suggest that, in using insurance agents and buying insurance coverage, the important consideration is how the insurance company handles claims. It is critically important that the information given to you by the agent be accurate and reliable. Try to confirm this information, and the information contained in the language of the policy, with other competitive companies and with an attorney specializing in insurance law. Finally, make sure that the insurance company has an excellent reputation for paying claims. The policy might well cost you more in premiums, but it will be far less expensive in the unlikely event that you have a substantial claim.

Incidentally, the firm involved in the claim detailed above is a prestigious national firm with an excellent reputation. I am sure that the majority of the readers would recognize the name. The insurance brokerage firm is also a well-known and respected firm. I can only conclude that being well known does not necessarily mean that the firm will have a good history of claim payment. And even a good history of claim payment is no assurance that you won't encounter difficulty in collecting on your claim.

STOCKBROKERS

Who? What do stockbrokers have to do with real estate investments? Increasingly, real estate, especially major projects, is purchased by limited partnerships formed by national syndication firms. Units of equity ownership in these partnerships are sold by stock brokerage firms. Stockbrokers also sell products that compete with real estate investments, including other tax-sheltered investments like oil and gas limited partnerships. The real estate investments sold by stockbrokers are strictly for the passive investor. Because of the many fees involved, they are not generally very high-yield investments, but they may be reasonably good tax shelters.

Stockbrokers are securities salespeople. That is all they are. They think of themselves as financial experts or at least as investment experts, but they aren't. Instead, stockbrokers are subject to a rare and debilitating disease known as "stockbroker's disease." The disease is pervasive in the industry and affects the mental functions of its victims by causing a swelling of the head. Novice stockbrokers are college graduates with a bachelor's degree in economics or business administration. Some may have MBAs. They are hired by the national stock brokerage firms on what is basically a commissioned sales basis. They start out with absolutely no experience in securities sales, and their inititial income level is very modest for college graduates. In addition, they are required to endure the very frustrating experience of placing thousands of cold calls. During the first year, the broker's compensation will be poor; the second year, better; the third year, better still; and by the fourth year, the broker's salary will be substantial. When stockbrokers are paid $70,000 per year or more, they begin to think that they are actually worth that kind of money. The brokerage firm makes them vice presidents and actually solicits their opinions on administrative matters. They have endured the hardship of establishing a business and clientele, and they have become very familiar with the securities marketplace and the investment vehicle available. For four years, these stockbrokers have been pretending and telling people that they are experts in all phases of investments. They have come to believe the misrepresentation. In fact, they have become more familiar with securities, but they are still basically securities salespeople—highly compensated salespeople. They are familiar with their product and are a valuable source of information for investors interested in a passive investment in a real estate limited partnership, but they aren't real estate investment experts. And you should never lose sight of the fact that they always have something to sell to you, regardless of whether or not the product is particularly appropriate for you.

If you are interested in buying stocks and bonds, go see a stockbroker. If you are interested in purchasing real estate investments, you will be in the wrong store.

MANAGEMENT COMPANIES

If you buy investment real estate but have no desire to manage it yourself, you will find it necessary to hire either your own employees or a management company. For several reasons, I prefer the former arrangement (see Chapter 7 for details), but if for some reason you decide to go with a management company, there are some things you should know.

The amount you must pay the management company depends on the services you wish it to perform and the amount of competition in the marketplace. In general, you will have to pay all the costs of on-site management: the salary of the resident manager and maintenance people and all the materials and supplies necessary for them to perform their work. You will probably also find that part of the manager's compensation is in the form of a free apartment or, in a small complex, reduced rent. In addition, you will have to pay a fee for the "management" of the complex. The fee is a percentage of the rent collected and is paid for the office functions associated with management. The fee is also compensation for the supervisory functions of the on-site management, as well as the assumption of the responsibility for the management of the property. Management fees may be as little as 3 percent of gross rent or as much as 10 to 12 percent of gross rent. Typically, fees range from 5 to 8 percent. If you have a large apartment complex that the management company wants very much to manage, you may be able to negotiate a lower fee.

The problem with hiring management companies is that there is a prevailing mediocrity in the quality of service. Management responsibilities are those of solving the problems associated with owning the property. It is not a glamorous activity. And the fees, regardless of how substantial they appear to the property owner, are not high enough to encourage a high level of performance. To make money in the property management business, a company must manage a large amount of property. When you hire a management company, you are just one of many property owners that the firm services. If the prevailing vacancy rate in your area is 5 percent, the management company will probably be happy if it can match this level. If the company has an overall vacancy rate of 5 percent, the individual projects may range from full to 10 percent vacant. You wouldn't complain if your project was full, but you might be very concerned if your property is 10 percent vacant. Yet the averages may work out satisfactorily for the management company.

In addition, management companies have varying attitudes about rent increases. It is important for your project to have optimum rent levels. Optimum rent levels are those that will maximize the receipts of the property over a period of time. If your property is full in an economy that is averaging a 5 percent vacancy, you may have good management, or your rents may be too low. If your property is 10 percent vacant, you may have poor management, or your rents may simply be too high. The vacancy could also be caused by factors other than rent levels or management. However, many management companies are reluctant to raise rents because this increases the problems associated with management. It is easier to leave things as they are than to increase rent, have some of the tenants move out, and have to work to get the property rerented. And rent levels are just one of the many areas in which management companies will not maximize the potential of your property. There are numerous other examples. If you want management done right, you must do it yourself.

If you must hire a management company, interview several and hire the one that you feel will do the best job of managing your property. As part of the management company review, get references for the companies from property owners that they service and contact those references. Ask those references the problems they have had with the management company or if there is anything that annoys them about the way the management company conducts its business. Another important part of the management company reference procedure should be getting references from the management company for projects that it manages. Obtain permission from the company to talk to the on-site managers.

Look over the projects that the company manages and see how well they are kept. Talk to the managers and maintenance people that the company has hired and consider how these individuals reflect on the business judgment of the management company. Are these the kind of people that you would like to have managing your property?

After you have hired the management company, don't ignore the property. It is still your property, and the fact that someone else is managing it doesn't relieve you of your obligation to pay the bills and be responsible for the property. Review the work that the management company is doing on a regular basis and work with the company at correcting the problems that you perceive. If the company is unable or unwilling to correct the problems, do not hesitate to hire a replacement company. Be aware, though, that disruptions in management are harmful to the property. Do your best to make sure that there is continuity in the management of the property. Change management companies only when it is impossible to get the company to perform in accordance with your requirements, despite you best efforts to change the situation.

INCOME TAX CONSIDERATIONS 13

The income tax law has become so complex that many accountants and lawyers specialize in dispensing federal income tax advice. The Internal Revenue Code and treasury regulations alone number thousands of pages. Add to that the internal revenue regulations and extensive case law, and you begin to see the complexity of the federal income tax law. Why is the federal income tax law so complex? Its purpose is to collect the revenue to run the government, isn't it? That function shouldn't require thousands of pages of law. It doesn't. The reason for the complexity in the law is that the revenue collection function has become polluted with a plethora of social legislation. The U.S. Congress has recognized that it is much easier and more effective to *encourage* people to do things than it is to *require* them to do things. The Internal Revenue Code encourages, among other things, oil and gas exploration, investment in airplanes, and the rehabilitation of old buildings. Among the things that the tax law discourages are thrift and savings, investment in secondhand equipment, and marriage. With all the valuable social functions that the tax law performs, is it any wonder that it occupies pages and pages of law? Another purpose of the tax law is a full employment bill for accountants and tax attorneys. Although the majority of the American public endorses the concept of a flat-rate income tax, how likely do you think it is to pass in a form that provides any significant reform? There is so much legislation in the tax law that virtually every special-interest group would have to be concerned with a scrapping of the Internal Revenue Code. Also, congressmen and senators tend to be upper-bracket taxpayers with tax-sheltered investments. Many are lawyers, and virtually all have an interest in maintenance of the status quo. Don't bet on any major reforms of the tax law. A section discussing the pending legislation and the effects of proposed changes in the law can be found at the end of this chapter.

The tax law is changing every day. It is evolving with judicial interpretations, with legislation, and with creative interpretation by tax professionals. This dynamic change is the bread and butter of the tax professional. If you are not a tax professional, you must actively seek the advice of one to keep up to date on changes in the tax law and how those changes affect your business. When the tax law changes through legislation, the change will generally be prospective only. So, if you buy long-lived assets like buildings, the tax law that will be applicable to your ownership is the law that is in effect on the date of your purchase. For example, if you purchased a new apartment building in 1979, you would be depreciating that building over 40 years or more. If you purchased the building in 1982, you could depreciate over 15 years. The building purchased in 1985 would be depreciated over 18 years. The depreciation method used in 1982 and 1985 allows for a more rapid write-off than was available in 1979. So, if you purchased a building in 1979, you are stuck with a long life on the asset for depreciation purposes, even though subsequent legislation increased the tax benefits for new purchasers. On the other hand, if you buy the property when the tax law is favorable (as it was in 1982), you are allowed to continue to take advantage of the favorable law even after Congress has decreased the benefits for new purchasers.

Changes that occur as a result of court cases are somewhat different. Officially, the court doesn't change the laws but merely interprets them. Actually, the court often causes profound changes. But, since the courts officially interpret the laws, their changes may well have retroactive application. In interpreting the law, the court is saying that the law as interpreted was the rule in effect since enactment, regardless of how the taxpayers and IRS were interpreting the law.

In considering the tax law as it applies to real estate, we must consider how much detail is appropriate here. As an investor; you should have a general knowledge of the applicable tax law. But, because of the nature of the subject matter, you will want to contact a CPA for specific details and updates on changes in the law. This chapter addresses general income tax rules as they apply to real estate. It doesn't purport to advise the CPA or tax attorney; instead, it is intended to be a primer for investors, and this information shouldn't be relied on for any period of time. The tax law changes, and nothing will date and age this book faster than the tax laws.

THE ONE TRUE TAX SHELTER

Real estate is sometimes called the one true tax shelter. But what does it take to be a tax shelter, let alone the one true tax shelter? Tax shelters, or tax-sheltered investments, are investments that yield a return that experiences some tax benefit. But there is more to it than that. Municipal bonds are not subject to federal income tax, so they are investments that have a return that experiences tax benefit. Still, municipal bonds are not considered tax shelters because they do not shelter income other than the income that they generate. So tax shelters are investments that shelter the investor's income from other sources. Not only does the investor not generate any additional taxable income from the tax shelter, but he or she shows losses from the investment or tax credits from the investment that will reduce his or her other income and thus income tax liability.

Such is the nature of a tax shelter; for income tax purposes, it shows a loss. Unfortunately, tax-sheltered investments often show a loss for other purposes as well, because every investment has a degree of risk. When someone is selling the idea that an investment will show losses for tax purposes, chances are that the degree of risk associated with the investment is relatively high. If you lose money in your business investments, the loss will produce tax benefits, but the cost may exceed the benefits. You are able to write off the amount of your loss, and the loss will be reduced by the tax savings. So, if you are in the 50 percent tax bracket, the after-tax loss will be only half of the loss before income tax considerations. If you are in the 30 percent marginal income tax bracket, you will reduce your loss by 30 percent and suffer a loss equal to only 70 percent of the actual investment loss.

Ideally, a tax shelter will show a loss for tax purposes but not actually experience a loss. How is this possible? It is possible where one is allowed to write off certain deductions for tax purposes when those deductions or expenses, or losses, are not really experienced. What does this mean? Do you lie to the government? Well, in a way you do lie to the government, but there is nothing illegal or unethical about it. You play the game according to the government's rules. You are not fooling anyone. The government recognizes that the losses that are being reported on tax-sheltered investments may not be real, but the social policy served by the tax law is considered more important than accurately reporting income.

So, in summary, a tax shelter is an investment in which the government allows you to write off expenses for tax purposes that you do not actually experience. The government, for reasons of its own, wishes to encourage certain activities and to promote certain investments. So, it allows for fictitious deductions to accomplish those objectives. But that's not all there is to it. There also must be some economic purpose for the investment. You will want to write off the investment for income tax purposes, while experiencing an actual gain. If the investment does particularly well, the tax benefits may be reduced. The income from the investment might partially or totally offset the fictitious deductions. This is hardly a bad situation, since you should be better off with the income from the investment than with the tax benefits. But the investment will not have produced the type of return you anticipated.

Real estate, more than any other investment, has attributes of tax shelter. The fictitious deduction is called *depreciation* or, in the new terminology, *accelerated cost recovery.* Sometimes tax credits are involved. And generally, if the property is maintained, it will tend to appreciate. What more could you want? How about preferential tax treatment on the gain that you realize on the sale of the property? Yes, real estate provides that, too. As detailed later in this chapter, real estate losses will generally be ordinary losses for tax purposes, but the gain will be long-term capital gain or a combination of some ordinary income and some long-term capital gain. Long-term capital gains are taxed at a much lower rate than ordinary income.

THE TAX SHELTER TRAP

There is a lot of interest in income-tax-sheltered investments. Each year around April 15, the financial press is full of stories about how many rich people pay either no money or very little money in income tax. Many people are envious of those who "get away with" paying very little money in taxes despite substantial incomes, and there is a temptation to try to emulate them. So, many middle- and upper-income investors are in the market for tax shelters. This is a mistake. They are approaching the matter in a manner that is likely to result in the loss of their money because tax shelters are a trap. If you are looking for investments that show a tax loss, you will be tempted by those exotic shelters that show "multiple" write-offs. In other words, more write-off is better than less write-off. Promoters, being aware of this, have attempted to produce investments acceptable to the IRS that allow the investor to write off several times the amount invested. If the taxpayer is in the 50 percent tax bracket, and the write-off from investment is three to one, not only will the taxpayer have the entire investment financed by money that would have otherwise been paid to the government in taxes, but also he or she will avoid paying taxes equal to an additional 50 percent of the investment.

To illustrate, assume that the investor buys a $10,000 unit of an investment that provides a three-to-one or 300 percent write-off. For the $10,000 invested, the taxpayer will be able to write off or deduct $30,000. If the taxpayer is in the 50 percent marginal income tax bracket, he or she will experience $15,000 worth of benefit after tax from the $10,000 investment.

This appears to be very attractive, but there are several problems with it. First, the IRS disallows deductions from investments that do not have a substantial economic purpose. It is considered an abuse of the tax system when the sole purpose of the investment is to produce tax shelter. You are allowed to take deductions only from investments that you enter into to produce a profit. The profit may not in fact be realized, but you must at least intend for the investment to realize a profit.

How does the IRS measure something as intangible as your intention with respect to an investment? Well, for one thing, it looks at the project with 20/20 hindsight and considers the likelihood that the scheme could have produced a profit. Then it looks at whether it was reasonable for the prudent, or even ignorant, investor to think that the investment might have produced a profit. Finally, although probably not last, it looks at how the investment was promoted. Were the promoters emphasizing the tax shelter from the investment and ignoring any potential income that the investment might produce? Were they soliciting investors in such a way as to obtain those who are interested in making a profitable investment, or were they soliciting those investors who want only tax shelter, who don't care if the investment ever makes economic sense? The analysis is not necessary if the investment has shown a profit. In considering what the IRS has come to label "abusive shelters," I believe that the service probably targets those that look like abusive shelters in their advertising. Frequently, in the *Wall Street Journal* and other financial publications, you will see suspect advertising promoting tax shelters that are unlikely to pass

IRS scrutiny. The promoter will advertise such things as "5-to-1 write-off," "tax shelter," and "never pay taxes again." This kind of promotion is something akin to writing a personal letter to the IRS saying "please audit me." The service will be more than happy to oblige.

The problem in shopping for tax shelter is that, as a general rule, the better the tax shelter and the greater the write-off, the worse the investment. So, in your effort to buy the best tax shelter available, you will be seeking out what is probably the worst investment. It is difficult to buy an investment that appears to produce a maximum loss for purposes without experiencing a real economic loss. The goal of some investors is to stretch the rules as far as possible without having losses that are disallowed by the Internal Revenue Service. This is a poor and unnecessary strategy. It is playing with fire, and you are bound to be burned. You need not flirt with the edge of the law in order to gain maximum return after tax. A good real estate investment that is reasonably leveraged will yield a high rate of return after tax without the exposure of having the losses disallowed. Since the losses shown by the exotic or abusive shelters are really all that they have to offer the investor, you will have nothing left if the losses are disallowed.

Even if you are not risking the actual loss of your investment, if you are investing for shelter rather than economics, you will have a tendency to make foolish investments. Maximizing shelter does not necessarily equate to maximizing return on investment after tax. You should be interested in the latter, not the former. Don't overpay for property to generate a better tax shelter at the expense of the after-tax return on investment.

A final element in the tax shelter trap is the sobering realization that it is dependent on the whim of the government. When a property is depreciated over 18 years rather than 15, it is simply not worth as much as a tax shelter. The government makes the tax law, and the government can change it. Those of us who have investments that we are depreciating over 15 years must face the fact that the property is not worth as much as a tax shelter to a new purchaser as it was us for tax shelter purposes when we bought it, and the value as a tax shelter might be further reduced if the pending tax legislation (addressed later in this chapter) is enacted.

The seriousness of this problem depends on your investment strategy. If your investment makes economic sense, and the tax shelter is only one of the elements you are considering, the change in the tax law is not as serious a setback. In addition, if you have a long-term holding period, you will find that the law will fluctuate better or worse over your holding period and will largely net out.

If you bought the property in 1983, and for whatever reason must sell it now, the decrease in the tax benefits from real estate may well have a devastating effect on your return on investment. You also must consider what can be expected as far as changes in the tax law in the future. The government deficits are likely to cause further retrenching of the tax benefits of tax-sheltered investments. On the other hand, the lobbyists are constantly working on getting still more benefits for the industry. What will be the net effect? The result is uncertain, and I for one am not willing to bet the future of my investments on the outcome.

ORDINARY LOSS AND CAPITAL GAIN

Since we have considered how the 1984 tax legislation had an adverse effect on real estate investments by extending the depreciation period from 15 to 18 years, it is only appropriate to mention that the legislation also had a major positive effect on the treatment of assets that could be sold for a capital gain. Specifically, the legislation shortened the holding period required to obtain the benefits of long-term capital gain treatment on the property from one year to six months. It is now possible to buy property in May, for example, and sell it in December, and realize a gain that will be characterized as a long-term capital gain. With the transaction costs involved, however, it is unlikely that the change in the law will have much effect on real estate. In fact, the small amount of benefit that might have been realized from sales at capital gains rates for property held six months to one year will be offset by stock sales held for a like period. Stocks are much more likely to experience the kind of value fluctuation over six to 12 months that will enable the investor to benefit from the changed law. Does this mean that investors are more likely to favor stocks for investment over real estate? Probably not, but it is one element that favors a competitive investment.

Real estate experiences, particularly advantageous tax treatments, not only can be sold at long-term capital gains rates, but also the losses from operations will offset ordinary income. In fact, some think that the conversion of ordinary income into long-term capital gain is motivation enough in itself to make real estate investment worthwhile. At this writing, long-term capital gains are taxed at a rate that is only 40 percent of the rate on ordinary income. Thus, to the extent that you can convert the status of your income from ordinary income into long-term capital gain, you can reduce the tax on that income by 60 percent. I should think that, given this treatment, taxpayers would want to convert as much income as possible into long-term capital gains. The IRS thinks so, too. Therefore, there are some limitations on the amount of tax benefit you can obtain. If you have a lot of long-term capital gains and other tax preference items, you may be subject to the alternative minimum tax. Don't lose sleep over it. If you are getting near a situation to which the alternative minimum tax might be applicable, you should be in a financial situation that enables you to afford a CPA for professional advice. At any rate, the alternative minimum tax is not a problem for investors until they have substantial investments.

DEPRECIATION RECAPTURE

Another limitation on the benefits of long-term capital gains is what is called *depreciation recapture*. Depreciation recapture limits the amount of income that can be converted from ordinary income into long-term capital gains by providing that some of the income on the sale be "recaptured" as ordinary income. The rules are intended not to prevent the conversion of ordinary income into long-term capital gains, but rather to limit the benefit.

To understand the rules, you have to understand how depreciation works. When you buy investment property, you will usually buy land, buildings, and personal property. You can't depreciate the land. At this writing, you can depreciate the building over 18 years and the personal property over five years. In other words, the amount of the purchase price attributable to the buildings and personal property may be expensed over the applicable period. There are special rules for the personal property, with half-year conventions and modified half-year conventions and the like, which I believe should be considered beyond our scope.

The principal depreciation of consideration in real estate investments is the depreciation on buildings. For example, if the value of the buildings is $1,000,000, you will expense part of that $1,000,000 over each month or part of a month that you own the property over the following 18 years. In 18 years there are 216 months. The easiest depreciation to understand is straight-line depreciation. With straight-line depreciation, you depreciate the property by an equal amount each month. For each month of ownership, the owner will deduct $1/216$ of the purchase price of the property or, in our example, approximately $4,630 per month, or approximately $55,555 for each full year of ownership. If you depreciate the property using the straight-line method, you will not have depreciation recapture. However, you may choose to depreciate the property using an accelerated method. The period is still 18 years, but the method allows you to write off more of the cost of the property during the early years of the property ownership. It is advantageous to write off the property as rapidly as possible so that you can take advantage of the deductions and tax savings. Everything else being equal, you would prefer to take deductions now rather than in five years or ten years, if for no other reason than that you would be able to invest the tax savings.

Under current law, you are allowed to write off up to 175 percent of the straight-line rate on the declining balance of the property. The calculation is somewhat complex, but the IRS has published simplifying tables as it did with the 15-year depreciation in effect for 1981 through part of 1984. For our purposes, it is enough to note that the property may be depreciated over a period of 18 years, but with more of the depreciation in the earlier years if you so elect. If you hold the property for the full 18 years, you will not suffer any penalty as a result of taking more of the depreciation deduction in the earlier years. But, if you sell the property in less than eighteen years, which in all likelihood you will, you will have to recapture the difference between the depreciation deductions using the accelerated method and the depreciation you would have been allowed had you used the straight-line method, if the building is residential. If the property is not residential, and you have elected to use the accelerated depreciation method, you must recapture all of the depreciation taken, as ordinary income.

If you are depreciating residential property, you will almost always benefit from the use of accelerated depreciation, despite the depreciation recapture. (But beware of the new provisions for installment sales considered below.) If, on the other hand, you are depreciating nonresidential property, you will almost always be better off using the straight-line method. The penalty in the form of depreciation recapture for nonresidential property is simply too great to make the election to use the accelerated method of depreciation worthwhile.

INCOME TAX CREDITS

Income tax credits are a relatively new innovation in the income tax law. They are more potent and valuable than deductions. Deductions reduce the amount of income subject to tax. Their value is equal to their face amount times the tax rate. Thus, if you are in the 50 percent marginal income tax bracket, a deduction is worth 50 percent of its face value in terms of tax savings. If you are in the 30 percent tax bracket, the deduction is worth only 30 percent of its face value. Income tax credits, on the other hand, reduce the tax liability, not the income subject to tax. So, income tax credits reduce the tax liability dollar for dollar and are worth their face value in tax savings. A $10,000 income tax credit will save you $10,000 in income taxes. If you don't owe $10,000 in taxes before the credit, you may carry back the credit and recover taxes that you paid during the prior three years. If you have reduced your tax liability for the current year to zero, recovered the taxes you paid during the prior three years, and have still not used up all of the credit, you may carry over the unused credit for up to 15 years into the future. It is only after this 19-year period (the current year plus three years back plus 15 years forward) that the income tax credit will lapse unused. (Income tax deductions may also be carried over if you are unable to use them in the current year, but each year it will reduce taxable income rather than reducing the tax directly.) So, income tax credits are valuable and versatile. If you are able to generate the tax credits through your investments, you will in all likelihood receive the benefit of their use. But recent changes reduced the benefits of the investment tax credit by providing that the depreciable basis of the property must be reduced by one-half of the credit claimed.

Another element in income tax credits that is particularly attractive to the liberal social planners is that, while deductions favor the rich, being more valuable to those in higher tax brackets, tax credits do not favor those in a higher tax bracket. In fact, there are limitations on the amount of income tax credit that may be used for taxpayers that would otherwise have a tax liability in excess of $25,000. The limitation is a percentage of the income tax liability. With the limitation on the income tax liability that the higher-bracket taxpayers may offset with the income tax credit, the credit actually favors lower-bracket taxpayers. Also, since income tax credits cannot be used to reduce the alternative minimum tax, they tend to be of more benefit to lower-bracket taxpayers.

THE INVESTMENT TAX CREDIT

Income tax credits were introduced to encourage investment in personal property in manufacturing companies. The credit called the *investment tax credit,* was equal to 10 percent of the cost of personal property bought and used in the business. Credit was earned when the property was first placed in service in the business. It was also considered more desirable to encourage investment in new rather than in used equipment. New equipment would have to be manufactured, and the economy would experience not only the benefit of the new equipment's being put to productive use, but also the benefit of manufacturing the new equipment.

However, it was determined that some benefit would also be obtained from placing used equipment in production. So, the credit was allowed for used property as well, but it was limited to $100,000 worth of property subject to the credit.

It was also planned that the credit be used to encourage the purchase of long-lived equipment. So, originally, to get the full 10 percent credit the property had to have a life of at least seven years. The credit was reduced if the life of the asset was less than seven years and was eliminated if the life of the asset was less than three years. It is not worthwhile to dwell on the specific provisions of these laws since they are subject to change and are frequently modified. Get specific advice when you consider an investment that may be subject to the credit.

In summary, the salient features of the investment tax credit are the following:

• It applies to personal property only, not buildings or fixtures.

• There was a $100,000 limitation on the used property (it is now $125,000 and is scheduled to increase to $150,000 in 1987, provided that the pending legislation proposed by the Reagan Administration is not enacted).

• Although it may apply to personal property purchases in conjunction with commercial property, it does not apply to residential property except for coin-operated vending machines, laundry equipment, and the like.

RENOVATION CREDIT

Income tax credits have also been used for many other purposes and to encourage many other activities. From providing employment for certain groups of individuals that are not generally well employed (from minority members to convicts), to investments in energy equipment, there has been a great expansion in the use of income tax credits. In the context of real estate investments, tax credits have been used principally to encourage the renovation of older and historic properties. If you are considering investing in property that is over 20 years old, that hasn't been renovated within the last 20 years, and your investment objective includes renovating the property or changing its use, you will want to contact your tax advisor for details on the applicability of the renovation credit. This is especially appropriate if you are considering investment in a certified historic structure. The credits available are substantial in terms of the percentage of expenditure, equal to 20 to 25 percent of the remodeling expenditures.

There are specific rules about the relative amount of remodeling expenditures required to qualify the expenditure as a substantial remodeling and the amount of the building's original walls that must be maintained in the remodeled structure to qualify for the credit. These rules were also changed by the 1984 legislation. Under prior law, a three-tier system of rehabilitation credits was provided for qualified expenditures in connection with qualifying buildings. A building qualified if 75 percent of the external walls were retained after completion of the rehabilitation. Under the new law, a rehabilitation can qualify if at least 50 percent of the external walls are retained in place as external walls, at least 75 percent of the external walls are retained in place as either external or internal walls, and at least 75 percent of the building's internal structure framework is retained. This explanation is illustrative of the complexity of the law. The law is not only complex, but also dynamic and changing. Should you become involved in anything exotic, like the remodeling of an older building, it is important to coordinate your activity closely with your tax advisor.

LIKE-KIND EXCHANGES

Another interesting provision in the tax law that has special applicability to real estate investments is the rules related to like-kind exchanges. As the term implies, like-kind exchanges involve the exchange between parties of property that is considered of a like kind. What kind of property is considered of a like kind? Generally, the property will have the same or a similar purpose. The IRS would prefer to apply the rules only where the property is identical. But, if there are not some differences in the property, there is no motivation for an exchange. So, there is the practical problem of identifying property that is close enough to be considered of like kind but still different enough to motivate an exchange.

Pragmatic problems like the identification of what property is of like kind are not new in the context of like-kind exchanges. In fact, it is pragmatic considerations that caused the introduction of the like-kind exchange rules in the first place. If the property used in business is exchanged between businesses so as to improve the utilization of the property in the businesses, it is questionable whether the Internal Revenue Service should intervene and discourage such transactions by taxing them. Collecting the tax might prove to be a problem, since like-kind exchanges may not involve the transfer of any cash and maybe neither party has cash to pay the tax on any gain they might be considered to have been generated. Measuring the gain is certain to be controversial. We know that the parties consider the property to be of approximately equal value, but what is that value?

These are pragmatic problems that are not without solution. One solution to part of the problem is not to impose tax on like-kind exchanges, and that is the general rule. Like-kind exchanges are generally not taxed, and there is no adjustment in the basis that the parties have in their assets. In other words, if I trade assets with you, my basis in the asset that I acquire from you will be the same as the basis I had in the asset that I traded, and your basis in the asset that you received from me will be the same as the basis you had in the asset that you traded.

Now, if that were all there was to it, you would seldom see like-kind exchanges. The property I have that I might want to exchange will seldom be of equal value to the property that you might want to exchange with me. In recognition of the desirability of encouraging like-kind exchanges and the fact that the value of the properties will seldom be exactly equal, the law provides that like-kind exchanges may include property that is not like-kind property to equalize the value. The property that is not like-kind property will usually be cash, but it may be other property. In that context, the property exchange may be largely untaxed but still partially taxed. The receipt of non-like-kind property, or "boot" might result in the recognition of a taxable gain up to the amount of the boot, if such a gain is realized. Generally, the party that is trading up will not experience a tax liability, but the party that is trading down may experience some benefit, as in the relief of a greater amount of debt, which results in the transaction's being partially taxable.

Again, it is not the purpose of this book to give detailed tax advice and discuss such items as boot and basis adjustment. Such discussions are best left to income taxation books and an audience of accountants and tax lawyers. For our purposes, assume that if you trade up you will not have a taxable transaction, but if you trade down you will. Get professional advice before consummating the transaction, but recognize that this will be the general treatment. Your basis in the asset will be the same as your basis in the traded asset, plus the increased debt in the asset you acquired over the amount of the debt in the asset you traded, plus any cash and your basis in other assets you contributed in addition to the exchange property.

There are still likely to be few like-kind exchanges, especially in the context of real estate, because it is unlikely that I will have property that is wanted by another party who has property that I want. It is true that the range of prospective exchange parties is greatly increased by allowing other property in an exchange to equalize the value. But parties that are interested in exchanging property are usually interested in deferring income recognition while their property base is growing. It is difficult to find parties who want to trade down. Those who have property that they are interested in selling want to do just that, sell the property, not exchange it for a smaller property. In fact, the seller may not be able to trade down. For example, if both parties have equal equity in their property, that may not be enough. If one party has a building with a value of $1,000,000 and a mortgage of $800,000, he or she might have depreciated the building down to a basis of, say, $600,000. If the other party has a free and clear building worth $200,000, you would think that the parties desiring an exchange could make one since both have $200,000 worth of equity. But the party trading down from the $1,000,000 to the $200,000 property has a significant problem. He or she would not receive cash in the transaction but would have a taxable gain equal to the difference between his or her basis and the amount of debt relief—in this example, $200,000 ($800,000 less $600,000). This could cost the party $40,000 in taxes as a long-term capital gain, assuming that the taxpayer is in the 50 percent tax bracket, or even more if depreciation recapture is involved. In addition to this, following the transaction, the party would have no basis in the smaller building. Under these circumstances, how likely do you think it is that you can structure an exchange between the parties? It is not very likely, unless you can find some help.

THREE-WAY EXCHANGES
Help will be found in the form of a third party. You might expect that a three-way like-kind exchange would be more difficult to construct than a two-way exchange, since the needs and objectives of three parties rather than two must be satisfied. In fact, a three-way like-kind exchange is much easier to put together. This is because only one of the three parties has to be interested in exchanging. Typically, the exchange motivator is the one who wants to trade up. In our previous example, this is the party with the free and clear building worth $200,000.

The second party is the person with the $1,000,000 building, $200,000 in equity, and $800,000 debt. The second party wants to sell the building and cash out his or her equity. Since this party has basis equal to only $600,000, the sale will produce a long-term capital gain of $400,000 and result in an income tax liability of $80,000. The second party wants to cash out his or her interest to net $120,000 after tax.

The third party is one who is interested in buying the smaller property. This party probably doesn't want to pay $200,000 cash but may be able to pay $40,000 down and refinance the property for a new debt of $160,000.

To accomplish the exchange, the third party technically purchases the larger property and exchanges it with the first party for the smaller building. The transactions are accomplished with simultaneous escrows and closings so the parties don't have to worry about getting stuck with something they don't want halfway through the transaction. In this way, all the parties get what they want with a minimum of inconvenience. By allowing three or more parties to participate in like-kind exchanges, the government has provided rules designed to facilitate and encourage exchanges.

STARKER EXCHANGES

Despite the resistance of the Internal Revenue Service, the courts provided still another facilitating provision. Now the party desiring the tax benefits of a like-kind exchange need not have identified the exchange property he or she wishes to acquire at the time of the "sale" of the property. Sometimes referred to as *Starker exchanges,* after the leading court case on this subject, these transactions allow a person to sell property and place the funds in a trust over which he or she has no authority or control except for the capacity to direct the purchase of property by the trust for exchanges for his or her property. In the Starker case, the court allowed for acquisition of replacement property over two years after the first sale (exchange), but recent legislation has substantially reduced the time period during which replacement property must be identified. In either a three-way like-kind exchange or a Starker exchange (which may involve two or more parties), the cooperation of the parties to the transaction is necessary. The other parties should not object, since accommodating your needs for a like-kind exchange will not cost them anything. However, the other parties might not be cooperative for one reason or another. It is best to make your intentions with respect to a like-kind exchange known early in the negotiation. Don't just assume that the other party or parties will go along with the plan simply because it doesn't cost them anything. Such assumptions are likely to cost *you* something.

SALE OF PRINCIPAL RESIDENCE

If there is anything that warms the hearts of congressmen and other elected officials, it is the family home. It is as American as apple pie and baseball. Part of the American dream is to own the family home. The tax law favors property ownership over rental by making the interest expense on mortgage payments an itemized deduction, while rent payments made by tenants are not deductible. However, it is not enough simply to make the interest expense deductible to facilitate home ownership. It is also recognized that home ownership is more feasible in a mobile society if the government defers taxing inflationary gains in property values. It is also recognized that for many people their home is their primary asset. After their children have grown, they will want to sell "the big house" and move into something smaller. In recognition of these desirable home ownership attributes, Congress adopted two rules that deserve elaboration. These rules may facilitate certain investment strategies, but the principal reason for elaboration of these rules is because they will, at one time or another, affect nearly every homeowner.

DEFERRING GAINS

The first rule defers the recognition of gain on the sale of the principal residence of the taxpayer, in part or in full, if the taxpayer reinvests in a new principal residence by either buying or building a new principal residence and occupying it within two years. Part of the rule involves a measurement of the gain that is to be deferred. The basis in the house being sold is its original purchase price and the capitalized costs of the purchase, plus the cost of improvements to the property. The IRS also allows you to add in the fixing-up expenses of decorating and repairing the property to aid in the sale. These fixing-up costs are allowed only if incurred within 90 days before the contract to sell was signed and paid for within 30 days after the sale. The basis calculation is intended to measure what you have invested in the property. The property must sell for more than this amount, or you don't have a gain to measure.

The next step is to determine the amount you receive from the purchaser. Your starting point is the contractual selling price for the property. However, you won't get the contractual selling price. Your proceeds will be reduced by the commissions and other expenses of the sale. This includes sales commissions, advertising, attorney and legal fees, etc., incurred in order to sell the old residence. Loan charges, such as loan placement fees or points charged the seller, are selling expenses, but moving costs are not. Moving expenses may be otherwise deductible if you are moving over 35 miles in order to take a new job, but they are not deductible in the calculation of the gain on the sale of the principal residence, and the rules for the deductibility of moving expenses are beyond our scope.

So, you start with the selling price and deduct the costs of the sale to arrive at the net amount that you realize on the sale. From this you subtract your basis in the property and the fixing-up expenses to calculate the gain. Note that at no point in the calculation have we considered the cash you have realized in the sale. The reason is that it is irrelevant to the calculation. For the calculation of the gain on the sale of the principal residence, the IRS doesn't consider the amount of cash you received. It doesn't matter if you have cashed out or if you received nothing down on the real estate contract, or somewhere in between. So, it is conceivable that you could have a taxable gain even though you received no cash in the transaction. There is some relief from this possibility as a result of the installment sales rules, which are detailed later in this chapter.

Now, the government, in taxing the gain on the sale of personal residences, has a somewhat strange attitude. If you experience a gain, it asserts that it is taxable unless the gain is deferred. But, if you suffer a loss, that is your problem. The loss is a personal expense and not deductible. To defer recognition of the gain on the sale of the old house, you must either buy or build a new residence and occupy that residence within two years before or two years after the sale of your old residence. This provision enables you to buy a new residence and move your family into the property, while offering the old residence for sale. If you are financially able, you need not sell the old residence before purchasing the new residence. To defer recognition of all of the gain on the sale of the old residence, the cost of the new residence must equal or exceed the adjusted sales price (the sales price less commissions, other sales expenses, and fixing-up costs) of the old residence. The cost of the new residence includes cash payments for the new residence plus the amount of any mortgage or other debt on the new residence plus the commissions and other purchase expenses and the cost of construction or improvements made within two years before and two years after the sale of the old residence. If you pay less for the new residence than you realized on the sale of the old residence, the gain on the sale of the old residence will be taxable to the extent of the difference. Your basis in the new residence will be reduced by the gain not recognized in the sale of the old residence. So eventually, when you sell and do not reinvest, the gain will be taxable. However, you may be able to take advantage of the second rule in the sale of personal residence to avoid recognition of this gain.

EXCLUDING GAINS

The second rule affecting the sale of personal residences provides an exclusion of part of the gain on the sale of a residence even where you do not reinvest the proceeds. To qualify for excluding the gain from taxation, you must be aged 55 or over on the date of the sale. You must elect to exclude the gain from taxation. And you may exclude a maximum of $125,000 if you are single or married, and $62,500 if married and filing a separate return from your spouse. If the gain on the sale of the property exceeds $125,000, it will be taxable to that extent. If the gain is less than $125,000, it will be fully nontaxable; however, the election can be made only once. Therefore, if the gain is, say, $40,000, you must seriously consider whether or not the exclusion election should be made. If you elect to exclude the current gain of $40,000 and subsequently realize a gain of $100,000, your exclusion will be used up and not available to exclude the larger gain.

The exclusion is designed for the situation in which you are selling the family house with the intention of moving into a retirement home or apartment. Its applicability extends beyond this scenario, but you must consider whether the rules were intended for your situation. How likely is it that you will again be investing in a house and that it will appreciate so that you will have a gain that is in excess of the current gain? How soon is that gain likely to occur, and is it worth giving up the current tax benefits available in the exclusion? Will you be in a position to defer the gain recognition under the first rule considered above instead of using up this once-in-a-lifetime exclusion? Once the election is made on a filed income tax return, it cannot later be rescinded. So, if the gain that is to be excluded is not substantial, you should not make the election without consideration of the alternatives.

IMPUTED INTEREST

Normally, the IRS does not have to regulate such things as the price and terms on property. The market determines what the price and terms will be, and the buyer and seller have opposing interests that will dictate a reasonable compromise. But, as interest rates began to climb into the stratosphere in the 1970s, and more and more sellers found it necessary to carry the financing on their property in order to sell, the buyers and sellers discovered that it might be in the interest of both parties to distort the contract in their mutual best interest. To illustrate the possibility of manipulation, consider the following example:

1. The seller and purchaser have agreed on the price and terms on a six-unit apartment at $125,000 with $25,000 down, and the seller is to carry $100,000 for 30 years at 12 percent interest.
2. The total payments on the property will be $25,000 down plus $1,028.62 per month for 30 years. Three hundred sixty payments of $1,028.62 equals total payments of $370,303.20. So, including the down payment, the total amount the purchaser will be paying for the property is $395,303.20.
3. One party approaches the other about modifying the contract so that the sales price is $395,303.20 and the terms are $25,000 down and $1,028.62 per month with zero interest.

Should the parties be interested in so modifying the contract? In the absence of any IRS regulation, the answer is yes. It is in the interest of both to modify the contract. From the seller's point of view, if the sales price is increased, when the contract payments are received he or she can treat the gain as a long-term capital gain rather than having to treat the interest portion as ordinary income. Since the seller can elect to report the gain using the installment sales method (see below), he or she will be able to recognize the income as it is received, just as he or she would have without the modification. But the change from ordinary income to long-term capital gain means that the seller will be able to recognize 60 percent less income. The buyer will not be able to deduct the interest portion of the contract payments, but he or she will be able to deduct the depreciation expense on the much greater purchase price. Under current law, the buyer will be able to deduct the expenses much sooner than if he or she were required to deduct only the interest portion on the contract payments plus the depreciation deduction on the original purchase price.

So, the IRS finds that it is in the best interest of both parties to state a low rate of interest offset by a higher sales price. It was determined that the potential for manipulation should be addressed and the loophole, if you want to describe it as that, should be closed. Therefore, the IRS adopted the rule that, if the interest rate on the sale of property was stated at a rate less than ten percent or not stated, it would be imputed at 11 percent. The IRS did not purport to change the agreement between the parties, and the contract would determine their relationship, but for tax purposes the IRS would recalculate the contract price and the payments to determine what the value of the property would be and the interest and principal if the unpaid principal would be bearing interest at 11 percent. In our example, an 11 percent rate of interest would yield a purchase price only slightly higher than the $125,000 on which the parties had agreed. Since the government has recognized that related parties (primarily family members) might be even more inclined to conspire to defraud the government, or at least conspire to manipulate the tax laws, there are special rules for imputed interest applicable to transactions between related parties. Also, the imputed interest rates are adjusted from time to time to relate more closely to market interest rates by using a complicated formula in the Internal Revenue Code.

INSTALLMENT SALES

Another rule that grew out of the pragmatic considerations faced by the tax collectors was the rule for installment sales. The rule constitutes a grace provision on the part of the IRS. Basically, it recognizes that, as the seller of property, you might not receive all of your proceeds on the closing of the property. In fact, you might receive little or none of the proceeds at that time, and it may be some time before you are cashed out. If the IRS attempts to collect cash from you when you have received none, it might well find the collection to be difficult or impossible. In addition, it will discourage contract sales, since sellers might not be able to sell the property if they have to recognize the gain. So, the installment sales rule was introduced.

Originally, it imposed a limitation on the amount of the purchase price that could be received in the year of the sale and still allow the sale to qualify as an installment sale. But it was later determined that this limitation was counterproductive in that it artificially imposed leverage requirements on transactions (i.e., no more than 30 percent down). It was a trap for the unsophisticated seller, who might not realize that the principal portion of the monthly payment was additional principal received in the year of the sale, and it reduced the receipts of the IRS that would be collected if the provisions were expanded so that more sales would qualify.

The basic rule is that, if you have a gain on the sale of property, and you carry back a contract or otherwise provide the financing for the property so that some of your interest is not cashed out, you may recognize the same percentage of the gain as the proceeds you receive bears to the total price. In other words, if you receive 30 percent down in the year of the sale, including the principal portion of the contract payments, you will have to recognize 30 percent of the gain that you have realized on the sale. You will still have to recognize the remainder of the gain, but it will be recognized as you receive the principal proceeds on the transaction. The rules become more complex in those 95 percent-plus instances in which the property is encumbered by debt.

Questions relate to whether or not you are relieved of the debt and whether that debt relief should be considered part of the proceeds of the sale. There are legal questions involved here, as well as complex accounting calculations of your gain. The best approach is to get legal or accounting advice when contemplating an installment sale. When it is properly structured, you may be able to defer a large portion of the gain until you receive the contract principal payments. When it is improperly structured, the IRS might assert that you have received much more benefit in the form of debt relief than is appropriate. If you receive a small amount of cash in the sale and are facing a large income tax bill, it is hard to see how much benefit you have realized. And the larger income tax bill is much more likely under new rules that modify the installment sales rules to provide that, if you have ordinary income from the sale due to depreciation recapture, you must recognize all of that income in the year of the sale, regardless of the amount of cash received.

CONSTRUCTION PERIOD INTEREST AND TAXES

Another example of the regulators' seemingly infinite capacity for overkill is the rule regarding construction period interest and taxes. Under normal circumstances, interest and property taxes are deductible expenses. The rule for the deductibility of expenses is that expenses are deductible if no future benefit is to be realized from the expenditure. If, instead, an expenditure either augments the value of the property or extends its useful life, it must be capitalized and depreciated along with the property. On this basis, if you paint a property or perform other routine maintenance, you may deduct those expenses in the year incurred. However, if you add a new wing to a building, the new construction has increased the value of the structure and must be capitalized (added to the value of the structure) and depreciated over the appropriate period (now 18 years). Interest and property taxes are currently deductible since they are current expenses that do not improve the value of the property or affect its future life.

But someone determined that there should be a different rule applicable to construction period interest and taxes. It wasn't argued that construction period interest and property taxes were somehow different from other interest and taxes in that they somehow affected the value of the property. Rather, it was argued that the construction period interest and property taxes were part of the overall construction project expenses, and that the overall project would have to be capitalized. It is hard to argue that the construction costs don't include the interest expense necessary to obtain the money to construct the building. Similarly, the property taxes on the property are part of the overall costs of building that will hopefully sell at a profit or operate profitably. But it seems a bit petty to disallow these deductions. And heaven forbid that we should be subject to any rules that encourage construction projects that by their very nature require more than a year to complete. But that is the rule; construction period interest and taxes must be capitalized in the value of the building.

OWNERSHIP IN CORPORATIONS VERSUS PARTNERSHIPS

Various legal entities may acquire the ownership of real estate: individuals, corporations, partnerships, estates, and trusts. In considering corporate or partnership ownership, you might find it initially curious that most property that is not owned by individuals is owned by either limited or general partnerships. Why is this so? Corporations would shield the individual investors involved from some of the legal exposure they would suffer as a result of partnership ownership. The problem is that the corporation does more than shield the investors from legal exposure; it also locks in the tax benefits.

INDIVIDUAL OWNERSHIP

If property is owned by an individual, the cash flow from the property, as well as the income or tax loss, will be considered as that of the individual. The individual does not file a separate income tax return for the property, but instead includes the property on his or her income tax return, reporting the income or loss therein. The individual will detail the income and expense from this property, and any other property owned, on Schedule E of Form 1040.

PARTNERSHIPS

If a partnership owns the property, it will file a Form 1065, on which it reports the income and expense from the property it owns and from any other business activity it has. Form 1065 is described by the IRS as an informational return since no tax will be due with the return. Instead the return must be filed so that the IRS is informed of the income that should be reported by the individual partners. That is how partnerships work. The partnership itself has no income or loss on which to pay tax. The income or loss of the partnership flows through to the individual partners. It is this flow-through of the income, and more particularly the tax losses and credits, that makes the partnership form of ownership so attractive for real estate. Generally, improved real estate is a tax shelter, and, if the property is owned by a partnership, the individual will be able to benefit from the tax advantages of owning the property.

Limited partnerships often are formed for the purpose of investing in real estate, for several reasons. As with general partnerships, limited partnerships are a means of combining the money of several investors in order to accumulate enough money to invest in a property that would be beyond the means of any of them separately. And, even if the investors would have the capacity to invest in the property alone, they may choose to form a partnership because none of them wishes to undertake the obligation without the company of others.

Partnerships are a means of spreading the risk and rewards of the investment. They may spread or split up the rewards, but it is questionable that they spread the risk. In a general partnership, each of the partners is jointly and severally liable for the whole amount of the obligations of the partnership. As a practical matter, anyone suing the partnership will target the deepest pocket among the partners. That partner might be legally entitled to contribution from the other partners for their share of the judgment. But, if they are without money, that partner may be without practical recourse. Also, it is far from convenient to have the partners suing one another.

A limited partnership has the advantages of a general partnership, without the risk exposure for the limited partners. The limited partners are entitled to their share of the partnership's profits and tax losses and tax credits. But their loss exposure is limited to the amount that they have invested in the partnership plus the amount they have obligated themselves to pay in the future or be assessed to pay. The liability limitation gives the investor the advantages of the corporation with the tax benefits pass-through of the partnership. In addition to the tax advantages of this investment vehicle, there are practical advantages that were explored in more detail in previous chapters.

CORPORATIONS

If the property is owned by a corporation, it is the corporation and not the shareholders who will receive the tax benefits of ownership. The corporation will file a Form 1120, on which it reports the income from the property together with the income from any other property it owns and any income from other business activities. On the basis of this reporting, the corporation will determine its tax liability. Having tax-sheltered investments in corporations is questionable for several reasons.

First, corporations are subject to different rules for income tax reporting than individuals and, as a general rule, pay tax at a lower rate. Second, new corporations, like any new business, are unlikely to generate large amounts of income during their first few years. Therefore, corporations are unable to utilize the tax shelter that real estate can provide. Third, corporations are generally formed to carry on business activity. That activity may or may not be consistent with investing in property. You may feel that it is worthwhile for the business to own its operating or office facilities, but it is probably not worthwhile for the business to make other investments. In fact, owning tax-sheltered investments could restrict the options available to the board of directors by unnecessarily absorbing working capital.

S Corporations

Small business corporations or S corporations (formerly Subchapter S corporations) are taxed in much the same way as partnerships in that they pass on the income or loss of the corporation to the shareholders. However, S corporations are subject to a special tax on their passive income. Rent is considered passive income. So corporation's rental income may be subject to this special tax. As a rule, an S corporation may be an appropriate ownership entity during the period in which the real estate shows tax losses, but not when that property begins to show gains. Because of this restriction and lack of flexibility, and because S corporations were previously restricted substantially in the amount of passive income that they could have, S corporations seldom own very much investment property.

THE ALTERNATIVE MINIMUM TAX

Were it not for the alternative minimum tax, it would be quite possible, even easy, for anyone, regardless of income level, to avoid paying any income tax through investments in income tax shelters. If your goal is legally to avoid the payment of any income tax, and you don't care too much about the quality of your investments in those tax shelters, you can avoid the payment of income taxes. However, the alternative minimum tax puts some limitation on the benefits of income tax shelters for high-bracket individuals who have substantial investments that produce what is called *tax preference items*. The tax is designed to limit the advantages of tax shelters and thus to limit their use.

TAX PREFERENCE ITEMS

Tax preference items are defined in the Internal Revenue Code and include several items of income exclusion and deductions that produce substantial tax benefits. Some are quite obscure and seldom utilized (more for pragmatic reasons than for legal reasons); others are used frequently and are the substance of tax shelters. The items of tax preference are as follows.

1. Adjusted itemized deductions, which include most itemized deductions except medical and dental expenses and deductible casualty losses and sometimes state and local and foreign taxes.
2. Accelerated depreciation on real property. If an accelerated depreciation method is used to calculate the depreciation deduction, this is the amount by which the depreciation deduction exceeds the straight line rate.
3. Accelerated depreciation on leased personal property.
4. Amortization of certified pollution control facilities.
5. Amortization of railroad rolling stock.
6. Stock options—the amount by which the fair market value of the shares of stock at the time of exercise exceeds the option price when an option is exercised pursuant to the rules for a qualified stock option or a restricted stock option.
7. Reserves for losses on bad debts of financial institutions.
8. Excess depletion on oil and gas investments.
9. The excluded portion of long-term capital gains; the 60 percent of the gain that is excluded from income tax recognition.
10. Amortization of child-care facilities.
11. Excess intangible drilling costs in oil and gas investments.

As you might observe, many of these items are not likely to be encountered with any degree of frequency. Real estate tax shelters produce primarily item number two from the list, accelerated depreciation on real property; item number nine, the excluded portion of long-term capital gains; and item number one, for the interest deduction and real estate taxes on the taxpayer's home, which are deductible as itemized deductions.

APPLICATIONS OF THE ALTERNATIVE MINIMUM TAX

The alternative minimum tax is a tax that might be imposed on the taxpayer as an alternative to the regular income tax. The IRS requires you to pay the higher amount of the alternative minimum tax or the ordinary income tax. The tax is not imposed if the regular income tax on your income is greater. To calculate the applicability and amount of the tax, the items of tax preference are added back to the taxable income otherwise reportable by you. The amount of income thus calculated is then subject to a tax at the following rates: zero to $40,000 (applicable to married taxpayers filing a joint return), 0; $40,000 and over; 20%.

Unless you have made significant use of tax-sheltered investments, your regular income tax would be much higher than that imposed by the alternative minimum tax. So, the alternative minimum tax will be inapplicable for most investors. But, if you are in the position to generate long-term capital gain from the sale of some real estate or other investments, or you have substantial investments that produce other tax preference items, you should consider the applicability of the tax. If the tax is applicable, you will find that there is no longer much purpose in the purchase of additional tax shelter. This is because there is little purpose in further reducing your ordinary income tax obligation by using tax preference items. You won't be paying ordinary income tax, you will be paying the alternative minimum tax.

REGULATION OF APPRAISERS

An interesting provision in the 1984 income tax legislation calls for the adoption of rules regulating appraisers. In recognition of the fact that under prior law there were no regulations to bar appraisers who commit grossly negligent acts from practicing before the Internal Revenue Service, the act provides that regulations will be issued to monitor the conduct of professional appraisers in proceedings before the Internal Revenue Service. I wish the service luck in its attempt to clean up the appraisal profession in its practice before the service and in tax court. I have been quite frank about my dissatisfaction with the status of the profession. I am curious to see if the regulations have any teeth in them and whether or not they accomplish their objective. The profession, which refuses to self-regulate in any meaningful way, deserves whatever regulation the government imposes.

PENDING LEGISLATION

Most real estate investment books contain very little discussion of the income tax law. As important as the tax law is to real estate investments, I thought this was a curious omission until I attempted to write about real estate investments in the environment of changing tax legislation. Legislation enacted during 1984 made substantial changes in the tax law, but those changes were trivial compared to the changes proposed during 1985. Add to that the uncertainty surrounding whether any of the proposed changes will be enacted, and you begin to see the difficulty in discussing them.

If it is difficult to discuss the pending changes and consider the likelihood of their adoption and impact, consider how difficult it is to invest in such an uncertain environment. The proposed changes have caused chaos in the real estate investment markets as investors must consider whether they should dump their investments now or wait for legislation that might result in a substantial decline in their value. It is important for the government to recognize the disruptive effect of substantial changes in the tax law and approach such a substantial overhaul of the system with caution. Among the proposed changes and their likely impact are the following.

THE FLAT-RATE TAX
The proposed legislation is intended to simplify the tax law. It has been labeled a *flat-rate tax,* but it actually involves three brackets over the zero bracket amount. The proposed tax rates of 15 percent, 25 percent, and 35 percent are being considered. With the highest marginal income tax rate of 35 percent, the advantages of tax shelters will be reduced significantly, and their value will decline.

CHANGE IN LONG-TERM CAPITAL GAINS
Originally, it was proposed that the lower tax rates for long-term capital gains be eliminated, but the current administration has backed down on that proposal by suggesting that the new excluded gain be 50 percent for an effective maximum rate of 17.5 percent (35 percent tax on 50 percent taxable). There has also been

some discussion of indexing the gain measurement for inflation and giving the taxpayer a choice between capital gains rates and ordinary income tax rates on the indexed gain, to avoid the anomaly of taxing artificial gains. As currently proposed, the changes would have little impact on the treatment of long-term capital gains on stocks and bonds but would significantly change the rules for real estate. The proposed changes would exclude depreciable assets like buildings from long-term capital gains treatment. The gain on the sale of those assets would be taxed at ordinary income tax rates, but the proposal is to index the gains for inflation. In theory, if the gain does no more than reflect inflation, it will not be taxed.

CHANGES IN DEPRECIATION RULES

The treasury's flat-rate tax proposal suggested that the depreciable life on real estate be changed from the current 18 years to the economic life of the asset, which for buildings would be about 60 years. If this proposal is adopted, within about a four-year period we would have seen the depreciable life on buildings adjust from about 40 years down to 15 years and up to 60 years. It is very difficult to plan investment activity given this kind of disruption and instability.

The president's proposal is somewhat better in that it would depreciate buildings over 28 years at four percent of the declining balance (as indexed for inflation). If the rate of inflation exceeds 4 percent, the depreciation deductions would presumably increase over the years. How this affects basis and gain measurement remains to be seen. The depreciation in excess of economic depreciation would be a tax preference item and could result in alternative minimum tax.

ELIMINATION OF TAX CREDITS

Even its supporters acknowledge that there is no evidence that the investment tax credit accomplishes its objective of encouraging business capital investment. Instead, it appears to have provided for a windfall for manufacturing companies and big businesses. Given this perception, it is likely that the investment tax credit might be repealed. If the credit slashing extends beyond the investment credit, the real estate credits may also be eliminated. The president's tax plan would eliminate both the investment tax credit and the real estate renovation credits.

ELIMINATION OF CERTAIN ITEMIZED DEDUCTIONS

Of relevance to real estate are proposals for elimination of state and local taxes as an itemized deduction and the reduction of interest expense as an itemized deduction, with the exception of home mortgage interest. Both of these changes could make investment property less valuable; however, most real estate investments would not be impacted since their deductions are above the line and not itemized deductions.

CHANGE IN THE AT-RISK RULES

Under the current law, real estate enjoys a favored status over all other tax shelters in that the at-risk rules do not apply. What this means is that investors in real estate investments are permitted to write off more than the amount of money they have invested in the property plus the amount of debt on which they are liable. In other words, if the acquisition is structured properly with nonrecourse financing, the investor is able to write off losses for tax purposes, even though there is no possibility that those losses will be realized. The advantages of nonrecourse financing in this context were considered earlier. The president's proposal would apply the at-risk rules to real estate in the same way that they are applied to other investments, limiting the amount of the write-off to the amount that the investor invested in the property plus the amount of debt for which he or she is personally liable. If this rule is enacted, nonrecourse financing will cease to have its preferred tax attributes for real estate investments, and future real estate investments will have to be restructured so that the investor can experience the write-off. And, as recourse debt replaces nonrecourse debt, the risk of the investments will increase.

EVALUATION OF PENDING LEGISLATION

President Reagan asserts that his proposed changes would promote simplicity, growth, and fairness (not necessarily in that order) in the federal income tax law. And the president has a lot of popular support for the proposals. Who wouldn't support simplicity, growth, and fairness? To be opposed to the plan would appear to be in favor of complexity, stagnation, and inequity. In fact, that is exactly the assertion that is being made by the president as he attempts to sell his program to the American people. The presidential rhetoric includes suggestions that the current tax law is unfair and un-American and encourages otherwise honest people to cheat on their taxes.

While there are many faults with the tax system, I resent the assertion that those of us who engage in tax planning to reduce our tax bills are un-American or fraudulent. This is especially annoying when the president's proposal is being touted as a major reform. While the changes proposed are substantial, the assertion that the changes promote greater simplicity, growth, and fairness does not stand up under close scrutiny.

Simplicity

The changes do not promote simplicity. Of the itemized deductions, only state and local taxes are to be eliminated, and the deduction for interest other than home mortgage interest is to be reduced. The capital gains and depreciation rules become more complex, as does the entire corporate income tax. The proposed legislation has illusions of simplicity in the form of fewer tax brackets, elimination of some credits and deductions and income averaging, and rounded zero bracket amount ($4,000 for married filing a joint return) and personal exemption ($2,000). But using fewer brackets does not make the law simpler. The typical taxpayer calculates his or her taxable income and looks up the tax on the tax table or schedules. This procedure will not change; only the tax indicated will be different. Fewer people will itemize deductions because the zero bracket threshold will increase (to $4,000 for married filing jointly) and the deduction for state and local taxes is to be eliminated. But most people will have to continue keeping the records necessary to determine whether itemizing is applicable. The calculations will not be simpler; they will just be less worthwhile. And even the nice round numbers, which appear to appeal to the administration, will be short-lived as they are adjusted for inflation.

Growth

Predicting how the proposed tax law will affect growth is quite precarious. Many of the incentives to capital construction, such as the investment tax credit and rapid depreciation, are being eliminated or reduced. Other incentives, such as the research credit and some of the special advantages for the oil industry, are being retained. Tax shelters are being deemphasized, but with the highest tax rate declining and the long-term capital gains rate declining, there may be greater incentive to invest.

President Reagan claims to be ushering in the "age of the entrepreneur." But other than cheerleading, he offers very little in the way of incentive. Also, if the entrepreneurs do business in a corporation, they will likely find that they would be paying more tax under the president's proposal than under prior law.

Fairness

Fairness, like beauty, is in the eyes of the beholder, and whether the new tax proposals are fairer than prior law is a matter of personal opinion. Is a flat-rate tax, where nearly everyone pays a similar percentage of income in tax, with few deductions, fairer than current law? Some will suggest that fine-tuning the current law to reduce the abuses would be a better alternative to the proposed wholesale changes. Others will certainly note that the beneficiaries of the proposed law once again are the rich and poor at the expense of the middle class, and some might also note that, if the pending legislation is passed during the Reagan administration, the highest marginal income tax rate will have been cut in half from 70 percent to 35 percent. Some will certainly suggest that a graduated-rate tax, which taxes according to the ability to pay, is more equitable than a flat-rate tax. Others will also note that the reasons the tax law favors certain investments is intentional and by design, to encourage certain activity, and utilizing tax shelters is not an abuse of the Internal Revenue Code. But there appears to be a widely held opinion that, since some high-income individuals utilize tax shelters to pay little or no income tax, the system is corrupt and subject to abuse. In a relatively efficient market, the price of these tax-sheltering investments reflect all their attributes, including their tax attributes, so it is difficult to make the case that these investments are abusive. But the general public perception is that they are abusive, and that is all that matters.

If the tax benefits are reduced, either the investments will be worth less than before or the return from other elements of the investment, like cash flow, will have to increase. In fact, some economists have predicted that the proposed changes will result in increased rents. But, as noted elsewhere, whether or not rent will increase is more a function of local market conditions than federal income tax law. However, the property would be less attractive as a tax shelter, so there will be more pressure to improve the economics of the investment.

I have already expressed the opinion that under current law the tax shelter provided by real estate investment is overemphasized at the expense of economic considerations. To the extent that the proposed legislation increases the economic emphasis of investments, its long-term benefits might offset the short-term costs. However, if fairness is what is being measured, consider how fair the law is to real estate investors.

During President Reagan's first term, his Economic Recovery Tax Act of 1981 increased the tax benefits of real estate investment to lure investors into these investments. Many good people responded to the incentives for legitimate, if selfish, reasons by making real estate investments. If the tax benefits of real estate are reduced substantially, these investors are likely to find that their equity, perhaps representing their life savings, is reduced or eliminated. What have these investors done wrong? Nothing much, really. They responded to incentives provided by the government and made investments for tax shelter purposes, under the mistaken belief that they could rely on their government and their president to be consistent.

THE *PENDING* IN PENDING LEGISLATION

Keep in mind that the pending legislation may not pass or may pass with substantial modification. Over the years, I have noted that, in income tax matters, the pending legislation often passes in a form far different from the initial proposals or fails to pass altogether. Indeed, the president's proposal, released in May 1985, varied substantially from the treasury proposal issued in the fall of 1984. The legislation being considered will have to run the gamut of the Senate and House of Representatives and is unlikely to come up for a vote until very late in 1985 or in 1986, if at all. The pressure to maintain the status quo will be tremendous, and if the legislation didn't have the support of the president, its chances of passing would be remote. But here we have a popular president endorsing a popular issue of tax reform and simplification. It doesn't matter that the law neither reforms nor simplifies, provided that the American people think it does.

The president and the Republican Party cannot lose on this issue if the facade of tax reform is maintained. If the legislation passes, the president and his party will claim credit for having introduced popular tax reform. If the legislation fails or is substantially modified, the president can blame the Democrats in the House of Representatives for killing a bill that the American people want. Under these circumstances, I would expect some kind of legislation in which the Democrats and Republicans attempt to share the credit for tax reform.

WHEN THINGS GO RIGHT AND WRONG | 14

At the risk of dwelling on the negative, this book has focused on the problems to be encountered in real estate investment. In carrying this theme to its logical extreme, it should be noted that there are problems to consider even when things go right. However, if you had a choice between the problems detailed here and those in the latter portion of this chapter, there can be little doubt that you would choose the problems associated with success. That doesn't make the problems any less real, but perhaps the advantages associated with success (minor considerations like wealth) will make the problems tolerable.

THE PROBLEMS OF SUCCESS

THE SUCCESS TRAP

Like growth, success is intoxicating. It is more fun to be a success than it is to fail. It's also self-satisfying to see your plans and ambitions realize their intended success. In an environment where you call the shots and employees respond, where the business discipline is controlled and orderly, it is easy to become oblivious or even intolerant of problems in your personal life. If you are having problems with elements of your personal life, your business activity will give you plenty of excuse to ignore them. A workaholic will feel right at home.

Initially, your business will require a considerable amount of your time and energy. Later, the amount of time and energy necessary depends largely on your management style and the quality of the people in your organization. One of my former business acquaintances used to pride himself on his ability to delegate. I considered him to be among the laziest people I have known, yet he seemed to accomplish his objectives through the work of other people. Unfortunately, the propensity to delegate is unusual among real estate entrepreneurs. Real estate entrepreneurs tend to attempt to do it all themselves. They recognize the inadequacies of their employees, even where those inadequacies are largely imagined, and prefer to do things themselves. The result is an incredible work load.

This work load actually does not make the workaholic unhappy—quite the contrary. The work is not unpleasant; in fact, the real world is far less pleasant. Successful businesspeople can retreat from the problems of their personal life by spending more and more time at work. Rather than face the personal problems with the same zeal they apply to business, they tend to avoid recognizing personal problems because personal problems are far more complex and perplexing than business problems. Also, the problems are not given to easy and quick solution. If an employee is not performing to expectations, you attempt to determine why. Is the problem that the employee and the job are ill-matched? Is the employee lazy or simply unmotivated because he lacks challenge? What can be done to improve the situation? In this context, a problem is identified, a range of corrective solutions determined, and a decision made. At one extreme is the option of firing the employee; at the other extreme is the decision to ignore the problem. In between the two extremes are a variety of remedial actions designed to correct the problem. The action will be implemented, and its success will be reviewed at a later date. If the remedial actions do not meet with the anticipated success, the employee will eventually be dismissed.

How does this neat, cut-and-dried procedure apply to the personal life of the businessperson? Not at all. Problems in your personal life are not corrected by decisions and delegation; instead, they are corrected through a continuous process and personal involvement. If your son is not doing well in school, is a heavy drug user, and is engaging in other disruptive behavior, no decision on your part is going to correct the problem. And, if he doesn't improve, you can't just fire him. He deserves your time and attention. At some point, his behavior might be recognized as a plea for attention. If you fail to respond to the plea, the rejection is likely to be mutual. And at that point, you have lost him. He can't wait

until after the Sacramento deal is closed or until after the tax returns are filed. There will always be something in the business that
prevents you from enjoying a personal life if you allow it to do so.
And a personal life unattended gradually diminishes. If you marry
your job, you may expect very shortly to have a monogamous relationship with it.

Another problem with success is that it tends to equate with
growth. Many people enter the real estate investment business in
the hope of achieving a certain amount of success and wealth, and
then retiring to a life of comfort, wealth, and leisure. The problem
is that, in order to achieve the level of wealth desired, you must
build an organization. You must employ capable and competent
people in the management of your property, in your partnership
syndication business, and in various other capacities to accomplish your goals. To hire quality employees, you are going to have
to provide them with a future in the organization. If there is no future or long-term benefits in working for you, the quality employees will take their skills elsewhere. It is inconsistent with plans to
terminate the business after a period of, say, ten years to provide
long-term employment and security for your employees. Therefore, if you achieve the level of success to which you aspire, you
must create an organization that has a longer duration and greater
capacity than are necessary to accomplish your goals. You may
find that you have created a business empire that can be sold. Or
you may find that the business you have created is so dependent
on your personal involvement as to be a success trap.

SUCCESS-GENERATED TAX PROBLEMS

When your business starts to realize success, you will find some
interesting characteristics of tax shelters. The first that will become painfully obvious is that tax shelters have only a limited duration during which significant shelter will be generated. In fact, it
is likely that the real estate bought as an investment, rather than as
just a tax shelter, will produce taxable income within about five
years. The taxable income will grow over the holding period of the
property. So the tax shelter will shortly become a tax liability. During the growth phase of the business, the diminishing shelter will
not prove to be a problem because you will be expanding your
property base. In other words, as your property base grows, you
will be replacing shelter at a faster rate than you are using it up.
However, should you slow your rate of growth, attempt to maintain a fixed size, or reduce the size of your business, you could
find that you are experiencing tax problems.

While the tax shelter decreases over the life of the investments, debt principal paydown typically will increase over the life of the debt on the property. So, there will be less write-off, and what income is generated will be used for reduction of the debt rather than being available for the payment of income tax. Rapid paydown on the debt can produce substantial tax problems as well as substantial practical problems. When the debt paydown exceeds the noncash deductions (depreciation and amortization primarily), the income from the property will exceed the cash flow from the property. It is bad enough having taxable income; it is worse having taxable income without cash flow to pay the tax. In considering the advantages of refinancing property, we noted that the refinancing principal proceeds were not currently taxable. This is advantageous, since you want to use the proceeds of refinancing for things other than the payment of taxes. However, the flip side of the advantages of new debt principal's not being taxable is that when you make payments to reduce the debt, they are not deductible. It is ironic that in extreme cases it may be necessary to put new higher-interest debt on the property to pay the income tax, augmented by the fact that the lower-interest underlying debt is being paid down at such a rapid rate.

In addition to the tax problems associated with the diminishing shelter and the debt paydown, as a successful real estate investor you are also likely to be subject to the alternative minimum tax since you will have substantial investments that produce tax preference items. Chapter 13 gives you a general description of the rules for the alternative minimum tax and puts you in a position where you can see whether the tax is applicable or nearing applicability. If you are reaching the point where tax shelters that produce tax preference items are no longer of benefit to you, you will want to concentrate your investment activity in investments that do not produce tax preference items. One example is commercial buildings that are, as a practical matter, depreciable using the straight-line method only. They will then produce the tax shelter without also producing the preference items. So long as you don't produce preference items, you won't be subject to the alternative minimum tax, regardless of how little tax you pay.

ILLIQUIDITY PROBLEMS

Every year, the government comes up with statistics on how many millionaires there are and where they are located. Sometimes, information is also available on how they acquired their wealth. The best-selling issue of *Forbes* magazine each year is the issue that includes information on the 400 richest people in the United States. Forbes acknowledges the difficulty in wealth measurement, and disclaims responsibility for the accuracy of the information, but profits substantially from our societal preoccupation with wealth. But who am I to point fingers? Obviously, this book will be purchased by many people who aspire to make money through real estate investment.

The statistics on the number of millionaires actually is of very little value. A million dollars is not worth nearly as much as it used to be worth. And although many people are considered millionaires, most of that wealth is merely on paper. Many people have assets or equity in assets that are supposedly worth over $1,000,000 but couldn't cash a check for $10,000. Being a millionaire doesn't mean that you have $1,000,000 in cash. If statistics were published on the number of people with $1,000,000 in cash or liquid assets, you would find the number to be much smaller. One reason for this is that you don't make $1,000,000 by putting your money in a savings account. Instead, you make it by investing it in generally illiquid investments. It's true that many people have made large amounts of money in the stock market, which can be both high-yield and liquid. But more money has been made through illiquid investments, including businesses and real estate. So it is not uncommon for someone to be a millionaire and have cash flow problems. It is not uncommon for someone to have over $1,000,000 on paper and yet be penniless. This is particularly true in an environment of high interest rates, where property owners are unable to withdraw some of the equity out of their investments through the use of refinancing.

So, what is it worth to be a millionaire if you can't use the wealth that you have attained? Obviously, it is worth something less than $1,000,000. If I were asked to measure the wealth of an individual property owner, I would not simply take the market value of the property that individual owns and deduct the debts of the property. This person will not realize this amount should he or she sell or refinance the property. Instead, I would reduce his or her net worth by the costs of selling the property, and I would recognize only the cash value of any contracts that he or she would have to carry back. This is the individual's liquid net worth, and that is far more meaningful than any speculative value that might be assigned to the market value of his or her assets. The individual's liquid net worth determines his or her capacity to handle adversity and also determines the lifestyle that his or her investments could generate. Both of these are more meaningful measures of the individual's net worth. Essentially, money is worth nothing in a vacuum; its value depends on what you can do with it.

If you are very illiquid, as many real estate investors are, your net worth on paper might prove to be of little worth to you. It might even prove to be of negative value, since you will feel the impotence associated with having supposed wealth but being unable to use it. Also, the supposed wealth may generate some other problems associated with being wealthy, and you won't even have the money to make the problems seem worthwhile.

PROBLEMS OF THE VERY RICH

What does it take to be rich, let alone very rich? Will $1,000,000 in cash do it? There are those who would suggest that the richest people may be those who have no money because they are rich in nonmaterial things. Others will tell you that rich people aren't happy. As a group, you will find that rich people are every bit as happy as middle-class people and considerably happier than the poor. Wealth may not contribute to the happiness, but neither is it a detriment. It is just one of many elements that define the person. The kind of happiness that money can't buy is better left to books by psychologists and sociologists, so here we'll consider the happiness that money *can* buy and how much money it takes to be considered rich.

Wealth is a relative measurement. It varies among individuals, depending on their background and expectations. Basically, I would define rich people as those who have enough money to maintain their desired lifestyle for the rest of their lives—people who have more than enough money to do anything that they want to do and to own anything that they want to own. Very rich people have more money still. To some extent, they are burdened by their wealth. They may feel the need to preserve the principal and pass it on to subsequent generations. They may also feel the need to increase the family wealth as did their predecessors. It they are to pass to their children a value comparable to the value they received from their parents, they must substantially increase the nominal value of the estate to offset inflation and the estate taxes that they must pay to make the transfer. They are trustees of sorts and feel all the burdens associated with the trusteeship.

The Need to Spend

Preserving wealth for the purpose of passing it to subsequent generations seems hardly worthwhile. Instead of enjoying the wealth, each generation is burdened with the responsibility of preserving it and passing it on to the generation that follows. But there is more to it than that. In our society wealth equates with power, and maintaining the wealth base is necessary to maintain the power base. Also, the rich families who are working to maintain their positions of wealth and power in our society are hardly suffering. Part of being wealthy and powerful is looking wealthy and powerful. The very rich find that they are able to maintain the family's wealth while enjoying a very pleasant lifestyle. But, it is not a lifestyle without problems, and some of those problems are unique to the rich, the very rich, and those who are perceived to be rich or very rich.

One problem with having money is the perception of a need to use it. Robin Williams said that cocaine is God's way of telling you that you make too much money. If you have the money to finance your vices, those vices are likely to flourish. Is alcohol or drug abuse any less damaging to your body simply because you have the money to pay for it? Any vice that you happen to have will be more easily obtained if you have money. So to avoid the problems associated with vices, the rich people have to have more willpower than the rest of us. If you are poor, it doesn't take any willpower to forgo those vices that you can't afford. But rich people have the power not only to obtain and use the vices, but also to conceal their use and increase their dependency.

Beware of Schemes

Another problem with being rich is that you are the target of every sales scheme and phony deal that comes along. You won't realize how many flaky people and phony schemes there are in the world until you have the capacity to finance them. At that point, they will come out of the woodwork. It should not prove difficult to develop sales resistance. If you had enough commonsense to build the wealth in the first place, you are unlikely to squander it on the schemes of some shyster. Of greater concern is the quantity of legitimate investments that you have that you really don't have the time to monitor adequately. Don't allow the problems in these investments to get out of hand. Seek and use professional help to keep an eye on your investment interests. In the long run, it will be more than worth the cost.

Loans to Friends

While you might find it easy to develop sales resistance for the schemes of promoters, a different kind of request is much more difficult to ignore or decline. After you have obtained wealth, you will find that many of your friends are in need of a loan. Suddenly, the friendly relationship that you had with them will cease to exist. They will not treat you as a friend; rather, they will approach you with hat in hand and show the proper deference that is shown by potential debtors when seeking a loan from a potential creditor.

What has happened to your friends? They have shown that they value the loan more than your friendship. They also appear to be questionable credit risks. Why aren't they seeking the loan from a bank? They are accepting the personal humiliation of seeking a loan from a personal friend because they are unable to obtain the loan from conventional sources. Those conventional sources recognize the likelihood of default on the loan and are unwilling to take the risk. That likelihood of default is only increased when the loan is obtained from a friend rather than a financial institution. You might find it surprising that friend would default on a personal loan before defaulting on a loan from a financial institution. But there are several reasons that the default is more likely.

First of all, recognize that these people are no longer your friends, but rather your debtors. They were the ones who chose to change the relationship, not you. Also, you probably don't have a lien against any of their property as security. They are far more likely to pay the secured creditors ahead of the unsecured creditors. In addition, they are relying on the friendship to influence the business relationship. If they should fall behind on the payments, they expect you to allow them more time and grace than would be appropriate in a strict business transaction. After all, your friendship should be "worth that much." When people decide to put a financial value on a friendship, that friendship ceases to have any real value. Also, if they fall behind on payments to you, it is unlikely to affect their credit rating since you are unlikely to report the default to the credit bureau. Finally, you will be the victim of your success. These people will rationalize that they need the money far more than you do, and that although they have every intention of making good on their obligations, it won't hurt you to wait a little while.

In addition to the financial burdens of your friends, you are also likely to share the personal burdens that have financial solutions. You will very shortly know which friends are behind on their alimony payments and which have children in expensive drug rehabilitation programs. You will be burdened with a variety of problems courtesy of your former friends. There is no good solution to this problem. If you refuse the requests of your friends, they will have embarrassed themselves for nothing and will resent you. If you loan them the money, you are in all likelihood throwing away your money and encouraging similar requests from other friends. Either way, the quantity and quality of your friendships will diminish.

The best advice is not to lend the money. If your friendship hinges on whether or not you make the loan, the friendship is not worth very much. In as polite a way as possible, inform your friends that their friendship is too valuable to you to be risked on a loan. Tell them that you know of many friendships that have been destroyed when the friends become creditors and debtors. Offer to introduce them to your banker or otherwise assist in helping them with their problems. But do not offer to guarantee the loan or otherwise enter the transaction in the position of a creditor or in any other official capacity. Offer moral support to your friends and attempt to maintain contact. Your relationship will be strained at first since they have confided in you and you have refused their requests for help. It is easy to lose contact with one another under these circumstances. But, if you make the effort to maintain the relationship, you may find that it can be restored.

The Shock of New Wealth

Friends seeking loans are just one example of the disruption that money causes in the personal life of successful investors. There are many other examples. You sometimes hear it said that money changes people, and inevitably it does. There are both positive and negative changes. We have already considered the capacity to indulge in your vices, but there is also the capacity to improve your lifestyle significantly. That improvement may come in the form of acquisitions of material goods, travel and other experiences, and social climbing. You may find that you are a fish out of water. You may feel uncomfortable with your new friends and unwilling to assimilate their pretentiousness. Should you move into a new house in a nicer neighborhood, you will have to build new friendships because your old friends are also likely to feel uncomfortable in your new surroundings. Complicating the problem is the fact that the wealth is likely to come quickly. After operating a marginally positive cash flow project for eight years, you sell the project and suddenly have $1,000,000 in cash. The shock of this event, although very pleasant, is likely to upset the patterns of your life. The orderliness and routine of your life are now bombarded by the capacity to do things you never could before. And you must decide if and how your life should change. The first thing asked of people who have won the state lottery is what they will do with the money. We all fantasize as to what we would do with sudden wealth, and we are curious as to what an actual recipient intends. There is the implied need to do something to improve the lifestyle. If the money and the changing lifestyle don't make you happy, there is the perception that there must be something wrong with you. In fact, change can be a shock, both mentally and physically. You can become physically ill from both positive and negative changes in your life. The important thing is to go slowly. Don't change your life immediately; make the change slow and gradual. Continue with as much of the routine of your life as it is possible to maintain. Then, in a comfortable and unhurried environment, decide what you want to do with your life and your money, then do it.

THE PROBLEMS OF FAILURE

Of far more concern than the comparatively trivial problems encountered when things go right are the problems to be encountered when things go wrong. The problems are serious in nature and long-term in duration. The risk associated with these problems should not be taken lightly. Prospective investors should consider the risks seriously prior to investing in real estate.

There is a tendency to approach the subject with a rather blasé attitude. If you start out with nothing, and you lose everything that you have created, what have you really lost? Are not the experience and the potential worth the risk? If you are young and unsuccessful, aren't you in a position to start over? It is difficult to be objective about the costs of failure. It is also difficult to measure the benefits of the experience acquired against the costs, both financial and personal, associated with a business failure.

I have often heard people who have had varying degrees of success in this business say that they would be better off if their business failed. They will make such a statement in the heat of a difficult situation, and it is not to be taken seriously; however, it does illustrate a problem. In the investment business, like any other small business, entrepreneurs are problem solvers. That is their primary responsibility. They are on the hot seat day after day in an environment of considerable pressure. They may have deadlines to make for closings, management problems, code violations, frivolous lawsuits, employee relations problems, cash flow troubles, and a variety of other problems. They must face the problems day after day. Sometimes they will solve the problems, but more often the solution will not be totally successful and the problem will recur. The more property you have and the larger the property, the more and greater your problems. An organization can be put together that addresses some of the problems, but the ultimate responsibility for the success or failure of the venture is that of the principal, and the ultimate decision-making authority can be nowhere else.

If you have never been associated with a business failure, you will have a hard time judging how you will react to your own. But, if you intend to have your investment activity grow to the point at which it has the capacity to make you wealthy, you must accept the fact that the business also has the capacity to fail. And the failure of a business tends to be a highly personal thing. In the business of investing in real estate, this is especially true. The business tends to be associated with and to assume the identity of the investor. So, if the business fails, the investor fails. This personal failure is difficult to live with.

The failure of the business is even difficult to recognize. At what point do you determine that the business is doomed to failure? Remember that the investments will show a taxable loss and may even experience substantial negative cash flow and still be wildly successful. So, how do you judge that a particular investment is unlikely to turn around and so should be abandoned? Since it is difficult to recognize when a business is failing, there is a tendency to struggle to make a success of the business for a long period of time. If the business does eventually fail, the effort will have been one of extreme protracted frustration. Just as it is exciting to be associated with success, it is very depressing to be associated with failure. For various reasons, that depressing state of affairs may continue for a long period of time.

A friend of mine who was president of a property management company and a partner in various unsuccessful real estate investments expressed the frustration this way:

"I spend ten hours a day staring at negative numbers, trying to think of ways to make them positive. I find that I am incapable of doing anything else. I can't eat. I can't sleep. I know that I am not much fun to live with. And my preoccupation with the problem properties is causing problems with those that are doing better. I just want to throw up my hands and walk away. But, unfortunately, that isn't possible either."

After fighting a losing battle for many months or years, it is difficult to maintain the positive mental outlook necessary for success.

LEGAL COMPLIANCE

Part of a business failure is lawsuits. Whether from creditors, contract sellers, investors, tenants, or the government, if your business fails, chances are that you are liable to many people for your failure to meet your obligations.

Disclosure to Investors

One question that is certain to arise is whether you are in compliance with the legal requirements for disclosure of pertinent facts to your investors. Real estate limited partnership units are offered for sale through a prospectus. The prospectus is required to include such information about the promoter and his or her track record so as to apprise the investors of the risk associated with the investment. Naturally, when the business fails the question arises as to whether or not the disclosure is adequate and accurate. There is also the question of what other representations were made to the investors apart from the prospectus.

The prospectus is used to advise the investors of what is being offered for sale, but its practical purpose is to limit the liability of the promoter. The prospectus will contain some self-serving language about how the investors are relying only on the information contained in the prospectus for their investment decision and about how the promoter has made no representations inconsistent with those disclosed in the prospectus. Technically, it is generally unnecessary to use a prospectus in the sale of private placement real estate limited partnership units, but the prospectus is a valuable deterrent to lawsuit. When a lawsuit is actually filed, the existence of the prospectus, and the self-serving language contained therein, will serve to undermine the plaintiff's suit. However, it is important that the information contained in the prospectus, particularly the financial information, be accurate. If, for example, the promoter has exaggerated his or her background and experience, it could be argued that the misrepresentation had the effect of misleading the investors as to the risk associated with the investment. A suit for rescission, in which the investors ask to get their money back (plus interest), is a distinct possibility. Whether the suit is successful depends on the nature and magnitude of the misrepresentation. If there is no prospectus, there is more question as to what representations were made in the sales effort. Also, investors expect to see a prospectus. They are unlikely to read the prospectus, but they still want to see one. The prospectus is written for lawyers and accountants, by lawyers and accountants. They are very difficult for the investors to read and are generally not read. But it is still important to have a prospectus that appears professional, since it gives the investors the impression that the offering is professional. You may give the investors plenty of reasons to doubt your professionalism later, but it is important to start out with a professional image.

Other elements of legal compliance include whether the partnership is registered properly with the state and the various regulatory authorities. Has the limited partnership registered properly with the state? Has the offering been properly registered with the state securities regulators? Are any of the investors from outside the state, requiring the limited partnership to be registered with the Securities and Exchange Commission?

If the investors wish to bring a suit for rescission, it is generally possible to make a credible claim. In addition to many technical filing and other legal requirements, they can always make the claim that the promoter has misrepresented the risk, either through the prospectus or despite it. Whether the suit can be won is another matter, and whether the victory will be worth anything is always a serious question. As will be seen shortly, often only the attorneys will profit from such a lawsuit.

COMMINGLING FUNDS

In addition to the question of legal compliance, the failing promoter is often guilty of commingling funds. This is a violation of his or her fiduciary duty to the investors and may result in both civil and criminal liability.

Commingling occurs when the funds invested in one partnership are used for the benefit of another partnership, without the authorization of the first partnership to so use the funds. Varying degrees of culpability are associated with commingling funds. Sometimes the commingling is accidental and comes about through sloppy accounting or banking policies. Other times there is evidence of intentional acts on the part of the promoter to make unauthorized use of the funds. But how does it come about that promoters commingle funds? What is the motivation? How culpable are the promoters?

Carrying Troubled Partnerships

Commingling occurs when the promoter has varying degrees of success with his or her projects. If all of the projects were doing well, there would be no reason to "borrow" from one project to help another. Similarly, if all the projects were failing, there would be little benefit to be obtained from commingling. So commingling requires a situation in which some of the promoter's properties are succeeding and some are not doing as well. This is a common situation. Frequently, the first few investments that a new syndicator makes will not be as good as those that are made later. This is because, hopefully, the promoter will have learned from his or her early mistakes and not duplicated them later. The quality of the investments will probably improve.

So, the promoter is faced with a dilemma. Assume that your early investments are not doing very well, but subsequent investments are doing better (or at least appear to be doing better; perhaps the investments haven't had enough time to fail). You are

entitled to certain fees for the organization and management of
the partnerships and their property. You have probably deferred
collecting fees from the troubled partnerships. They don't have
the capacity to pay the fees, and you don't wish to burden them
further. You must decide whether to advance to the troubled partnerships some of your fees from the successful ones.

Several factors will influence your decision. You will consider
the likelihood of the advanced funds doing any good. Is the negative cash flow on the project going to be of indefinite duration, or
will a short-term infusion of cash carry the partnership to a period
of prosperity? As noted earlier, buyers and investors tend to be optimistic, and they are likely to feel that they can turn the property
around given a little more time. Another consideration is the fact
that you are in the business of selling interests in new limited partnerships. How will the failure of an early partnership impact the
sales of subsequent offerings? It will certainly be regarded as evidence of substantial risk in the investment. The salespeople will attempt to emphasize the advantages of learning from prior
mistakes. But the investors are likely to prefer promoters who
have not made such significant mistakes over those who have
learned from them. So, you are motivated not to give up on the
early investments, despite the appearance that they will not be successful. You do not want your track record burdened by early failures. And at this point you haven't done anything wrong. You are
simply deciding whether or not to make a loan to a troubled partnership. The funds you intend to loan are your own. They are fees
to which you are entitled from the other partnership.

But carrying the troubled partnerships can be habit-forming.
The partnership that was initially carried because you felt that it
could be turned around in a short period continues to be carried
even after the turnaround period appears to be anything but short-
term. There may be some improvement that continues to provide
you with faint hope. The problem is that eventually the money
runs out, and you must face the possibility of default. If you have
a considerable amount of successful properties and only a limited
amount of problem property, you may choose to carry the property indefinitely rather than face up to the reality of your failure
and its effect on your track record. But a problem comes when the
money runs out, because the money *doesn't* run out. Only the legitimate money runs out. You remain in control of what might be
considerable working capital in other partnerships. The profitable
partnerships might not need the working capital and may even be
looking for short-term investments to make the working capital
productive. You may even have the legal discretion, provided in

the partnership agreement, to loan the partnership's excess working capital. These are not reasons; they are justifications and rationalizations.

It is a mistake to advance the funds of one partnership to another even if it is arguably legal to do so. It is impossible to maintain your fiduciary responsibility to both partnerships when you are loaning money from one to the other. It is one thing to loan your money; it is quite another to loan someone else's money. It is still worse to loan that money without the prior consent and approval of the limited partnership. And at what rate would you loan the money? How do you objectively consider the credit risk? Consider why you are loaning the partnership money. You are advancing it money to carry negative cash flow property. You are advancing it in the hope of turning the property around. But why are *you* loaning the partnership money? You aren't a bank. You are loaning the partnership money because it can't borrow the money anywhere else. What does that say about the partnership as a credit risk? What does that say about the propriety of the loan? If the partnership has the capacity to borrow its needed working capital, get the loan.

Another alternative is to level with the limited partners and ask for their input into the undesirable situation. If enough of them feel it is worthwhile to continue to support the investments, they will honor a partnership assessment and will continue the ownership. Those are the only circumstances that justify continued ownership if you are unprepared to loan the partnership your own money. The limited partners are likely to have differences of opinion as to the propriety of continuing ownership. Those who choose not to participate in the assessment will lose their interest in the partnership. The remaining partners are likely to have considerable input into and interest in the future of the property.

You must also face the distinct possibility that the partners will blame you for the failure of the investments. Whether or not their impression is accurate is not really relevant. The point is that they prefer to manage the future of the property without you. Without the limited partners' involvement, the partnership property has no future for your investment group. It is only appropriate that, if the investors want you out, you withdraw gracefully.

The temptation to commingle and the availability of funds for that purpose will prove too much temptation for many promoters. Blind ambition is as debilitating a disease as you will encounter. Some will embezzle funds for fun and games; others will do so to service diseases. The disease may be alcoholism, drug abuse, or blind ambition. When it comes time to pay for the embezzlement, the fun and games embezzler will have had the fun to justify the cost. Those who have embezzled to service a disease will have only the grief. If you have commingled funds, your business has failed; you just don't realize it yet.

Accidental Commingling

While intentional commingling is certainly culpable, accidental commingling is sometimes considered less damning. Accidental commingling might occur in those circumstances in which a promoter combines the receipts of several properties or partnerships within one account. I was once negotiating an apartment acquisition from a seller who I found to be commingling funds unintentionally. On my review of source documents, I examined a checking account into which were deposited the receipts of several buildings. The promoter maintained meticulous records of the income and expenses of the various buildings. It appeared that the motivation for the combining of the accounts was one of banking convenience more than the desire to commingle the funds of the partnerships. However, one of the partnerships had a credit balance in its account. In other words, one of the partnerships owed money to the common pool. The other partnerships were effectively loaning money to the debtor partnership. Regardless of the intentions of the parties, the promoter was allowing an unauthorized use of the funds. It could be suggested that this promoter was less culpable since he appeared to lack the intent to commingle funds illegally. But I would be more concerned with his apparent lack of regard or consideration for the rules affecting the separation of partnership assets. The purpose of the rules is to provide the investors with the assurance that their funds will not be misused. It is apparent that the promoter in question does not appreciate the importance of the rules and does not feel compelled to comply with them.

FRAUD

When a business is not doing well, and especially when a business fails, it is often suggested by the investors that they were misled about the risks associated with the business. After the failure, it is apparent that the risks were significant. One is always in a better position to evaluate the risks after the fact. And, although salespeople will acknowledge the possibility that the business might fail, they will also express optimism that the efforts will be successful. So, have the investors been misled? Each case will have its own unique facts and circumstances that will determine whether the investors have been fraudulently misled. The facts and circumstances will also determine whether the fraud is substantial enough to warrant legal remedy.

To avoid the assertion that they are defrauding the investors, promoters provide substantial disclaimers as to experience and expertise in the prospectus. They will also print the statutory warning in bold print on the cover of the prospectus as follows:

> This offering of securities involves a high degree of risk and is suitable only for long-term investment by persons with adequate financial means and substantial taxable income who have no need for liquidity with respect to this investment.
>
> Neither the Securities and Exchange Commission nor the securities division of the (STATE) department of licensing has passed upon the merits of these securities, nor have they passed upon the accuracy or completeness of this offering circular or other selling literature.
>
> Prospective investors are not to construe the contents of this memorandum as legal or tax advice. Each investor should consult his own counsel, accountant, or other advisors as to legal, tax, and related matters concerning the investment described herein and its suitability for him.
>
> Participants may not resell or otherwise transfer an interest in securities offered hereby unless such interest or the subsequent offer or resale thereof is either registered and/or qualified as set forth in the securities act of 1933, as amended (STATE LAW SECTION) of the securities act of (STATE), or is exempted from such registration and/or qualification.
>
> No person has been authorized to give any information or make any representation not contained in this memorandum except as provided by the general partner of (NAME OF PARTNERSHIP) upon request, and if any other information or representation is given or made, it must not be relied upon as having been authorized.
>
> Prospective investors should recognize that the acquisition of these investment interests involves a high degree of risk (see "Risk Factors"), substantial fees to the general partners and affiliates (see "Compensation to General Partner and Affiliates"); and is subject to various conflicts of interest (see "Conflicts

of Interest"). These securities are offered only to
bona fide residents of the state of (STATE).

There are variations on the wording of the disclaimer, and not
all the elements above may be applicable. But it is generally advisable to be as thorough as possible. It is better to warn the investors
of dangers that don't occur than to fail to warn them of risk factors that result in the business failure. If the risk factor has been
addressed and disclosed adequately, the fraud case will be difficult
to support. But if the risk has not been addressed, and it results in
the failure of the business, the investors may well have a cause of
action against the promoter.

The carefully worded disclaimers are prepared by the attorneys
to limit the legal exposure of the promoter. You might think that
such disclaimers would scare the investors away, but this rarely
happens. Sophisticated investors know that disclaimers must be issued to protect the promoter and general partners, and the disclaimers tend to be disregarded. Another reason that they tend to
be disregarded is that they really don't say anything about the investment. All investments of this type are required to disclose that
they have a "high degree of risk," regardless of the relative risk of
the investment. Since neither the SEC nor the state's securities de-
partment passes on the degree of risk in the investment, the offerings aren't allowed to differentiate degrees of risk. Since the
disclaimers always say approximately the same thing, the sophisticated investor tends to ignore them.

The securities salespeople tend to do more than ignore the disclaimers. When asked about them by concerned investors, the
salespeople respond with, "Oh, don't worry about that. We are required to include the disclaimer to sell the securities. All securities
have such a disclaimer; it doesn't mean anything." I am sure that
the attorneys appreciate the salespeople's undermining their efforts to avoid legal exposure as much as the salespeople appreciate
the attorney's insistence on writing in a clause that has a negative
impact on sales.

The prospectus will also include information on the promoter,
his or her track record, and his or her experience, including educa-
tional background. It will also contain information on the property to be purchased or the type of property to be purchased by a
blind pool. It is important that this information be accurate and
conservative. Don't overstate your experience or the performance
of the property previously acquired. Once again, investors expect
to see disclaimers. They tend to make the investment decision on
the basis of their relationship with the salesperson or their knowledge of the promoter's success through prior dealings or through

references of friends and business acquaintances. The prospectus will have very little to do with the investors' investment decision. Therefore, although its official purpose is to appraise the investors of the opportunity and to solicit their investment, its practical purpose is to limit the liability of the promoter and to counter the claim of investors that they were fraudulently induced into making the investment.

WHO ARE ALL THOSE ANGRY PEOPLE?

You put together a partnership whose limited partners are investing with you to realize a profit. Whether it is a tax shelter in their eyes or an investment depends largely on the time of year. Near the end of the year, or near April 15, they are interested in how much write-off the investment will produce. However, during the rest of the year they want to know how their investment is doing. When your investments don't work and the property is lost, the otherwise friendly investors will turn into people you don't recognize. If you were to describe the investors in two words, they would be *disappointed* and *angry*. They are disappointed that the investment didn't work out the way they had hoped, and they will be angry that they can't do anything about it. They can file suit if they wish to hassle you, but the suit is unlikely to result in any recovery for them. They have simply made a bad investment. Some will recognize this unfortunate reality, but most will complain loudly. If investors are without legal remedy, and you give them the opportunity to express their anger, which is desirable, they will express that anger. But, from your point of view, it is better to give the investors the opportunity to express their displeasure in a non-litigious setting than to have that anger manifested in a lawsuit. Don't be cute or evasive. Explain those circumstances beyond your control that contributed to your failure. If you choose to admit to making investment or operating managerial mistakes, limit your admissions to honest mistakes. If you have arguably made mistakes for which you might be legally culpable, don't discuss these mistakes without competent legal advice.

KNOW WITH WHOM YOU ARE DEALING

It is important in the context of a failing business to know with whom you are dealing. Whether you are considering creditors of the business, investors, or other parties, it is important to recognize who they are and of what they are capable.

Business owners with struggling or failing businesses are in a delicate position. Obviously, they have disappointed the investors and creditors. They may have even engaged in legally questionable

activity and be legally culpable to the investors. This is particularly likely in the final days before the fall of the business. At that
time, the promoter might be driven by the desperate situation to
do things that he or she wouldn't have thought possible. This will
be considered shortly; here we are concerned with the other parties that the failure affects and what their reaction is likely to be.

It is important when you form the partnership to determine
that the investors are people with whom you would like to share
success and wouldn't mind sharing failure. The principal reason
that I advise against forming partnerships with family and friends
is not that you will not want to share success with them but that
you will experience psychological difficulty in sharing failure with
them. So, there are many people with whom you would not want
to be involved in the event that the business fails.

There are others with whom you can't share failure. If you
choose to become involved with underworld figures, and your
business fails, you may know before anyone else what happened
to Jimmy Hoffa. It is important to know with whom you are dealing. A lot of underworld money is invested in legitimate businesses. It seems reasonable that some of the promoters receive
these questionable investments unaware of the background of the
investors. The event of a business failure is not the time that you
want to find out about your investor's association with the crime
syndicate. There are also enough legitimate investors interested in
real estate investments that there is no reason to become know-
ingly involved with the mob.

Even if the investors are not so notorious as to have underworld
connections, it is important to consider the extent to which they
might attempt to seek other than legal remedy for their grievances.
If the business has failed, and you have no assets beyond the business, or if your other assets are somehow shielded from attack by
creditors, the investors and creditors will probably be without adequate legal remedy. The question is the extent to which they will
seek other than legal remedy and what that remedy is likely to be.
When you are facing angry investors and creditors, it is important
to placate them and not antagonize them to the point of seeking
other remedy.

In our society, debtors are no longer imprisoned. In fact, the
status of the debtor is no longer regarded as being worthy of apology. It is recognized that our society is fueled by the business activity that is generated by prudent use of debt. However, defaulting
debtors are still regarded with a certain amount of disdain. They
may be considered morally as well as financially bankrupt, and it
is unlikely that they will get a lot of sympathy if they are "roughed
up" by a disgruntled creditor. So, choose your alliances carefully.

And, in the event of a bankruptcy, don't flaunt your lack of exposure to creditors and investors.

THE TRAUMA OF A BUSINESS FAILURE
Because of the personal relationship between promoters and their investments, the failure of a business often equates with the personal failure of the promoter. This is unfortunate since it increases the already heavy burden that the promoter must carry. The reaction to this failure depends on the personality of the promoter. Some bounce back and are out promoting new deals before the dust settles on the old failures. Others withdraw into a very depressed state that has been known to result in suicide. Between the two extremes are the bulk of promoters' reactions.

If you find yourself in this position, you will probably be less than anxious to start over. Your experience has not been pleasant, and the last thing that you want to do is go out and do it again. It will also be difficult to start over because, regardless of your experience, your reputation is tarnished. It will probably be difficult for you to raise the money to put together new partnerships, having failed on previous partnerships.

The trauma of a business failure is difficult to describe to those who haven't experienced it. Some businesses fail before they really get started, as when a manufacturer fails to get the contracts needed to get started or the small store is undercapitalized and never realizes its potential before closing. But real estate investments don't tend to fail in this manner. Their failure tends to be slower and more painful. The reason for the failure is almost always negative cash flow. Some would suggest that negative cash flow isn't a cause but rather a result of other causes, like poor management or excessive debt service requirements. But, this is a semantic argument. The point is that the property is unable to pay its operating expenses and debt service.

Actually, negative cash flow doesn't always result in immediate abandonment of the property. In fact, that is seldom the result. Instead, you as the owner will attempt to economize the operations of the property. You will repair appliances rather than replace them, mow the lawn every other week rather than weekly, and defer discretionary improvements. If you have the capacity to loan the property money, you will feed it. And those payments that you must make will be deferred as long as possible. So the payments will be late, the creditors will receive their payments very slowly, and the property will probably suffer from a lack of necessary maintenance. More and more repairs will be deferred, until the property begins to look run-down.

If the property is not making money by that time, the problems will accelerate. You won't be able to pay the employees what their service is worth, so you will have difficulty in keeping quality help. The lack of maintenance will cause tenant problems. You may find yourself unable to refund the tenant deposits on time. If the management is not concerned with maintenance of a quality appearance, the tenants can't be expected to take pride in the place where they live, so they will be less likely to maintain their apartments. Quality tenants will move, and you will be left with lower-quality tenants. You will find yourself unable to implement planned rent increases, and your vacancy rate will climb. All of these factors worsen the cash flow problem.

To correct the problem and realize the potential of the property, it is necessary to infuse the money to make the deferred repairs. The property, in a depressed condition, will not support additional debt. It may be necessary for a new purchaser to provide the cash infusion. But a new purchaser will want a substantial discount on the purchase price for at least three reasons. First, the purchaser will have to be compensated for the cost of repairs necessitated by the condition of the property. Second, the purchaser will recognize the problem situation and will want to take advantage of it. Third, the property will not merit the selling price desired since it would not have the rent history reflecting its potential.

This whole process of failure and decline may well take years to complete. It is not an inevitable process. Often, the decline is headed off by an improving market. You work and hope that your efforts will pay off. For years, you will work in the depressing environment of the problem property. Your hopes will grow fainter with each passing month. You may have everything you own invested in the property, in your share of the equity and in subsequent personal loans. When you face the loss of this property, is it any wonder that you might resort to unauthorized loans from partnerships within your control? Also, the depressing situation may cause you to do things you wouldn't have thought possible, like contracting for repairs for which you are unable to pay. Extreme measures may be rationalized in the name of survival.

When failure does finally come, you will find that you have lost far more than money. Your reputation and good name will have suffered through the months of bad debts and unkept promises. Your depression may have grown to unbearable levels, or you may finally experience the relief that comes with resignation and recognition of the inevitable.

BANKRUPTCY PROVISIONS

The purpose of the bankruptcy laws is to recognize that you can't get blood out of a stone. It would be very disruptive to business if creditors were allowed relentlessly to pursue and harass debtors that have no real prospect of being able to honor the debt. Also, the prospect of such treatment would discourage business-people from taking risks, creating goods and services, and fueling the economy. It is recognized that, while many businesses fail, it is in the best interest of the country to encourage new business activity. It is necessary to balance the legitimate claims of creditors against the needs of the country and the practical limitations of the debtor.

The bankruptcy laws were intended to be a shield to protect debtors from the actions of creditors and to give debtors a new start. These days, however, many debtors use the bankruptcy provisions more as a sword than as a shield. The protection of the bankruptcy court has been used (some would say abused) by some companies to dissolve labor contracts and by others to defeat tort claims from people who have been injured by the company's products. But, while the abuses of the bankruptcy laws are newsworthy, the provisions have many legitimate applications. And the abuses by creditors, in their attempts to collect on problem loans, are not newsworthy because they are so commonplace. Many of the collection practices regularly engaged in by collection agencies are of questionable legality. The agencies are relying on the fact that debtors are normally too embarrassed about the debt to complain about the abuses of the creditors. But abuses by the collectors do not impact the legitimacy of the debt. Even the bankruptcy laws do not deny the legitimacy of the debt. Bankruptcy recognizes the legitimacy of the debts and the desirability of encouraging the payments of debts, but it also recognizes the practical impossibility of collecting the claim from insolvent debtors.

The bankruptcy laws protect debtors in two different ways. Some of the provisions do not eliminate the debt or reduce it at all but rather restructure the payment arrangements so that the debtor has the capacity to make the payments. In order to accomplish this, the bankruptcy provision stops any collection procedures on the part of the creditors until such time as the debtor submits a plan for paying the debts that is satisfactory to the court. In this circumstance, the individual or business remains under the jurisdiction of the bankruptcy court until either the debts are paid or the plan fails. When the plan fails, or if it is determined that attempting a payment plan would not be worthwhile, the debt forgiveness provisions of the bankruptcy laws will apply. Under the debt forgiveness provisions of the bankruptcy laws, the debtor doesn't lose everything, just almost everything. The law permits the debtor to keep a certain amount of equity in his or her house and personal property. If the debtor has any assets beyond those that he or she is allowed to retain, the assets will be split among the creditors. Payment will be made first to the secured creditors, then to the general creditors, then to the equity investors. The secured creditors have to be paid off completely before the general creditors receive anything, and the general creditors have to be paid off completely before the equity investors receive anything. As a practical matter, if the equity investors were going to receive anything, or the general creditors very much, a bankruptcy would probably not be filed. So, under most circumstances, if a debtor files bankruptcy, the general creditors and the investors will receive nothing, and the secured creditors will probably receive only a percentage of their debt.

The potential for abuse in the bankruptcy laws should be obvious. In the absence of limitations in the law, some debtors would be inclined to run up debts and file bankruptcy regularly. Businesspeople would find it impossible to advance credit and collect on a sufficient percentage of the debt to make the arrangements worthwhile. The availability of credit is also important to the economy. Therefore, the bankruptcy laws limit the frequency with which debtors may avail themselves of the protection of the debt forgiveness provisions of the bankruptcy laws. As a general rule, the bankruptcy provisions may be used no more frequently than every six years. If you feel the need to use the bankruptcy debt forgiveness provisions more frequently than that, you are not only out of money; you are also out of luck.

CONCLUSIONS 15

After reading the previous chapter and considering the problems that accompany failure in the business, you might well conclude that the potential benefits are not worth the risk. This book's emphasis on the problems that plague the industry would reinforce that perception. My intent is not to discourage but rather to caution. There are many problems with real estate investments and the real estate industry. Ignoring the problems will not make them go away, and what you don't know *could* hurt you. The problems with the industry damage not just the individual investor but also the real estate market and the overall economy. The need for reform is incontrovertible; the impetus for reform is nonexistent. This book does not crusade for reform. It certainly does not crusade for governmental intervention and regulation. What is needed is better personal responsibility and meaningful legal penalties for misrepresentation. The doctrine of caveat emptor must be abandoned. Rather than have the lax laws encourage misrepresentation, we must enforce civil liability penalties for the fraud perpetrated by sellers, their agents, and appraisers in whatever capacity.

REAL ESTATER'S DISEASE

The state of the real estate market prompted a friend of mine to label practitioners as suffering from "real estater's disease." There is so much phony financial information presented by sellers of real estate, and so much misrepresentation as to the quality of property, that you must assume the information to be incorrect. It is, of course, only prudent to investigate the information that you receive. But it seems unfortunate that the information you receive will more than likely be substantially misrepresented. My friend suggested that it appeared to him that real estate agents, sellers, and promoters would rather lie than tell the truth. This appeared to be true even in circumstances where the truth was very positive. Sometimes the lie actually made the property look worse than the truth would. We concluded that lies were preferred. They were easier to deal with because they weren't constrained by the facts. It was better to lie all the time than to shift between lies and the truth, which would only cause unnecessary confusion.

My friend identified this malady he called "real estater's disease" in response to the apparent preference for lies over the truth. The feeling is apparently that the truth has no relevance to the property or to investment decisions. The truth is an annoying nuisance that is best ignored. If practitioners occasionally find themselves flirting with the truth, that may be an unavoidable accident that, despite the best lack of effort, can't be avoided.

How do you determine if the people with whom you are dealing suffer from the disease? Well, there are several warning signs. Have they presented you with pro forma financial statements or round expense estimates? Do they always have an answer to your question and never admit to a lack of information? If they are caught in a lie, do they disregard it? Diseased real estaters will not let being caught in a lie slow them down. They will neither acknowledge the fabrication nor apologize for it. They may change the subject or continue to make their point despite the lie.

Anything that such people say is suspect. It is worthless to ask them questions, unless you are simply curious as to what their creativity will produce. It is morally corrupting to deal with such people. They will give you the false impression that their business ethics are acceptable and the standard of the industry. Unfortunately, they are likely to be successful. In much the same way as the real estate agent who "buys" listings is likely to do more business than those who don't, diseased real estaters are likely to be involved in more transactions than reputable practitioners. This is because the misrepresentations are likely to solicit a contingent offer. If the misrepresentations are not discovered until after the closing, there is little remedy for the purchaser. The purchaser is unlikely to do future business with the diseased real estater, but at that point it is too late. But, even if the misrepresentation is discovered prior to closing, it is unlikely to end the negotiations between an interested buyer and seller. The lies created interest in the property, and the property itself maintained the interest despite the lies. If an agreement is negotiated between these parties, the diseased real estater will have profited, at least in part, from the disease. Rather than discourage misrepresentation, the parties tend to encourage the lies to continue by continuing to negotiate. It is difficult to suggest that you shouldn't negotiate for property that interests you simply because you have been lied to by the seller or the real estate agent. However, that is exactly what I would suggest. It is important that both the law and the parties encourage a higher standard of truthfulness in the industry. The only way to do that is to refuse to deal in any manner with those who have provided you with inaccurate information.

THE TEN COMMANDMENTS OF REAL ESTATE INVESTMENT

In an effort to improve the standards of behavior and performance of the industry, and in an effort to summarize the advice offered in this book, I offer the ten commandments of real estate investment listed below.

1. Thou shalt not rely on the representations of others as to financial or other information, and thou shalt not tell a lie, regardless of the practices of the marketplace.
2. Thou shalt exercise extreme caution in investing in foreign jurisdictions.
3. Thou shalt beware of operating costs.
4. Thou shalt not buy negative cash flow property.
5. Thou shalt not pay a premium for the conversion value of property or the projected rents.
6. Thou shalt always maintain accurate and complete books and records.
7. Thou shalt take thy successes and failures with equal grace and humility.
8. Thou shalt always set up the subsequent sale on the purchase of the property.
9. Thou shalt recognize thy limitations and compensate for them with the use of professionals.
10. Thou shalt not allow procrastination to prevent realization of goals and ambitions.

THE BEST INVESTMENT IN AMERICA TODAY

Real estate is probably the best investment in America today. It is common for the investments to yield over 20 percent per year after tax, and rates of return in excess of 30 percent per year after tax are not unusual. How does this rate of return compare to that of other investments? This yield is many times superior to that offered by alternative investments. Over the last five years tax exempt municipal bonds have yielded between about six and 12 percent depending on maturity date and quality rating. Bank certificates of deposits have yields that vary with the term. Generally, the longer the period, the higher the rate. Bank certificates have yielded about seven percent to about 13 percent. Corporate bonds have yields that depend on their risk rating and have had yields comparable with or a little higher than bank certificates of deposit. First mortgages have yielded about 11 to 16 percent and second mortgages from about 12 percent to 25 percent. It is difficult to generalize about the yields on corporate stocks since they are usually purchased for both dividend yield and appreciation. Except for the tax-exempt municipal bonds, the interest and dividend income is subject to federal income tax, and the after-tax yield will be reduced by the tax. In other words, to yield 20 percent after tax, the return on investment before tax must be greater than 20 percent by the amount of the tax rate. If the investor is in the 50 percent tax bracket, the yield before income tax would have to be 40 percent to yield 20 percent after tax. Other investments are nowhere close to this yield. Of all the investments, real estate has the highest yield. The only other investment that might experience a comparable yield is that of the personal business. Occasionally, private business investments will experience this kind of yield, but high yield means high risk. In the real estate context, among the risk factors is the illiquidity of the investment. The bank bonds and other investments are likely to have much lower yields but are also much more liquid. Do not concentrate so much of your investments in real estate that you experience a liquidity crisis. Equity in your real estate investments won't buy you lunch. So, while I would suggest that real estate is the best investment in America today, it is also illiquid and high-risk.

Do not invest exclusively in real estate. The old admonishment, "Don't put all your eggs in one basket," applies not only to one investment but also to one type of investment. It is only prudent to include real estate in your rounded investment portfolio.

BE CAREFUL

If I were to sum up the advice of this book in two words, they would be: Be careful. Fantastic opportunity is available in real estate investment, but there is also opportunity for unlimited loss. Don't give up the opportunity simply because it is associated with risk. But don't disregard the risk. Don't be greedy; remember the pig theory. Be cautious of the quality of professionals in the industry, and be suspicious of the accuracy of financial information. Now, go out and buy a newspaper. Throw away everything except the classified advertising section and go to work.